# X POWER TOOLS®

*Chris Tyler*

Beijing · Cambridge · Farnham · Köln · Paris · Sebastopol · Taipei · Tokyo

**X Power Tools®**
by Chris Tyler

Copyright © 2008 O'Reilly Media, Inc. All rights reserved.

Published by O'Reilly Media, Inc., 1005 Gravenstein Highway North, Sebastopol, CA 95472.

O'Reilly books may be purchased for educational, business, or sales promotional use. Online editions are also available for most titles (*safari.oreilly.com*). For more information, contact our corporate/institutional sales department: (800) 998-9938 or *corporate@oreilly.com*.

| | |
|---|---|
| **Editor:** Andy Oram | **Indexer:** Ellen Troutman-Zaig |
| **Production Editor:** Mary Brady | **Cover Designer:** Marcia Friedman |
| **Copyeditor:** Mary Brady | **Interior Designer:** David Futato |
| **Proofreader:** Laurel Ruma | **Illustrator:** Robert Romano |

**Printing History:**

December 2007:     First Edition.

ISBN-10: 0-596-10195-3
ISBN-13: 978-0-596-10195-4
[LSI]

# Table of Contents

## Part II    X Clients

# Part IV  Using X Remotely

## Part V   Special Configurations

# Preface

This is a book about the X Window System, a technology that continues to amaze observers in many ways. It was released as open source software before that term was formally defined, it's more than 20 years old but has an installed base that is growing daily, and it maintains compatibility with decades-old software while still taking full advantage of the very latest hardware.

This software is so versatile and can be used in so many different ways that it's not easy to cover it in a traditional book format—so this book is written in the Power Tools format, as a collection of short, independent articles that are extensively cross-referenced.

This book is written for experienced computer users who need to manage, configure, and support the X Window System, whether on a single laptop, a network of hundreds of remote displays, or a public-access kiosk.

## How This Book Is Organized

Each article in this book is numbered by its chapter number and section number—so 3.2 is the second article in Chapter 3. There are 15 chapters.

### Part I: The X Server

Chapter 1, *Introduction to the X Window System*
    Covers the origin, history, and structure of the X Window System.

Chapter 2, *Starting a Local X Server*
    Outlines how the X server can be executed in different ways to meet a wide variety of needs.

Chapter 3, *Basic X.org Configuration*
    Deals with the server configuration file for the most widely deployed X Server.

Chapter 4, *Advanced X.org Configuration*
Covers multiple-device configuration: multiple screens, multiple mice, or multiple keyboards.

Chapter 5, *Using the X Server*
Describes keyboard sequences and mouse actions that directly affect the X Server.

## Part II: X Clients

Chapter 6, *X Utility Programs*
Discusses the often ignored but very useful utility programs that are distributed with the X Window System.

Chapter 7, *Running X Clients*
Deals with starting X clients—programs that draw on the display.

Chapter 8, *Session Managers, Desktop Environments, and Window Managers*
Covers software that works with the X Window System to provide a full-fledged graphical user interface and desktop environment.

## Part III: Colors, Fonts, and Keyboards

Chapter 9, *Color*
Describes how color is represented and managed within X.

Chapter 10, *Core Fonts: Fonts the Old Way*
Explains the traditional font system available in all versions of the X Window System.

Chapter 11, *Pango, Xft, Fontconfig, and Render: Fonts the New Way*
Gives the detail of the new client-side font rendering used in almost all new X-based applications.

Chapter 12, *Keyboard Configuration*
Deals with the configuration of keyboards for the global environment, where the user may use several different languages with different character sets.

## Part IV: Using X Remotely

Chapter 13, *Remote Access*
Covers the safe and effective use of X's powerful remote-display capabilities.

Chapter 14, *Using VNC*
Explores the incredibly flexible *Virtual Network Computer* cross-platform display technology, which can be used with X in many powerful ways.

## Part V: Special Configurations

Chapter 15, *Building a Kiosk*
> Discusses how public-access GUI systems can be built using X Window technology.

# Conventions Used in This Book

The following typographical conventions are used in this book:

Plain text
> Indicates menu titles, menu options, menu buttons, and keyboard modifiers (such as Alt and Ctrl)

*Italic*
> Indicates new terms, URLs, email addresses, filenames, file extensions, pathnames, directories, commands, and Unix utilities

`Constant width`
> Indicates options, variables, values, the contents of files, and the output from commands

**`Constant width bold`**
> Shows commands or other text that should be typed literally by the user, as well as important lines of code.

*`Constant width italic`*
> Shows text that may be replaced with user-supplied values to adapt a command to a particular circumstance

 This icon signifies a tip, suggestion, or general note.

 This icon indicates a warning or caution.

# Using Code Examples

This book is here to help you get your job done. In general, you may use the code in this book in your programs and documentation. You do not need to contact us for permission unless you're reproducing a significant portion of the code. For example, writing a program that uses several chunks of code from this book does not require permission. Selling or distributing a CD-ROM of examples from O'Reilly books *does* require permission. Answering a question by citing this book and quoting example code does not require permission. Incorporating a significant amount of example code from this book into your product's documentation *does* require permission.

We appreciate, but do not require, attribution. An attribution usually includes the title, author, publisher, and ISBN. For example: "*X Power Tools,* by Chris Tyler. Copyright 2008 O'Reilly Media Inc., 978-0-596-10195-4."

If you feel your use of code examples falls outside fair use or the permission given above, feel free to contact us at *permissions@oreilly.com*.

## We'd Like to Hear from You

Please address comments and questions concerning this book to the publisher:

O'Reilly Media, Inc.
1005 Gravenstein Highway North
Sebastopol, CA 95472
800-998-9938 (in the United States or Canada)
707-829-0515 (international or local)
707-829-0104 (fax)

We have a web page for this book, where we list errata, examples, and any additional information. You can access this page at:

*http://www.oreilly.com/catalog/9780596101954*

To comment or ask technical questions about this book, send email to:

*bookquestions@oreilly.com*

For more information about our books, conferences, Resource Centers, and the O'Reilly Network, see our web site at:

*http://www.oreilly.com*

## Safari® Books Online

 When you see a Safari® Books Online icon on the cover of your favorite technology book, that means the book is available online through the O'Reilly Network Safari Bookshelf.

Safari offers a solution that's better than e-books. It's a virtual library that lets you easily search thousands of top tech books, cut and paste code samples, download chapters, and find quick answers when you need the most accurate, current information. Try it for free at *http://safari.oreilly.com*.

# Acknowledgments

Thank you to the X developers for creating such a powerful and enduring technology, engineered from the beginning with sufficient flexibility to withstand changes that could not be forseen.

I'd like to thank Andy Oram, David Brickner, and Isabel Kunkle from O'Reilly for working with me on this book. I'd also like to thank Matt Frye, Jim McQuillan, and Josh More for their detailed technical review; and my colleague John Selmys at Seneca College for his review and feedback on the early chapters.

My deep gratitude to my loving wife Diane and my girls Saralyn and Laura for their patience and understanding as I started this book, interrupted it to write another, and then resumed work on this volume. It's been a long haul, and I couldn't have done it without their love and support.

And most importantly, I give my humble thanks to God for His love—may any skill or understanding that He has given me be used to His glory.

# Part I

# The X Server

# 1

# Introduction to the X Window System

## 1.1   The X Window System

The X Window System is a *portable, network-based display system*. That short definition contains three of the keys to X's success:

*Portable*
> The X Window System is primarily used on Unix, Linux, and BSD systems, but it can also be used on Microsoft Windows, Mac OS X, and many other systems—in fact, it can be used on just about any modern operating system. It supports a wide range of hardware, from PDAs and standalone terminals to multimonitor workstations and information displays. Technology may be mixed and matched to suit user preferences, needs, and budget.

*Network-based*
> Programs can display anywhere on the network, and windows from programs running on machines several time zones apart can be displayed side-by-side on one screen. With X, users have complete freedom to work wherever they want.

*Display system*
> X is not a graphical user interface (GUI), but it provides a solid foundation for building one. GUI developers can escape from dealing with the intricacies of the display hardware and focus on user interface design, and legacy applications written for decades-old X-based GUIs will continue to work with modern ones.

Although most users of Unix (or Linux, or FreeBSD, or Darwin) often take X for granted, a good understanding of how it works opens up a world of possibilities, from speeding up remote access to building personal video recorders to configuring multiuser computers and information kiosks.

In this book, I assume that you have used X and that you have a basic understanding of Unix. This chapter introduces some of the history and basic concepts of X as well as the hardware technology used in modern displays; this sets the stage for the rest of the book, which uses a hands-on approach.

# 1.2   The History of X

X originated at MIT in 1984. It was a part of Project Athena, a campus-wide, cross-platform system, and it was loosely based on the W Window System from Stanford.

Before long, Unix vendors started to gain an interest in X. They realized that X would make it easier to port graphical applications to new hardware, which in turn would attract independent software vendors (ISVs)—and the more software became available, the more systems would be sold.

After a brief flirtation with restrictive licenses, version 11 of the X Window system was released in 1987 under the MIT license, and a vendor-neutral group called *The X Consortium* was formed to manage development. This was one of the earliest examples of an open source project. In fact, it predates the term *open source* by more than a decade. Each vendor used the sample code from the X Consortium as a starting point and implemented a server tuned for their particular display hardware and operating system.

Control of X passed from group to group until 1999, when *X.org* was established by The Open Group to manage the technology. Unfortunately, official work on X had almost come to a standstill by that point.

However, one particular implementation of X for PCs, named *X386*, piqued the interest of many developers in 1992. When distribution of a commercial version of X386 began, the open source version was renamed *XFree86* (say both names aloud to realize the pun). Eventually, most X innovations were made within the XFree86 project rather than coming from the official guardians of the X standard.

But internal politics and a rigid organizational structure took their toll on the *The XFree86 Project, Inc*, and after a license dispute in 2003, some key developers decided that they'd had enough. They moved development back to the almost-defunct X.org, formed *The X.org Foundation*, and shifted work into high gear. Most open source operating system distributions adopted the X.org server in 2004.

In the end, active X development wound up where it had started, the successor to the XFree86 project replaced the sample implementation of X technology, and a revitalized developer community started to once again steadily advance the state of the technology.

# 1.3   The Renaissance: New X Versus Old X

I recently skimmed through the 1994 book *X User Tools*, by Linda Mui and Valerie Quercia (O'Reilly), and the 1993 *UnixWare* user documentation. It was a fun and nostalgic stroll down memory lane, because the X Window System I used in the early-to-mid 90s was very different from X today. Many of the changes have been introduced so gradually that it's only by looking at old screen dumps that I realize how far we've come.

I have started to think of X development in terms of two eras: *Old X* (1984–1996) and *New X* (2000–present). Old X was characterized by the development of the core protocols, essential extensions, and Xt-based toolkits. New X development was kicked off by the release of the RENDER extension in 2000, which, along with Xft, OpenGL, the COMPOSE extension, and non-Xt toolkits (Qt and KDE), is causing large portions of the core X protocol to fall into disuse. Between these two eras, X development almost came to a standstill.

Here is a summary of some of the key differences in the technology of the two eras:

| Element | Old X | New X |
| --- | --- | --- |
| Fonts | Bitmapped fonts and scalable fonts without anti-aliasing, rendered by the core font capabilities in the server. | Scalable fonts with full anti-aliasing, managed on the client side by fontconfig, and displayed by the Xft library using the REN-DER extension. |
| Desktop environments | No standard desktop environments (though HP Vue morphed into CDE and made a late appearance). Consequently, window managers played a much larger role than they do today. Panel bars were rare—icons for minimized windows sat directly on the desktop (or, sometimes, in a separate icon box window). Clients were usually started through root-window menus or by typing commands in an *xterm*. | Two widely used desktop environments (KDE and Gnome) and a lightweight desktop (Xfce) with well-integrated root desktop, menu, and panel-bar operation. |
| Toolkits and configuration | Lots of Xt-based toolkits, including Motif, OpenLook, and the Athena Widgets. All of the toolkits could be configured through *resources*. | Xt has almost completely fallen into disuse; Qt and GTK+ have captured developer mindshare. Each provides their own configuration systems. freedesktop.org has coordinated shared standards for desktop menu entries and icons. |
| Display hardware | Entry-level desktop displays starting at 0.45 megapixels (800 × 600) and ranging up to 1.25 megapixels on the high end, with a typical resolution of 75 *dots per inch* (dpi). Common color capabilities ranged from monochrome to 256-color palettes, with very few high-end systems providing full-color capabilities. Palette management issues were a major headache. 3D hardware was rare and very expensive. LCD displays were rare except on laptops, which seldom exceed 0.75 megapixels (1024 × 768). | 24-bit palette-free color with 3D capabilities, and hardware acceleration is standard issue. 0.75 megapixel resolution (1024 × 768) is considered entry level; high-end systems have multimegapixel displays at resolutions up to 200 dpi. 1.25 megapixel and higher laptop displays are common.<br><br>Hand-held systems sport resolutions of 320 × 400 and up. |

| Element | Old X | New X |
|---|---|---|
| Client appearance | Low-resolution, high-contrast (to work with the display hardware) with minimal customizability. | Shading, gradients, and fine visual details take good advantage of hardware capabilities. Themes provide extensive opportunities for easy customization. |

# 1.4   X by Any Other Name

The X Window System goes by many different names, and sometimes this is a source of confusion. According to the manpage, X should be referenced using one of these names:

- X
- X Window System
- X Version 11
- X Window System, Version 11
- X11

Notice that "X Windows" is not on that list; this omission was originally due to concern about confusion with Microsoft's Windows product line.

This has been used as a shibboleth for many years; anyone referring to "X Windows" was considered an outsider or a beginner. Fortunately, this pedantry is waning, but you should probably avoid saying "X Windows" if you find yourself in the company of an industry old-timer.

The version number is almost never mentioned in modern usage, since the previous versions were experimental, and Version 11 has been in use for almost two decades (though the release number keeps going up).

The dominance of the X.org implementation has led a number of people to refer to X itself as *Xorg* or *X dot org*.

# 1.5   Seven Layers of an X-based GUI

It is Unix tradition to assemble solutions out of many small programs rather than to use a single, monolithic program. This approach gives more flexibility, since these smaller building blocks may be combined in different ways to meet different needs.

GUIs based on the X Window System follow this same philosophy—they're built in layers that can be mixed and matched as needed.

Figure 1-1 shows a simple model of the seven layers found in most X-based GUIs.

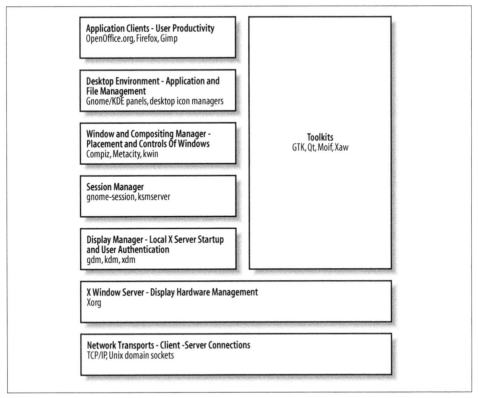

*Figure 1-1. The layers of an X-based GUI*

Elements at the top of the diagram are the most visible and important to the user, and the components at the bottom of the diagram are the least visible. From the bottom up, these layers are:

*Network Transport*

Enables the other layers to communicate. This layer almost always consists of TCP/IP plus a faster connection scheme for local clients (Section 1.14), but many older or proprietary network transports can be used, including IPX/SPX and DecNET.

*X Window Server*

Consists of the software that manages the display (which normally consists of a keyboard, video screen, and mouse) and runs on the computer connected to the display hardware. All of the layers above the X server are considered *clients* of that server and may be located anywhere on the local network, or even over the Internet.

*Display manager*

Enables a user to log in to the system graphically. Most display managers ask the user to type his user ID and password, but it's possible to use almost any authentication scheme, including biometric scanning.

*Session manager*

Tracks application state across login sessions, starting standard clients such as the window manager and desktop environment components, restarting applications that were active at the end of a previous session, and optionally restarting applications if they crash.

*Window and Compositing manager*

Manages window placement and provides *window decorations*. This includes window title bars, borders, and controls for common operations such as resizing, maximizing, minimizing, moving, and closing windows. When the COMPOSITE extension is available, the window manager also acts as the compositing manager. The X developers tried separating them, but in order to work really well, the compositing manager needs access to information about the windows that only a window manager knows. A window manager is considered to be a special class of client, and only one can be active on a display at a time.

*Desktop environment*

One or more programs that provide a desktop paradigm for the user. This may include menus to start programs, trays or panels to indicate currently running programs, icons that represent files or programs on the desktop background, docked applets, and other useful tools and utilities.

*Application clients*

Programs that enable the user to perform useful work. They are spreadsheets, word processors, web browsers, media players, video editors, and so forth.

*Toolkits*

Programming libraries that are used to simplify the task of writing clients that communicate with an X server. Toolkits are not a layer per se, but they do support and simplify the construction of the client layers.

The software used in any layer can be changed without affecting the other layers. For example, you can switch from the *XDM* display manager to the *GDM* display manager without making any changes to the other layers.

The bottom two layers (Network Transport and X Server) are mandatory; the other layers are optional. This provides a lot of flexibility in the way that the GUI operates.

For example, the user of an automated teller machine doesn't need to log in with a user ID, to move or resize windows, or to manage files and start programs, so the display manager, window manager, and desktop environment layers are not needed; the ATM application can directly take control of the entire display space.

---

Or, if X is started after the user logs in (Section 2.9), the user has already been authenticated, so the display manager is not needed and may be left out.

## 1.6    Where Is the Server?

In most network terminology, the *client system* is the one that is on your desktop, in your hand, or on your lap, and the *server* is the computer in the closet down the hall.

But in X terminology, the computer in front of you runs the server, and the client programs may be located on the computer in the closet.

As confusing as this may seem at first, it makes sense if you think in terms of the resource being served. A file server is located where the files are stored; a print server is located at the printer; and a display server is located at the display.

The specific resources managed by an X server include video cards and monitors, pointing devices (such as mice, trackpads, and touchscreens), and keyboards. These are each located at the physical machine running the X server.

## 1.7    Why Windows Look and Act Differently

The programs that access and use display resources are the clients. They may be on the same computer as the server, or they may be located down the hall, or they may be on the other side of the planet.

One of the early tenets of the X Window developers was that X should provide a mechanism for implementing a GUI, but should not impose any policy on how that GUI should operate. This has been both a blessing and a curse throughout the history of X.

Since X does not define policy, the look and feel of applications has been left up to application and toolkit developers, and there is a tremendous variation between programs. The advantage is freedom to experiment and innovate; the disadvantage is confusion for users.

On one of my systems, I have three different calculators available: *xcalc*, *kcalc*, and *gnome-calculator*, as shown in Figure 1-2.

As you can see from this screen dump, each calculator looks different: the fonts, colors, button sizes, menu options, icons, and status bar vary from program to program. They also use different visual effects when buttons are pressed.

Fortunately, the toolkit developers have assumed responsibility for many policy issues, and programs based on the same toolkit generally operate in a consistent way. Programs using different toolkits still behave differently, but the most popular toolkits have converged in their look and feel; notice the similarities between the 3D buttons and the fonts used by *kcalc* (center) and *gnome-calculator* (right).

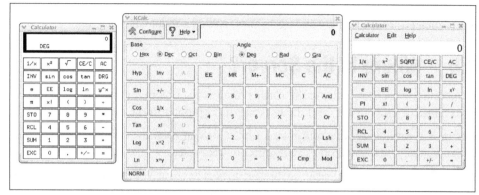

Figure 1-2. xcalc, kcalc, and gnome-calculator

One more thing to note in Figure 1-2: each window's title bar, border, and window controls are the same—because they are being drawn by the window manager, not the individual application programs.

# 1.8   Toolkits and Desktop Environments

There are three main toolkits currently in use, and desktop environments have been based upon each one:

| Toolkit | Original programming language | License | Open source | Desktops built with this toolkit |
|---|---|---|---|---|
| GTK+ | C | GPL | Yes | Gnome, Xfce |
| Qt | C++ | GPL | Yes | KDE |
| Motif/OpenMotif | C | Open Group Master Software License/Open Group Public License | No | CDE |

Most of these desktop environments are distributed with a display manager, window manager, and some application clients, but you can mix and match components from different environments. The use of one desktop environment does not prevent you from using applications built with another toolkit or distributed with another desktop environment, so you can use KDE along with GTK+ apps, or Xfce with Motif applications.

Almost all new development is now based on the GTK+ and Qt toolkits, primarily because they are open source (*http://opensource.org*) and therefore more accessible to developers.

However, Motif continues to be an important toolkit for legacy applications, especially in some financial and scientific niche markets. Motif and OpenMotif are essentially the same product, distributed under different licenses. While the Open Group Public License does permit OpenMotif to be freely distributed, this is for use only with open source operating systems such as FreeBSD or Linux, so the license does not meet the *Open Source Definition* (*http://opensource.org/docs/osd*) or the *Debian Free Software Guidelines* (DFSG, *http://www.debian.org/social_contract#guidelines*). Therefore, Motif is not included in most open source operating systems. The Open Group has stated that it intends to switch to a more open license, but it has been slow to do so; meanwhile, the LessTif project (*http://www.lesstif.org*) has reimplemented most of Motif's functionality under the GPL.

Motif is the last widely used toolkit based upon the *X Intrinsics Toolkit* (Xt), an object-oriented library written in C. In addition to Motif, there were *widget* (user-interface object) sets from the Athena project (Xaw), 3D versions of the Athena widgets (Xaw3d), Sun's OpenLook (Olit), Motif-OpenLook crossover widgets (Moolit), and others. All of these have fallen into disuse, but you may encounter them in older programs from time to time.

## 1.9   The Role of Freedesktop.org

There's more to a desktop than just a display—there's also sound, filesystem integration, on-the-fly hardware discovery, and much more. All of these bases must be covered in order to produce a desktop environment that can compete with commercial offerings such as Microsoft Windows or Mac OS X.

Recognizing this, developers have rallied around freedesktop.org, creating an informal consensus-building forum for desktop-oriented technologies. Freedesktop.org (the web site address is the same as the project's name) hosts much of the work of the revitalized X.org project, coordinates standards between Gnome and KDE, and supports the development of complimentary technologies such as D-BUS and HAL.

freedesktop.org's lightweight organization and focus on collaboration have made it the centerpiece for most desktop-oriented open source software development.

## 1.10   Display Hardware

Let's take a look at the hardware typically managed by an X server. It generally has the following components:

- Zero or more pointing devices (mice, trackballs, touchscreens).
- Zero or more keyboards.
- One or more video cards, each connected to one or more monitors.

The entire collection of hardware is called a *display* and is managed as a single unit, intended to be used by one person. It is possible to have multiple displays connected to one computer, but a separate X server needs to be run for each display.

# Pointing Devices

Pointing devices fall into two general categories: *relative* and *absolute*:

*Relative pointing devices*
> These send only movement information to the display. A new pointer position is calculated by taking the previous pointer position and updating it with the indicated movement. Mice, trackpads, and trackballs fall into this category.

*Absolute pointing devices*
> These send an exact screen position to the display. Touchscreens, graphics tablets, and light pens are all absolute devices.

It is possible to have multiple pointing devices connected to one display. This is common on laptops; some have two built-in pointing devices, and some users add a traditional mouse to compliment a built-in pointing device. The devices act in parallel, and any can be used to move the pointer on the screen (Section 4.8).

A display is rarely configured without a pointing device, but this may be done for an information-only display that does not permit user interaction.

Pointing devices are connected to the computer using a USB, PS/2, serial, or bluetooth connection. The data rate is very low, so USB pointing devices always run at low speed (1.5 Mbps) even when they are certified to USB 2.0 standards. PS/2 and serial interfaces are electrically identical but have different connectors; you can buy adapters to convert one to the other.

A few years ago, there were dozens of communication protocols used by mice. Fortunately, almost all mice now use an extended version of the PS/2 mouse protocol, regardless of how they are connected, though graphics tablets, touch screens, and the other more exotic pointing devices still use unique protocols.

By far the most popular pointing technology is now the optical mouse. Invented by Agilent (formerly HP), an optical mouse contains a simple high-speed monochrome video camera, a *Digital Signal Processor* (DSP), and interface electronics, all on a single chip. The video camera acquires images of the desk or mousepad at the minimum rate of 1,500 frames per second, and the DSP compares each frame with the previous frame to detect movement. When movement is detected, it is communicated with the host computer through the interface electronics, which may be serial- or radio-frequency-based (RF). Buttons and a rotary encoder for the scrollwheel round out the unit. Although optical mice outperform mechanical mice in most environments, they require a slightly textured or speckled surface to work well (hence, the sudden popularity of speckled and woodgrain patterns on office furniture instead of the solid colors popular a few years ago). I've found that they may be sensitive to bright light at a low angle (such as sunlight at sunrise or sunset), which may cause them to skip or temporarily stop functioning.

The memory and raw processing capability of many modern optical mice exceeds that of the first computer used to run Unix!

## Keyboards

Like mice, keyboards are sometimes used in parallel. This is most common on laptops, where an add-on numeric keypad may be used along with the built-in keyboard, or a larger external keyboard is used in preference to the internal one.

Keyboards typically have PS/2 or USB connectors; USB versions always operate at low speed (1.5 Mbps). The keyboard sends a *scancode* corresponding to a button location when that button is pressed, and sends another code when that button is released. This permits the system to detect how long buttons are held down and in what combination.

In order to convert these scancodes into characters, the system needs to know which symbol is associated with which key. This is done through a keyboard map. Since most English North American keyboards have a standard layout, one standard keyboard map usually suffices; but outside of English North America, additional symbols will appear, either supplementing or replacing the English North American symbols. For example, a U.K. keyboard layout will include symbols for the Euro and pound.

The layout of the basic roman letter symbols will also vary; in North America, the top row starts with QWERTY; in Germany, it often starts QWERTZ; and in France, AZERTY. Nonroman alphabets obviously have their own distinctive layouts as well, but typically provide some way to type roman letters for email addresses, URIs, and code.

Some languages use large numbers of accented characters. Keyboards set up for these languages often use *dead keys,* which don't actually type a character, but which cause the following character to be accented. This handling is performed by the system and not by the processor in the actual keyboard, so the operation of dead keys can be reconfigured as needed. A *compose key* is a special type of dead key that builds a character based on two subsequent keypresses. So, the user might press **compose, /, c** to produce the cent symbol (¢) or **compose, c, comma** to produce the letter c with a cedilla (ç).

The most complex keyboard input methods are required for Asian languages, which have very large alphabets of *ideographs* (idea-pictures). Input methods for Asian languages typically involve entering several keystrokes to phonetically or structurally describe the desired character; if this does not narrow down the selection to a single glyph, then the final selection is performed graphically. Although these input methods require multiple keystrokes per character, each character conveys more meaning, so the average typing speed can be similar to that attained in languages with smaller alphabets.

Most keyboards contain a simple microprocessor and a serial or USB interface, and have three LEDs to indicate keyboard status.

# Monitors

All video systems work by scanning dots (or *pixels*—picture elements) from left to right, top to bottom on the display. For each pixel on a color display, three pieces of information are sent: the individual brightness levels for the red, green, and blue (RGB) components of that dot. The monitor combines the appropriate amount of red, green, and blue light to form the specified color on the screen. Additional signals are used to synchronize the horizontal and vertical scanning so that pixels are drawn in the correct position.

### Cathode ray tube (CRT)

CRT monitors draw pixels by shooting electron beams at colored phosphor dots coated onto the inside of the front glass panel, which then glow. It takes a significant amount of energy to create the electron beams, and X-rays are produced as a side effect. In order to shield the user from these X-rays, a significant amount of lead is embedded into the glass of the CRT. Large electromagnets are used to bend the electron beams as the display is scanned.

CRTs are a proven, reliable, and inexpensive technology, and they present a clear image over a wide range of viewing angles. However, their large size, the use of lead in their construction, their high energy usage, and concern over X-ray and electromagnetic radiation has caused many people to consider alternatives.

### Liquid crystal display (LCD)

LCDs use light-gates made out of tiny liquid cells adjacent to a polarizing filter. By applying an electric current to the liquid, it can be polarized, allowing more or less light to flow through the light gate. Each pixel is made up of three liquid crystal cells, each with a colored filter—one each for red, green, and blue. Fluorescent lights or white LEDs placed behind the LCD panel provide illumination.

LCDs use less power and space than CRTs, but have a narrower range of acceptable viewing angles, may wash out in bright light, and typically have a less durable front surface than CRTs. Some graphic artists prefer CRTs, claiming that they reproduce a wider range of colors with greater accuracy.

To display images of different resolutions on a CRT, the width of the electron beams is changed, making the pixels larger or smaller. On an LCD, each pixel has a defined location and size, so using a resolution other than the "native" resolution of the display requires some hardware pixels to show a blended color representing a portion of two or more pixels from the image. This results in an undesirable blurring, softening, or blocky presentation of the image, so it is always best to run an LCD at its native resolution.

## Other flat-panel technologies

Other flat-panel technologies available include:

*Plasma displays*
> These use charged gases to produce an image that is bright and that can be very large, but that has a high power consumption and whose brightness diminishes over time, so this type of display's market share is diminishing as large-format LCD manufacturing becomes feasible.

*Organic Light-Emitting Diode (OLED) displays*
> These are "printed" onto a flexible substrate. They are currently used on some cell phones and portable music players and hold promise for large, inexpensive display panels once manufacturing issues are refined.

*Electronic paper (or electronic ink) technology displays*
> These use thousands of tiny cells that can be placed in a particular color state and then stay in that state until changed. There are several different approaches to cell construction, but all electronic paper displays are reflective and use ambient light to illuminate the display. This results in a familiar experience for the user and offers very low power consumption for displays that rarely change. Electronic paper displays are used on some cell phones and e-book readers, and may eventually be used for certain types of monitors, signs, and even billboards.

## Video projectors

A video projector can also be considered a type of monitor. Projectors either use LCD technology or thousands of tiny mirrors mounted directly on a *Digital Light Processor* (DLP) chip. This is coupled with a high-power light, projection lenses, a cooling system, and control electronics.

The control electronics in video projectors are usually more sophisticated than the circuits found in CRT or LCD monitors:

- Images can be flipped left to right (for rear-projection applications) or top to bottom (for upside-down ceiling mounts).

- Keystone correction permits the sides of the image to be slanted (and the top of the image to be made smaller than the bottom, or vice versa) so that the image will appear rectangular when projected onto the screen at an angle.

- Image scaling and multiple video inputs enable a clear picture to be projected despite huge variations in the resolution, quality, and speed of the incoming signals.

## Video timing

When dealing with video signals, timing is everything. In order to display a stable picture and accurately locate each dot during the scanning process, the timing of the video signal must be very precise.

The speed of the video signal is dictated by the screen resolution and refresh (scan) rate. Resolution is defined in terms of horizontal and vertical pixels; scan rate is expressed in *Hertz* (Hz), or cycles per second. A scan rate of 70 Hz or higher is recommended for CRTs in order to reduce eyestrain for the user; the refresh rate is not as important for most LCD displays, because the decay time (the time it takes a pixel to change color) is longer.

The length of cable that may be used to connect a video monitor to a video card is directly limited by the scan rate. A cable stores a small amount of energy between conductors; this quality is called capacitance, and it limits the cable's ability to handle fast signals. The longer the cable, or the poorer the insulator, the more energy is stored. This restricts the maximum refresh rate that can be used without noticeable image degradation.

## Monitor connections

Monitors connect to a video card using one of these standard connection schemes:

*Television*

All of the color, luminosity (brightness), and synchronization information is encoded into a single *composite* analog electrical signal. This type of signal is most useful for connecting to consumer video equipment such as a VCR or television; the standard connector is a coaxial "RCA" plug.

One variation on a television video signal is S-Video, which separates the luminance and chroma (color) information onto separate wires; many video cards that have a "TV Out" feature use this type of connector. In Europe, a rectangular SCART connector is standard and may include a composite signal.

*VGA*

An analog connection scheme that uses varying voltages on three separate pins to control the RGB levels. Additional pins are used for synchronization and device probing. The most common physical connector for VGA signals is an *HD15*—a high density, 15-pin mini D-shaped connector. "VGA" comes from *video graphics array*, which is the name of the original IBM graphics card that used this connector.

*Digital Visual Interface (DVI)*

A modern connector that supports analog signals, digital signals, or both. DVI-D includes digital signals only; DVI-I includes both; and the unofficial DVI-A connector includes analog only.

DVI-I and DVI-A can be connected to VGA equipment through a simple adapter. Where possible, though, the digital signal should be used for greater accuracy and clarity.

DVI-D supports dual-channel connections for high-resolution displays (above 1.25 megapixels) and may use *high-bandwidth digital content protection* (HDCP) signal encryption.

*High Definition Multimedia Interface (HDMI)*

HDMI provides an easy-to-use single connector that incorporates a DVI-D compatible digital video signal and digital audio. It is common on high-definition television equipment and monitors, but so far is not used often on computers. HDCP may be used with HDMI. There are two connectors in use: Type A, which supports single-channel connections, and Type B, which has additional conductors to carry a dual-channel signal.

*DisplayPort*

An alternative to HDMI that provides a similar pure-digital audio and video signal with optional HDCP encryption. While HDMI was intended as a consumer specification for entertainment devices, DisplayPort initially targets computer systems. The *Video Electronics Standard Association* (VESA) backs the DisplayPort standard and has established compliance testing programs for it, which will ensure interoperability of DisplayPort devices. Offering support for color depths beyond 24 bits per pixel (16 million colors) and the potential of an easy future upgrade to fiber optic connection, DisplayPort is a strong specification. But, it is late to market, and it may be difficult to unseat entrenched standards such as HDMI.

## Video Cards

The circuitry that drives the monitor is contained on a video card or integrated into the system motherboard.

There are four main components in a video card, as illustrated in Figure 1-3:

*Memory*

An area of memory set aside to keep track of the image on the screen (the *framebuffer*) and other video-related data such as pixmaps, save-unders, and images that will be composed into the framebuffer by the GPU.

Historically, successive generations of video cards have swung back and forth between using a reserved area of main system memory for the framebuffer and using a completely separate bank of physical memory. Any memory over and above the memory used for the framebuffer may be used for fonts, off-screen rendering, save-unders (remembering what is underneath windows), and texture maps.

*Graphics processing unit (GPU)*

Performs graphics operations such as block moves, line drawing, area fills, shading, and texture mapping independently from the system's CPU. Most modern GPUs handle 3D operations, although some of the lower-end devices (typically built into motherboards) have very weak 3D performance.

*Bus interface*

Connects the host system bus to the memory and GPU. *PCI Express* (PCI-E) is the preferred connection path on most new systems; an *accelerated graphics port* (AGP) or legacy PCI interface may also be used.

*Video controller*

Generates the video signal by repeatedly scanning the framebuffer and converting the pixel information into the format required at the video connector. If an analog connection is used, multiple *digital-to-analog converters* (DACs) are incorporated to convert the digital brightness values into varying voltages; the DACs speed often limits the maximum refresh rate available at a given resolution. Some graphics systems with DVI, HDMI, or DisplayPort connectors incorporate encryption chips between the video controller and the video connector.

*Signal encryption*

This optional circuit encrypts the signal for content protection using HDCP or a competing protocol.

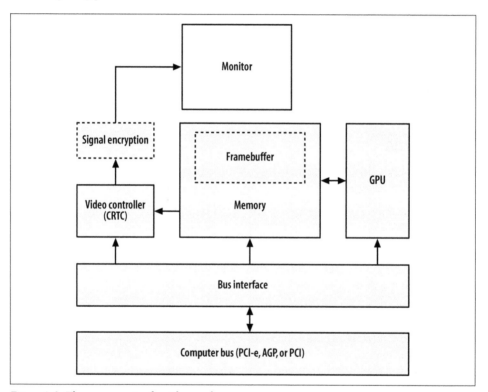

*Figure 1-3. The components of a video card*

The screen image can be represented in the framebuffer in one of two ways:

- The RGB information for each pixel can be stored in successive memory locations. On modern video cards, 8 bits (1 byte) of informaton is stored for each RGB channel, resulting in a total of 24 bits (3 bytes) of memory used for each pixel. This permits $2^{24} = 16$ million colors to be used simultaneously on the display. It is also fairly common to use 8, 15, or 16 bits per pixel, and less common (on specialized cinema-oriented hardware) to use 12 or 16 bits per RGB channel for a total of 36 to 48 bits per pixel.

- A color code for each pixel can be stored. This results in a "paint-by-number" scheme, where the video controller looks up each color code in a *palette* or lookup table to determine the RGB value. For example, the color code 3, when stored in the memory location for a given pixel, would instruct the video controller to look up entry number 3 in the palette and use whatever color is stored there.

Palette-based color is rarely used on modern PCs, but is common on smaller devices such as PDAs and cell phones. It may seem absurd to talk about PDAs and phones in a book about X, but they now have sufficient computing power to viably run an X server!

The size of a framebuffer in bytes is:

```
WidthInPixels * HeightInPixels * BytesPerPixel
```

Therefore, a $1280 \times 1024$ display with 3 bytes (24 bits) per pixel of color information would take:

```
1280 x 1024 x 3 = 3932160 bytes = 3.75 MB
```

Note that since most modern CPUs deal with memory in 32-bit words, many 24-bit video modes actually devote 32 bits to each pixel to simplify manipulation of the data. This wastes 8 bits per pixel, but the resulting increase in speed makes it worthwhile. If the video card in the preceding example used 32 bits per pixel, the memory required would be 5 MB.

# 1.11 Displays, Screens, and Xinerama

In X terminology, a *display* comprises the user interface for one person. That usually means one keyboard, pointer, video card, and monitor, but for some applications, more video "real estate" is required. Thus, a display can have multiple video cards and monitors, perhaps with different capabilities and resolutions—but this is where the terminology gets tricky.

All of a display's video cards and monitors can be combined to act like one giant video monitor. This approach is called *Xinerama* (Section 4.9) as a tribute to the old Cinerama multiprojector wide-screen movie format. Xinerama permits windows to span monitors and works especially well on multipanel LCD displays, video walls, or video projectors.

Alternately, a display's video cards and monitors may be configured as separate *screens*. Each screen is individually addressable, so windows can be directed to display on a specific screen. It is not possible to move windows between screens nor to have windows span screens, but the mouse pointer can be moved between screens. The use of screens predates Xinerama, but it is still useful for some dual-monitor applications, such as presentations where one monitor is used for control and setup and the second monitor displays live output to the audience. By using a two-screen configuration instead of Xinerama, windows from the control screen will be prevented from straying onto the publicly-visible display.

Some window managers, such as the LessTif version of the Motif Window Manager *MWM*, are not capable of managing multiple screens and will only register themselves as the window manager for one screen. On the other hand, some toolkits are not aware of Xinerama, so dialogs that are intended to be positioned in the center of a display always display in the middle of the Xinerama display—and therefore always span across monitors in a dual-monitor Xinerama configuration (which is very, very annoying).

Each display (regardless of the number of screens involved) is managed by exactly one X server process.

## 1.12  Display Specifications

Since X clients can connect to a display anywhere on the network, it is necessary to have some way of specifying the display to be used. This is done using a *display specification* (or *displayspec*).

A displayspec takes this form:

```
host:display[.screen]
```

The following list describes each element in a displayspec:

*host*
> The name or network address of the system running the X server. This may be:
> - A DNS hostname or IP address
> - Blank, or the word `unix`, indicating a local host connection (Section 1.14)
> - A DecNET, IPX/SPX, or other machine designation (extremely rare)

*display*
> The display number, greater than or equal to zero

*screen*
> An optional screen number within the display; screens are numbered starting at zero

Here are some examples:

*:0*
> Display 0 on the local computer, connected by a local connection scheme

*localhost:3*
> Display 3 on the local computer, connected by TCP/IP

*stealth.oreilly.net:2*
> Display 2 on the TCP/IP host *stealth.oreilly.net*

*172.250.12.7:4.3*
   Display 4, screen 3 on the host with IPv4 address 172.250.12.7

The displayspec can be passed to clients as an option value:

```
$ xclock -display displayspec
```

However, it is more common and convenient to use the DISPLAY environment variable. If you are using a shell that follows the Bourne syntax (sh, bash, ksh, zsh, or ash), you can set and export the DISPLAY variable like this:

```
$ export DISPLAY=displayspec
```

If you are a csh aficionado, use:

```
% setenv DISPLAY displayspec
```

Once the DISPLAY variable has been set, any new clients started will connect to the specified display by default. (Command-line options take precedence over the DISPLAY variable.)

# 1.13  TCP/IP Ports

Each X display uses a unique TCP/IP port so that multiple servers on the same system do not conflict. All of the screens managed by one display are accessed through the same port; screen selection is accomplished through the X protocol.

The standard port for an X server is *6000+display*, so display :0 uses port 6000, and display :15 uses port 6015. Since these port numbers are over 1024, the kernel permits anyone to open them—so you don't need to be root to run an X server. Large display numbers may conflict with other services (such as IRC at port 6667), so it is best to keep display numbers under 100.

# 1.14  Local Connection Mechanisms

TCP/IP is a great network transport, but it's overkill for connecting programs running on the same computer. Most X servers provide a faster alternative for local connections.

Unfortunately, there are at least five different local connection schemes in use, including Unix domain sockets, named pipes, and various types of Streams pipes. Open source operating systems use Unix domain sockets without exception.

A displayspec with a blank host field will automatically select the default local connection scheme; if the default isn't a Unix domain socket, then some systems permit a host value of unix to force a domain socket to be used.

Unix domain sockets for the X server are created in */tmp/.X11-unix* and are named according to the display number (therefore, */tmp/.X11-unix/X0* is the Unix domain socket for local display :0).

After a local connection has been established, the client and server can negotiate the use of shared memory for faster communication of large blocks of data; this requires the MIT SHM extension.

Binaries compiled for one platform but executed on another may not interpret a blank hostname field in the displayspec correctly. For example, binaries compiled for SCO Unix may default to a Streams mechanism. When running under Linux using the iBCS compatibility layer, this will cause a problem, because Linux doesn't support Streams. In this case, a hostname value of unix should force the use of Unix domain sockets; as a last resort, the TCP/IP local loopback mechanism can be used by specifying a hostname of localhost (however, this incurs the extra overhead of the TCP/IP stack—twice).

## 1.15  Server Extensions

The X11 protocol was designed to be enhanced by adding *extensions* to the X server. Clients can query the server to find out what extensions are available. This has enabled many features to be added through the years without significant changes to the core protocol (which explains why we're still using version 11!).

Extensions may be compiled in to the X server, or they may be loaded as modules. Because their presence is optional, the X server can be slimmed down for use on small machines by building it with a smaller set of extensions.

Here are some of the key extensions in widespread use (upper- and lowercase names are those reported by the extensions themselves using xdpyinfo (Section 6.2):

*MIT-BIG-REQUESTS*
> Permits client requests over 256 Kb, necessary to draw complex images.

*MIT-SHM*
> Offers shared memory for local communication of images.

*Composite*
> Enables off-screen rendering of windows, which are then combined (composited) into the final screen image by hardware under control of a compositing manager. This is usually integrated into the window manager. During composition, images can be distorted, blended, and resized, so the extension provides an easy way to add drop shadows, window transparency, icons, and thumbnails that are "live," smooth window resizing, and many other 2D and 3D visual effects.

*DAMAGE*
> Informs a client when one part of the display has been updated. Reduces unnecessary drawing and improves the efficiency of applications such as VNC (Section 14.1).

*DPMS*

> *Displays Power Management Signalling*. Enables the X server to reduce monitor power consumption when not in use (Section 3.11).

*GLX*

> *OpenGL extension for X11*. Enables clients to send OpenGL 3D commands to the X server, which then passes them on to 3D video hardware (or performs the 3D operations in software if necessary—which is very slow!).

*LBX*

> *Low-Bandwidth X*. Used with lbxproxy to reduce bandwidth requirements and latency for remote clients (Section 13.11).

*MIT-SCREEN-SAVER*

> The eye-candy extension! MIT-SCREEN-SAVER informs screensavers when to start and stop (Section 14.3).

*RANDR*

> Stands for rotate and resize. Notifies clients when the display is resized to a new resolution or rotated (useful on tablet PCs and LCDs on pivot mounts) and enables the hot-plugging of monitors (Section 5.2).

*RECORD*

> Permits X events to be recorded for later analysis or playback. Used to automate application testing and provide macro facilities.

*RENDER*

> Provides a digital image composition model. Render simplifies tasks such as alpha blending (combining partially transparent images) and high-quality anti-aliased text display (Section 11.1).

*SECURITY*

> Divides clients into two categories—*trusted* and *untrusted*—and prevents untrusted clients from accessing data held for trusted clients. Properly used, this can reduce the risk of compromise due to actions such as keystroke logging (to steal passwords) or remote screen dumping (to view sensitive information displayed on the screen). ssh now supports this extension (Section 13.10).

*SHAPE*

> Enables nonrectangular windows. The xeyes and oclock clients provide a good demonstration of this capability.

*SYNC*

> Makes it possible to synchronize the X display with external events—for example, keeping a movie soundtrack synchronized with the picture.

*XInputExtension*

> Provides support for specialized input devices such as graphics tablets, dial boxes/control surfaces, and 3D trackballs.

*XKEYBOARD*
Enables complex keyboard mapping and configuration (Section 12.1).

*XTEST*
Extends the X protocol to simplify performance benchmarking.

*XINERAMA*
Single-screen, multimonitor support (Sections 1.11 and 4.2).

*XVideo*
Enables video streams, such as those from a video camera or TV tuner card, to be converted, transformed, and then overlaid on the X display. This is done with hardware support and can dramatically improve video performance (Section 4.1).

*XVideo-MotionCompensation*
Utilizes hardware support for video decompression—useful for DVD viewing and other MPEG video playback.

# 1.16 Where to Draw the Line: Kernel Versus User-Space Drivers

The operating system kernel is usually responsible for managing all of the system hardware, and normal user-space programs access hardware only through the OS. This clear-cut distinction between the kernel and user-space programs has been very difficult to maintain when implementing X servers.

The problem is that video cards vary enormously in terms of their GPU capabilities and general architecture. It's hard to create a simple, well-defined interface between a video driver in the kernel and an X server in user-space that will work well for all video cards, though several attempts have been made. And of course the X server is too large and complex to safely place it directly into the kernel.

As it stands now, most kernel/X server combinations—including Linux with the X.org server—pretty much give the X server free reign when it comes to video card access, though some of the card drivers (such as the NVIDIA closed-source driver) use a small kernel module to assist them.

This will likely change in the future. The X server may eventually operate as one (of perhaps many) OpenGL clients, removing direct hardware access from the X server entirely. The Xgl server provides a preliminary implementation of this approach.

# 2

# Starting a Local X Server

## 2.1  One Size Doesn't Fit All

An X server can be started in different ways to suit different types of use. In this chapter, we'll examine the techniques available for starting X and discuss the best approach for some common scenarios, including:

- Presenting a graphical login display (Section 2.4)
- Configuring a home system with two graphical login displays, so that two people can alternately use it without disturbing each others' work (Section 2.7)
- Starting X on a server system only when it is really needed, in order to conserve system resources for more important uses (Section 2.9)
- Starting an X server that is displayed within another X server (Section 2.11)

We'll also take a look at how to use Virtual Terminals (Sections 2.2 and 2.10), how to simulate a mouse when a bad configuration leaves you without one (Section 2.12), and how to terminate X (Sections 2.13 and 2.14).

## 2.2  Virtual Terminals

Linux, FreeBSD, and many other modern Unix kernels support a *virtual terminal* (VT) (or *virtual console*) capability, which provides independent virtual video cards. The monitor, keyboard, mouse, and physical video card are associated with only one VT at a time, and each virtual video card can be in a different display mode—some may be in character mode while others are in graphical mode. This enables multiple X servers and nongraphical sessions to be active at the same time.

To switch virtual terminals on Linux, press Ctrl-Alt-F*x* (where F*x* is a function key from F1 through F12, corresponding to a virtual terminal from VT1 to VT12; you can also use Alt-F*x* if the current VT is in character mode). When you are connected to a virtual terminal that isn't running an X server, you can use Alt-LeftArrow to go to the previous VT and use Alt-RightArrow to switch to the next VT. Some Linux distributions also configure the Windows key to advance to the next VT; you can also switch virtual terminals using the *switchto* or *chvt* commands (Section 2.10).

By default, most Linux distributions boot up with six nongraphical logins on VT1–VT6 and one X server running on VT7.

FreeBSD provides a very similar VT capability, except that the VTs are numbered starting at zero, and the key combination to switch VTs when in character mode is Alt-F*x*. Virtual terminals are numbered one off from Alt keys, because there is no F0 key. Therefore, if you're on VT3 in character mode and press Alt-F1, the kernel will take you to VT0.

System V Release 4.*x* systems such as UnixWare use Alt-SysReq followed by F*x* to switch virtual terminals.

Although most kernels support more than 12 virtual terminals, this capability is rarely used because you can't usually use the keyboard to go directly to higher-numbered VTs.

# 2.3   Starting a Raw X Server Manually

The simplest way to start an X server is also the least-used technique: simply type the name of the server at a shell prompt:

```
$ X
```

Most Unix command and program names are lowercase, but the X server is an exception. You must enter "X" as a capital letter.

X is actually a symbolic link to the installed server binary, which is named *Xorg* if you're using the X.org server, *XFree86* if you're using the XFree86 server, and so on.

If an X server is already running on display :0, you will get an error message, because the network port will already be in use. In that case, you can give the new X server a different display number:

```
$ X :1
```

By default, the X server will start on the first unused VT (usually VT8). You can request a specific VT by specifying it on the command line:

```
$ X :1 vt10
```

You can also specify that a particular configuration file should be used, or a particular ServerLayout within a configuration file:

```
$ X :1 -config configFile
$ X :1 -layout layoutName
```

The downside to starting the X server this way is that no clients are started. Until you start some manually, you'll be left staring at a blank screen with only a mouse pointer to amuse yourself.

You can start the X server and a client at the same time like this:

```
$ X :1 -terminate  &  sleep 2 ; DISPLAY=:1 xterm
```

The -terminate option will cause the X server to exit when the last client disconnects, and the sleep 2 option ensures that the X server has time to start before the *xterm* client attempts to connect to it—not usually required, but it's good practice to ensure that your commands will work reliably. Note that this command line does not start a window manager or a desktop environment, so you will not be able to move or resize the *xterm* window, start additional programs (except by typing in the terminal), or set the keyboard focus.

The advantage of starting X directly is that you have precise control over the X server startup options and the list of clients displayed, which is perfect for a kiosk.

# 2.4   Using a Display Manager to Start the X Server

One of the possible layers of an X-based GUI is a display manager, which is the graphical equivalent of the login program. It is usually configured to start one or more local X servers to present a greeter dialog that collects the user's name and password. Once the user is authenticated, the display manager starts some preconfigured clients—typically a session manager that goes on to start a window manager and desktop environment such as KDE or GNOME. Many display managers let you select a session type, which will in turn activate a specific desktop environment. When the user exits the client(s), the process starts over again.

Three display managers are in common use. The biggest difference between them is the toolkit upon which they are built:

- GDM: GNOME Display Manager (built on GTK)
- KDM: KDE Display Manager (Qt)
- XDM: X Display Manager (Xt)

KDM and GDM offer some advanced features not present in the older XDM program, such as a picture-based face browser and the ability to select the desktop environment that will be loaded once the user authenticates.

You may be able to recognize the display manager used on your system by its appearance, since each toolkit has a distinctive look. Alternately, you can search the process table to see what's running, using the following:

```
$ ps -e | grep '[gkx]dm'
```

If you prefer BSD-style arguments, or if your version of ps permits these arguments only, use ps ax in place of ps -e.

## 2.5   Enabling or Disabling the Display Manager at Boot Time

Many commercial Unix systems and Linux distributions borrow a boot technique pioneered in Unix System V: the use of *runlevels* to start and stop software sets.

Table 2-1 lists the standard runlevels.

*Table 2-1. The standard runlevels observed by most System V Unix variants and Linux*

| Runlevel | Description |
| --- | --- |
| 0 | Halt |
| s, S | Single-user mode: no per-runlevel scripts executed; */etc/inittab* not required (emergency use only) |
| 1 | Single-user maintenance mode |
| 2 | Multiuser, nonnetworked mode (the default runlevel for Debian-based systems, including Ubuntu, but rarely used on other systems) |
| 3 | Multiuser, networked mode |
| 4 | Unused |
| 5 | Multiuser, networked mode with local graphical login |
| 6 | Reboot |
| 7, 8, 9, a, b, c | Unused |

Runlevel s or S is a special case: it's used internally by *init* and normally shouldn't be entered directly by the user, who can enter runlevel 1 for single-user mode instead. But it has a special quality: it's the only runlevel that does not require */etc/inittab* and is therefore useful in emergency recovery situations.

When you boot a Linux or Unix system into runlevel 5 (the default for most distributions except Debian/Ubuntu when an X Window server is installed), the display manager will start automatically. To prevent this, you can boot your system into runlevel 3 by editing the kernel boot parameters, either temporarily or permanently.

To temporarily change the boot into a different runlevel if you are using the *grub* bootloader, take the following steps:

1. At the start of the system boot process, access the boot menu (you may or may not need to press a key to do this—watch the screen prompts closely), highlight the menu entry you wish to use, and press A (to append kernel arguments).

2. You will be taken into an editor mode that lets you adjust the kernel boot arguments. Add the number 3 at the end of the argument line and press Enter to boot.

 If you are using a system that uses Xen virtualization, the kernel entry specifies the hypervisor instead of the Linux kernel. To edit the kernel boot parameters, press E (for *Edit*) at the main grub menu, which will display the details of your boot configuration. Select the module line that specifies the kernel file and press E. Add the desired runlevel (3) at the end of this line and press Enter to save your change, then press B to boot.

Or, if you are using the LILO bootloader:

1. At the start of the system boot process, access the LILO: prompt, then type the name of the boot configuration you wish to use (the Tab key will display the list of possibilities) and append the number 3 at the end (for example, linux 3).

2. Press Enter to boot.

You can change the runlevel of system *after* it has been booted by executing the *init* or *telinit* command with the desired runlevel:

```
$ init 3
```

To return to the graphical login state, switch to runlevel 5:

```
$ init 5
```

Permanently changing the default runlevel requires editing */etc/initab*. The runlevel is controlled by this line:

```
id:5:initdefault:
```

Change the second field to 3 to disable the automatic start-up of the display manager:

```
id:3:initdefault:
```

When you boot into any runlevel that does not start X automatically, you can start the display manager manually by typing the command name at a root shell prompt:

```
# gdm
```

 By default, Debian-based systems (including Ubuntu) start the display manager in all runlevels. You can easily disable the startup of the display manager in runlevel 3 by executing these commands:

```
# update-rc.d -f gdm remove
# update-rc.d gdm start 31 2 4 5 . stop 31 1 3 .
```

# 2.6   What Started the Display Manager?

Depending on your system configuration, the display manager may be started directly by *init*, or through an *init* script. It's useful to know how the display manager starts so that you can make changes and so that you know what will happen if the display manager exits (or crashes!).

## Started Directly by init

In some Linux distributions, the display manager is directly started by *init*. For example, in Fedora's */etc/inittab,* you will find this entry:

```
# Run xdm in runlevel 5
x:5:respawn:/etc/X11/prefdm -nodaemon
```

In the second line, the second field specifies that this command is executed only in runlevel 5, and the third field directs that it is to be respawned (executed again) if it exits.

The script */etc/X11/prefdm* will execute */usr/sbin/autologin* to automatically log in one user if that feature has been set up. Otherwise, it will start one of the display managers (GDM, KDM, or XDM) depending on the specification in */etc/sysconfig/desktop.* If that file does not exist, then the first display manager found in alphabetical order will be used.

Since *init* has been set up to respawn the display manager automatically, it is relatively easy to load and test changes to the display manager configuration file—just kill the display manager! If you're using XDM or KDM, you can kill the display manager by name:

```
# killall xdm
```

 Killing the display manager will also kill all the display manager's child processes, including X servers—so if you do this through the graphical interface, expect your session to disappear!

GDM is a wrapper script for *gdm-binary,* so if your system uses GDM, you'd have to kill the display manager with the following:

```
# killall gdm-binary
```

Alternately, you can restart GDM immediately using its restart script:

```
# gdm-restart
```

Or you can specify that a restart should take place as soon as everyone is logged out:

```
# gdm-safe-restart
```

In FreeBSD, the display manager is started by *init* but the configuration information is in */etc/ttys* instead of */etc/inittab*:

```
ttyv8  "/usr/sbin/xdm -nodaemon" xterm  on  secure
```

The fourth field can have a value of on or off to enable or disable the display manager.

## Started by an init Script

Some Linux distributions use startup scripts to execute the display manager. For example, on a SUSE system, the display manager is started by */etc/rc.d/rc5.d/S17xdm* (which is a symbolic link to */etc/rc.d/xdm*).

Similar to the *prefdm* script used by Fedora, this script finds your preferred display manager using a configuration file—in this case, */etc/sysconfig/displaymanager*—or it uses XDM if that file is missing.

Since this is a regular *init* script, it is executed only once at startup; when the display manager terminates, it will not be restarted. After editing the display manager configuration file, you can reinvoke the XDM *init* script using the restart option to put your changes into effect:

```
# /etc/X11/xdm restart
```

Or you can use the SUSE shortcut:

```
# rcxdm restart
```

# 2.7   Starting Multiple X Servers Using a Display Manager

On a home computer, it can be useful to configure the display manager to start two or more X servers. You can then flip between them using the virtual terminal mechanism (Section 2.2).

A few years ago, I used this configuration on my home computer, so that when I wasn't using it, other members of my family could change VTs and log in without disturbing my work. When they finished, I would just switch back to my VT and continue where I left off. (Now I've extended this configuration by adding additional video cards, keyboards, mice, and monitors so we can log in simultaneously.)

## Starting Multiple X Servers Using XDM (or Early Versions of KDM)

XDM and older versions of KDM (pre-3.4) use the *Xservers* file to configure the number of servers started by the display manager. The location of this file varies; try */etc/X11/xdm/Xservers* or */opt/kde3/share/config/kdm/Xservers*.

This is a fairly standard *Xservers* file:

```
# $Xorg: Xserv.ws.cpp,v 1.3 2000/08/17 19:54:17 cpqbld Exp $
#
# Xservers file, workstation prototype
#
# This file should contain an entry to start the server on the
# local display; if you have more than one display (not screen),
# you can add entries to the list (one per line). If you also
# have some X terminals connected that do not support XDMCP,
# you can add them here as well. Each X terminal line should
# look like:
#        XTerminalName:0 foreign
#
:0 local /usr/bin/X
```

Lines that start with # are comments. The active line, at the bottom, specifies that display 0 is a local X server, and gives the command line to be used to start that X server.

To start additional X servers, simply add lines at the bottom of this file:

```
:1 local /usr/bin/X :1 vt8
:2 local /usr/bin/X :2 vt9
```

Although it's not strictly necessary to specify the VT on these lines, it's a good idea, because then you will confidently know which display is paired with which VT.

If you wish to specify a different configuration file for one of the X servers, you can add a -config argument to the command:

```
:3 local /usr/bin/X -config configgile :3 vt10
```

This must all appear on a single line in the configuration file.

## Starting Multiple X Servers Using KDM

If you're using KDE 3.4 or higher, the local X server configuration is controlled by the *kdmrc* file (*/etc/X11/xdm/kdmrc* or */opt/kde3/share/config/kdm/kdmrc*). In the [General] section of that file, you can specify a list of local displays to be started by adding a StaticServers key:

```
StaticServers=:0,:1,:2
```

If this line is missing, the default is to start only display :0.

## Starting Multiple X Servers Using GDM

GDM is configured using two files; the first specifies default values, which may be overwritten when GDM is updated, and the second provides local values, which are never overwritten. The name and location of these files varies; on an Ubuntu system, the defaults are in */etc/gdm/gdm.conf* and the local settings are in */etc/gdm/gdm-custom.conf*, while on a Fedora system, the defaults are in */usr/share/gdm/defaults.conf* and the local settings are in */etc/gdm/custom.conf*.

There are two sections in the GDM default configuration file that deal with local X servers. The first defines the command to be used to start a new server, and it looks like this:

```
[server-Standard]
name=Standard server
command=/usr/bin/X
flexible=true
```

The name field is for your reference only. The last line enables GDM to start additional servers on-the-fly when instructed to do so by the gdmflexiserver command (Section 2.8).

Once it has been defined, the configuration is associated with a display number by a servers section elsewhere in the file:

```
[servers]
0=Standard
```

This will start a single server with a display number of :0. To configure GDM to initially start additional servers with the same configuration, add a servers section to the local configuration file:

```
[servers]
0=Standard
1=Standard
2=Standard
```

If you wish to use a different configuration for a specific display, you can add a new configuration section to the local configuration file:

```
[server-LowRes]
name=Low-Resolution Server
command=/usr/bin/X -config /etc/X11/xorg.conf-lowres
flexible=false
```

Then specify that configuration for one of your displays:

```
[servers]
0=Standard
1=Standard
2=Standard
3=LowRes
```

GDM automatically adds an argument to the X server command to specify the display to be used.

# 2.8   Starting Additional X Servers on Demand Using a Display Manager

Recent versions of both GDM and KDM are capable of starting additional X servers on demand. This is useful when you occasionally want to use multiple X servers but don't want the extra overhead when a single X server only is in use. The GNOME developers call these additional servers *flexible* servers; the KDE folks call them *reserve* servers.

## Starting Additional X Servers Using gdmflexiserver

The GDM display manager provides a command-line utility, gdmflexiserver, which communicates with a running *gdm* process and instructs it to start a new X server.

Assuming that you have flexible=true in at least one of your GDM server configurations (Section 2.6)—which is the default—the GNOME menu contains a New Login option on the System group. If you're not running GNOME, don't have a New Login option on the menu. If you prefer to use a shell prompt, simply run gdmflexiserver:

    $ gdmflexiserver

If more than one X server is already active, you will be given the option of switching to an existing session or starting a new one; otherwise, a new X server will be started and a new session login prompt will appear automatically.

Your existing X session will be locked automatically (via the screensaver) and can be unlocked with your password when you switch back to the original VT. If you don't want this automatic locking, add the -l option to the preceding command line.

gdmflexiserver can also start a nested X server (using Xnest) and present a session login prompt there:

    $ gdmflexiserver -n

## Starting Additional X Servers Using KDM

Although it doesn't provide a command-line interface, KDM can start new sessions. Before you can use this, you must edit the *kdmrc* file. In the [General] section, add a line that specifies some reserve servers:

    ReserveServers=:3,:4,:5

If you also have a StaticServers line (Section 2.7), make sure that no display numbers appear in both lists.

In order to start a reserve server, you must be running KDE as the desktop environment (this isn't a given, since you can run any desktop using any display manager). Select "Start new Session" from the Switch User menu group on the K Menu, and a new X server will start with a session login prompt. If you lock your session (either using the menu option or by configuring session locking for the KDE screensaver), a "Start new Session" button will appear on the locked-screen password dialog as well.

You can switch between open sessions—including character-mode VT logins—by using the Switch User options on the K Menu or screensaver password dialogs (as an alternative to using the switch-VT key combinations (Section 2.2).

# 2.9   Starting an X Server with Clients Only When Needed

Systems used primarily as network servers don't need to have an X server running all the time and should be configured to boot into runlevel 3. This saves some memory that is best used for network services. However, it's handy to run an X server when performing administration on a server system; for example, to start a web browser to search for documentation.

The xinit utility can be used to start an X server with specified clients, but the *startx* wrapper script provides a friendlier interface. After logging in at a character-based login prompt, simply execute:

    $ startx

startx permits you to specify which client is to be started as well as any options for the X server. A double-dash (--) is used to separate the client arguments (left) from the X server options (right).

You can explicitly specify a client to be started:

    $ startx /usr/bin/xterm -bg yellow -geometry 180x50

Or you can specify the X server options to be used. If an X server is already running on display :0, for example, you could specify that display :1 should be used for the new server:

    $ startx -- :1

Or you can specify both the client to be started and some server options:

    $ startx /usr/bin/xterm -bg yellow -geometry 180x50 -- :1 -config /etc/testconfig

When specifying a client for startx, the client command pathname must begin with a single dot or a slash; otherwise, it will be treated as an argument to the default client (typically *xterm*). Likewise, you can specify the pathname of the X server on the righthand side of the double-dash by using a pathname that starts with a dot or slash; if you omit the dot or slash, the value is treated as an argument to the standard X server (which is specified in ~/.xserverrc on a user-by-user basis or /etc/X11/xinit/xserverrc as the system-wide default). For example, *Xorg* would be interpreted as an argument to the standard X server, while ./*Xorg* or /usr/local/test/Xorg would be interpreted as the name of an alternate X server.

To start multiple clients, create a shell script and specify that shell script on the startx command line.

startx is usually used without any arguments. It will start an X server with a default set of clients. The clients are specified in the script ~/.xinitrc in your home directory, if it exists; otherwise, */etc/X11/xinit/xinitrc* is used. Most distributions ship with the default script configured to start a desktop environment (KDE or GNOME).

 Some SVR4x configurations and Fedora use a system-wide *xinitrc* script, which in turn looks for a script named *~/.Xclients*. If present, the *~/.Xclients* file is used to start a customized list of clients. Note that *~/.xinitrc* takes precedence over *~/.Xclients* (also note the difference in capitalization).

## 2.10   Switching VTs from the Shell Prompt

The Linux switchto or chvt command permits you to change the currently displayed virtual terminal. If you are logged into VT1 in character mode, you can change to an X server running on VT7:

```
$ switchto 7
```

Or:

```
$ chvt 7
```

You can run this using your normal user permissions from a character-mode VT. However, you must use *root* privilege to run switchto/chvt from a X session:

```
# switchto 1
```

You can log in from another machine and run this command even when you can't switch VTs using the keyboard. I've used it to remotely change the VT of a new Linux user while talking her through a problem on the phone (she had accidentally switched to VT4 and couldn't get back to her X session).

## 2.11   Starting X Within X

It can be a nuisance to continually switch VTs when testing an X setup. An alternative is *Xnest*, an X server that does not drive a video card. Instead, Xnest displays its output in a window on another X server's display.

The screen dump in Figure 2-1 is from a Fedora system and shows Xnest displaying a KDE session in a window within a GNOME session.

To start Xnest on the current display, use the following:

```
$ Xnest :1
```

It is necessary to specify the display number to prevent conflicts with the existing display.

To start Xnest with a particular client, you can use the startx script:

```
$ startx /usr/bin/startkde -- /usr/bin/Xnest :1
```

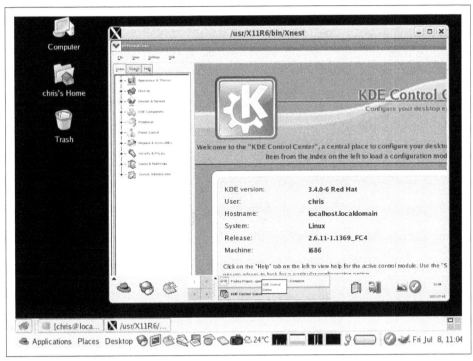

*Figure 2-1. A KDE session in a window within a Gnome session*

Since Xnest does not directly interact with any real hardware, you can set the screen size to any arbitrary value using the -geometry option. You can also test a multi-screen display using the -scrns option. To start Xnest with two screens of 600×400 pixels, use the following:

```
$ Xnest -scrns 2 -geometry 600x400 :1
```

The Xnest server has not been updated for several years, so it does not include current extensions such as RENDER. This may cause newer applications to operate poorly or to completely fail.

Xnest works by forwarding requests made of the nested server to the parent server. An alternative approach is offered by *Xephyr*, a server that renders onto an X image displayed in a window. The net effect is similar, but Xephyr can support extensions that are not provided by the parent server. It can also be used to build a multiseat solution.

## 2.12 No Mouse!

When testing and configuring an X server, it's not uncommon to find yourself without a working mouse. If your keyboard is working, though, there is a way to cope.

The X.org server (and some others) provides *mouse keys* capability, which permits the mouse pointer to be moved using the keypad. To toggle mouse keys mode on or off, press Shift-NumLock.

In this mode, the keypad buttons perform mouse actions, as illustrated in Figure 2-2.

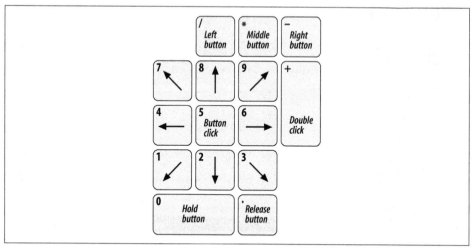

*Figure 2-2. Mouse actions on the keyboard*

The operation of the mouse buttons requires an explanation:

- Pressing the 5 key is equivalent to clicking a mouse button once.
- Pressing the 5 key twice in a row or pressing the + key is equivalent to double-clicking a mouse button.
- Pressing the 0 key holds a mouse button down (useful for drag operations), and the . (period) key releases it.
- The /, *, and - keys don't actually send a button click; they are used to select which mouse button will be simulated by the 5, +, and 0 keys. Pressing / will select left button clicks; pressing * will select middle button clicks; and pressing - will select right button clicks. The selected button remains in effect until a new one is chosen.

 Microsoft Windows and Mac OS each provide a similar mouse keys capability, but use a different hotkey sequence to enable/disable it.

In addition to rescuing mouse users when the rodent is uncooperative, mouse keys can be used as an accessibility tool, enabling the mouse pointer to be controlled using a mouth stick or a headpointer, or typing aid.

This feature may be difficult or impossible to use on laptop computers that are not equipped with a numeric keypad.

## 2.13 Bailing Out: Zapping X

Most X servers are configured with a keystroke combination that will bail out of the X server with no questions asked: Ctrl-Alt-Backspace. This is called *zapping* the X server.

This key combination should not be used lightly: since it immediately terminates the X server, client connections will be closed without warning, and most clients will subsequently terminate themselves. Any work-in-progress may be lost, and files may be left in an indeterminate state. Nonetheless, when the server is hopelessly messed up, zapping it may be your only available option short of a hard reset—and it is safe to do when no clients are connected.

Because this key combination can be dangerous, the X.org server permits you to disable it using the DontZap directive in *xorg.conf* configuration file.

## 2.14 Terminating X Automatically

By default, an X server will reset and continue running when the last client disconnects. The reset clears out the server memory, preventing new clients from accessing data from a previous session. This is an important security precaution.

For many applications it's desirable to have the X server exit when the last client disconnects. This is configured by adding the -terminate option to the X command line:

```
$ X -terminate
```

# 3

# Basic X.org Configuration

## 3.1  What Is There to Configure?

An X server manages a number of devices: keyboards, pointing devices, video cards, and monitors. The X server configuration determines how the display will be set up—which devices, in which operating modes, in which combination will be used.

For a simple configuration with one mouse, keyboard, monitor, and video card, using a reasonable resolution and scan rate, configuration is pretty straightforward. In fact, the X server can configure itself in the absence of a configuration file, or it can generate a default a basic configuration file (Section 3.4). But as soon as a special resolution or scan rate is desired or if multiple devices of the same kind are used, the complexity of the configuration can rise quickly. If there are two screens, the server needs to know which is on the left and which is on the right; if there are multiple mice, the server needs to know which ones you want it to manage.

Most distributions automatically generate a reasonable configuration file when they are installed, and also provide graphical tools for adjusting the configuration. However, none of these tools provides complete control over all of the configuration options—and if the display is misconfigured and unusable, it's hard to bring up a graphical tool to correct the problem!

 This chapter covers the configuration of the X.org server. Since this was forked from the XFree86 server, the configuration process is largely the same for both versions, except for minor differences in command-line options and filenames and features that have been added since the fork.

## 3.2  Why Only root Can Configure the X Server

Only the superuser, root, is permitted to configure the X.org server. This seems to be a serious limitation for a desktop system, but there are two critical reasons for it.

Since the X server pretty much has free reign over the hardware, it is possible to craft a malicious driver that would manage more than the display—it could manage other devices, snoop on system activity, or damage data. Any user who is given permission to configure the X server could install such a malicious driver; allowing a normal user to configure the server could permit a Trojan program to install a bad driver.

It's also possible to lock up the system by misconfiguring the X server. Worse yet, it's possible in some very rare cases to permanently damage the display hardware!

## 3.3 Places Your Configuration Could Hide

The X.org server configuration file is named *xorg.conf*. If you're using XFree86, the configuration file is named *XF86Config*. But where is the file located?

According to the X server manpage, it could be in any of 13 different locations:

- */etc/X11/cmdline*
- */usr/X11R6/etc/X11/cmdline*
- */etc/X11/$XORGCONFIG*
- */usr/X11R6/etc/X11/$XORGCONFIG*
- */etc/X11/xorg.conf-4*
- */etc/X11/xorg.conf*
- */etc/xorg.conf*
- */usr/X11R6/etc/X11/xorg.conf.hostname*
- */usr/X11R6/etc/X11/xorg.conf-4*
- */usr/X11R6/etc/X11/xorg.conf*
- */usr/X11R6/lib/X11/xorg.conf.hostname*
- */usr/X11R6/lib/X11/xorg.conf-4*
- */usr/X11R6/lib/X11/xorg.conf*

Where `cmdline` is the filename specified in the -config option on the server command line, `$XORGCONFIG` is the filename stored in the environment variable of the same name, and `hostname` is the computer's network hostname (as displayed by the hostname command). Unless you are the root user, the pathname given for `cmdline` or `$XORGCONFIG` must be relative and cannot contain a reference to a parent directory (it may not contain "..").

Translated into English, this means the following happens:

1. First priority is given to the filename specified on the command line, if present—but that filename must exist in the */etc/X11* or */usr/X11R6/etc/X11* subtrees. Those directories are normally writable only by root, so the configuration must be installed by the superuser.

2. The next possibility is a filename specified by the environment variable XORGCONFIG. The same directory limitations exist as above. To set this variable, use one of these lines (according to the shell you're using):

```
$ export XORGCONFIG=filename
% setenv XORGCONFIG filename
```

3. Next, */etc/X11* is searched, first for *xorg.conf-4* and then *xorg.conf*. The *xorg.conf-4* filename is a holdover from the XFree86 3.*x* to 4.*x* transition, when many users had both versions installed on their systems; if a different configuration was desired for the 4.*x* server, it was placed in the *-4* configuration file.

4. */etc* is next on the list, but only *xorg.conf* is sought in that directory.

5. */usr/X11R6/etc/X11* is searched. This directory may be a network share, so a machine-specific configuration file is sought first using the hostname as a suffix (*xorg.conf-hostname*). If the hostname isn't present, the X server looks for *xorg.conf-4* and then *xorg.conf*.

6. */usr/X11R6/lib/X11* is searched, using the same filenames as step 5.

When executing the X server as the root user, additional paths are searched:

- `cmdline` is searched before step 1. This may be relative or absolute.

- `$XORGCONFIG` is searched before step 2. This may be relative or absolute.

- *~/xorg.conf* is searched before step 3.

This permits the root user to specify any arbitrary pathname in `cmdline` or `$XORGCONFIG`—useful when testing a new configuration file (Section 3.4).

The standard configuration file location for most systems is */etc/X11/xorg.conf*.

To find out with certainty which configuration file the server is using, check the server logfile (Section 3.15).

If no configuration file can be found, the server will attempt to automatically generate a temporary configuration using the script *getconfig.pl*.

If you encounter a system that is using XFree86:

- The command-line configuration option is named `-xf86config` instead of `-config`.

- The environment variable is named *$XF86CONFIG* instead of *$XORGCONFIG*.

- The default filename is *XF86Config-4* or *XF86Config* instead of *xorg.conf-4* or *xorg.conf*.

- The standard configuration filename is */etc/X11/XF86Config*.

# 3.4 Let the X Server Configure Itself

The X.org server can, in most cases, probe, guess, and assume enough about the display configuration to start without a configuration file. Even better, it can generate a basic configuration file, if you specify the -configure option on the server command line:

```
# X -configure
```

If you're already running the X server, you can specify an alternate display number (such as :1) on the command line:

```
# X -configure :1
```

but it's probably best to attempt autoconfiguration when there is no server active.

The X server will gather as much information as possible by probing the hardware, and will then write the configuration file to */root/xorg.conf.new*.

You can test the configuration file by manually specifying it on the command line:

```
# X -config /root/xorg.conf.new
```

If the server appears to start and then immediately exits, while displaying the message *Fatal server error: failed to initialize core devices*, then your configuration may be fine except for the pointer device. Try telling the X server to continue even if the pointer cannot be opened:

```
# X -config /root/xorg.conf.new -allowMouseOpenFail
```

You can temporarily use mouse keys (Section 2.12) to move the mouse cursor. If the rest of the configuration is OK, you can correct the mouse pointer configuration (Section 3.7).

To exit from the server, zap it using Ctrl-Alt-Backspace (Section 2.13).

It's a good idea to save any working *xorg.conf* file before overwriting it with a new one, in case you find that you need to revert to a previous version:

```
# cp /etc/X11/xorg.conf /etc/X11/xorg.conf.original
```

You can keep as many versions of this file as seem practical (on many systems, you'll see multiple versions, such as *xorg.conf.original*, *xorg.conf.low-res*, *xorg.conf.videoprojector*, and so forth).

If the server appears to work properly and you wish to use it as the default configuration, install it by copying it to */etc/X11/xorg.conf*:

```
# cp /root/xorg.conf.new /etc/X11/xorg.conf
```

Even if the automatically generated configuration doesn't work, it is usually easier to start with that file and fine-tune it than to write a configuration file from scratch.

## 3.5 The xorg.conf Configuration File

The *xorg.conf* configuration file is divided into five basic sections (and there are eight optional sections; see Section 3.6). Knowing the purpose of each of these sections is the key to understanding the *xorg.conf* file.

ServerLayout
Defines how the screens and input devices are combined to form a display configuration.

Screen
Combines one video card (or Device in *xorg.conf* terminology) and one Monitor to form a screen. This section also defines the color depth and resolution(s) to be used on that screen.

Monitor
Describes the characteristics of the monitor—whether it supports DPMS and what scan rates are permissible.

Device
Configures the video card.

InputDevice
Contains configuration information for an input device. There are usually at least two of these sections—one for a pointing device and one for a keyboard.

These sections are arranged in the hierarchy shown in Figure 3-1.

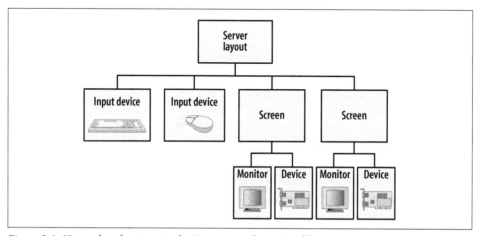

*Figure 3-1. Hierarchy of sections in the X server configuration file*

Each Screen section brings together a Monitor and Device section, and each ServerLayout section brings together one or more Screen sections with two or more InputDevice sections.

Multiple ServerLayout sections are used to handle alternate configurations—for example, a laptop configuration file could have one server layout for use on the road and a different server layout for use at the office.

A basic configuration looks like this (the order of the sections may vary):

```
# Sample xorg.conf file

Section "ServerLayout"
    Identifier    "Default Layout"
    Screen      0 "Screen0" 0 0
    InputDevice   "Mouse0"    "CorePointer"
    InputDevice   "Keyboard0" "CoreKeyboard"
EndSection

Section "Screen"
    Identifier    "Screen0"
    Device        "Videocard0"
    Monitor       "Monitor0"
    DefaultDepth  24
    SubSection    "Display"
        Depth     8
        Modes     "1280x1024" "1024x768" "800x600"
    EndSubSection
    SubSection    "Display"
        Depth     24
        Modes     "1280x1024" "1024x768" "800x600"
    EndSubSection
EndSection

Section "Monitor"
        Identifier   "Monitor0"
EndSection

Section "Device"
        Identifier   "Videocard0"
        Driver       "nv"
EndSection

Section "InputDevice"
        Identifier   "Keyboard0"
        Driver       "keyboard"
EndSection

Section "InputDevice"
        Identifier   "Mouse0"
        Driver       "mouse"
        Option       "Device" "/dev/input/mice"
EndSection
```

Notice that each section starts with the keyword Section followed by a quoted string describing the type of section, and that each section ends with the keyword EndSection. Lines beginning with # are comments.

The Identifier line in each section provides a name that is used when referencing that section from another section. The identifiers assigned by X -configure are pretty vague, but these can be changed to anything that makes sense; for example, in a two-screen configuration, you could name the monitors left and right or CRT and VideoProjector if that makes the file more readable.

The following sections offers brief descriptions of the main options in each code section.

## ServerLayout

The ServerLayout section of the file is optional—at least for most simple configurations—but it is almost always present in a configuration file. This is the ServerLayout section from our sample configuration:

```
Section "ServerLayout"
    Identifier     "Default Layout"
    Screen      0  "Screen0" 0 0
    InputDevice    "Mouse0"    "CorePointer"
    InputDevice    "Keyboard0" "CoreKeyboard"
EndSection
```

The entries in this section are:

Identifier

> The name given to this particular layout. This can be selected when the X server is started by specifying -layout *identifier* as a command-line option.

Screen

> Associates a screen with the display. To associate multiple screens with the display, use multiple Screen lines. The arguments are the screen number, the Screen section identifier, and the position of the screen (which is really only useful when using multiple screens together); see Section 4.4.

InputDevice

> Associates an InputDevice section with this display. The arguments are the InputDevice identifier, followed by the device type in double quotes. The device type must be CorePointer, CoreKeyboard, or SendCoreEvents (or the equivalent AlwaysCore). CorePointer and CoreKeyboard indicate the primary pointer and keyboard devices; SendCoreEvents identifies optional secondary devices, which should be used in parallel with the primary devices.

Option

> Any options that can be specified in the ServerFlags section may also be given here. The difference is that options in the ServerFlags section apply to all layouts, but options within a ServerLayout section apply only to one particular layout. Options in this section override options of the same names in the ServerFlags section.

# Screen

Here is our sample Screen section:

```
Section "Screen"
    Identifier      "Screen0"
    Device          "Videocard0"
    Monitor         "Monitor0"
    DefaultDepth    24
    SubSection      "Display"
        Depth       8
        Modes       "1280x1024" "1024x768" "800x600"
    EndSubSection
    SubSection      "Display"
        Depth       24
        Modes       "1280x1024" "1024x768" "800x600"
    EndSubSection
EndSection
```

There are three basic, required entries here:

Identifier
    The name of the screen, for reference from the ServerLayout section or the -screen command-line option.

Device
    A cross-reference to a particular video card's Device section identifier.

Monitor
    A cross-reference to a Monitor section identifier.

These entries are not required but are commonly used:

DefaultDepth
    The default *color depth* (bits per pixel) to be used. This can be overridden from the X server command line using the -depth option. Standard values are 8, 15, 16, and 24; I recommend using 24 on all modern video cards.

SubSection "Display"
    Specifies the available resolutions and other details for the display setup on this screen. This usually includes just two entries and is closed off with the keyword EndSubSection. The two entries are described as follows:

Depth
    The color depth (bits per pixel) for this SubSection. The SubSection with a depth that matches the server's color depth (which is usually the one specified in the DefaultDepth entry) is the one used by the server.

Modes
    A list of available video modes. The first entry in the list is the default mode. Most video modes are named with the resolution they provide (e.g., "640x480"). To find out which modes are available for a particular monitor and video card, consult the X server log file (Section 3.15).

## Monitor

The Monitor section is often quite simple:

```
Section "Monitor"
        Identifier   "Monitor0"
EndSection
```

In this example, the Monitor section contains only an Identifier entry. This will work fine if the actual monitor capabilities can be probed, which is the case for most modern monitors and some laptop screens. However, this will not work if the monitor is not on when the X server is started, the monitor does not report its capabilities, or special video hardware is in use, such as a splitter to connect both a monitor and a video projector, or a keyboard/video/mouse (KVM) switch. In those cases, the scan rates that the monitor can accept must be specified in this section (Section 3.14).

Because older monitors could be permanently (and sometimes spectacularly) damaged by sending a signal with the wrong scan rate, the X server is conservatively programmed and will exit rather than guess what scan rate to use.

## Device

The Device section needs only two basic entries:

```
Section "Device"
        Identifier   "Videocard0"
        Driver       "nv"
EndSection
```

The entries are:

Identifier
>    The name given to this video card, which is referenced by a Screen section.

Driver
>    The name of the device driver to use. This is determined automatically by scanning the PCI and AGP buses when you run the server with the -configure option. To see the X server's view of the buses, use the -scanpci option:

>    ```
>    $ X :1 -scanpci
>    ```

>    I used display :1 here to avoid conflicting with display :0 if it's already running. If you also have display :1 in use, choose a different display number.

In some cases, two or more drivers may work with one video card; the automatic configuration is usually the best choice, but there are times when you may want to override the configuration and choose a different driver manually.

Driver parameters may be specified in this section with Option entries (Section 3.12).

 If you have a video card and don't know which driver to use (or you don't have the right driver), use the vesa driver, which will enable basic operation with almost any modern video card at resolutions up to 800×600 and 16-bit color depths.

## InputDevice

In old configuration files, you may find Keyboard and Pointer sections instead of InputDevice sections. These section names are still recognized but may eventually be phased out, so they should be avoided.

Our sample configuration file has two InputDevice sections:

```
Section "InputDevice"
        Identifier   "Keyboard0"
        Driver       "keyboard"
EndSection

Section "InputDevice"
        Identifier   "Mouse0"
        Driver       "mouse"
        Option       "Device" "/dev/input/mice"
EndSection
```

There are three entries used here:

Identifier
> The name of the section, so it can be referenced from a ServerLayout section or from the -pointer and -keyboard command-line options.

Driver
> The name of the device driver, which is usually keyboard or mouse. Some specialized input devices use their own device driver, such as synaptics for Synaptics TouchPads (Section 3.10).

Option "Device"
> Specifies the device pathname. For the default BIOS-controlled keyboard(s) (whether PS/2 or USB), the device does not have to be specified. */dev/input/mice* is a special Linux device that merges input from all available mice into a single stream.

# 3.6    Optional Sections in the xorg.conf Configuration File

In addition to the basic, standard sections of the *xorg.conf* file, there are eight optional sections. Here is a brief synopsis:

Extensions
> These are options to enable or disable individual server extensions. Not all extensions can be controlled in this section; it was introduced to manage the *Composite* extension. To enable or disable an extension in this section, treat the extension name as a boolean option name (Option "Composite" "on").

Files

This is a list of various filenames and paths to be used by the server. The most common entries are:

FontPath

A comma-separated list of directories containing fonts (Section 10.2), or a font server specification (Section 10.3).

RGBPath

The pathname of the color name database (Section 3.13), which permits colors to be referenced by name instead of color code. The filename extension should be left off.

ServerFlags

These are flags that control the overall server operation. These flags control Zap (Section 2.13), Zoom (Section 5.2), and VT switching (Section 2.2) operations from the keyboard as well as enabling and disabling server features such as Xinerama (Section 4.2) and DPMS activations times (Section 3.11).

Module

This lists modules that should be loaded in addition to any device drivers; these are typically used to provide optional extensions (some extensions are built directly into the X server). The only entries permitted in this section are Load, which loads the specified module, and SubSection, which specifies options for a given module.

Mode *or* ModeLine

This describes the video modes in terms of scan rate, start/stop positions, and signal options. The server will consider using any video modes listed here that are supported by the hardware (monitor scan rate, framebuffer size, and DAC speed).

It is a bit tricky to construct a valid mode. Fortunately, the server has built-in entries for the common modes defined by the *Video Electronics Standard Association* (VESA), so it is no longer necessary to specify modes except for special cases (such as TV-out or ultra-high resolutions) above 2048×1536.

DRI

This offers configuration information for the *Direct Render Interface*, which shares 3D hardware access with applications. DRI is accessed through the device nodes */dev/dri/cardN*. Two options are used here:

Group

Specifies the group that should own the DRI device nodes. To limit DRI access to specific users, create a group for this purpose and place the selected users in that group (either by editing the */etc/group* file or by using the appropriate command-line tools, such as groupadd and usermod -G under Linux).

Mode
> Specifies the file permission mode for the DRI device nodes. Using a value of 0666 will enable every user of the system to access DRI (which is not necessarily safe, but is the default).

VideoAdaptor
> This is used to configure video streams for the Xv extension. I've never seen this section used.

Vendor
> This is vendor-specific configuration information. This is rarely used, except that some distribution-specific configuration tools use this section to identify that they created the configuration file.

# 3.7 Configuring the Pointer Device

X -configure does a very basic job of configuring the mouse pointer. It assumes that */dev/mouse* is a symbolic link to the actual mouse device.

On a Linux system, the physical mouse is usually connected to one of these devices:

*/dev/psaux*
> The PS/2 mouse port.

*/dev/input/mice*
> All USB mice merged together.

*/dev/input/mouseN*
> A specific USB mouse (*N* is the mouse number starting at zero).

*/dev/ttySN*
> A serial port (*N* is the serial port number starting at zero; the DOS/Windows device COM1: is */dev/ttyS0*).

For USB mice under NetBSD/OpenBSD, use the device */dev/umsN* (*N* is the mouse number, starting at zero).

You can create the */dev/mouse* symlink with the command:

```
ln -s /dev/mousedevice /dev/mouse
```

However, some distributions (such as Ubuntu) are starting to use a volatile */dev* directory—one that is not saved on disk, but created on-the-fly when the system is booted. The symbolic link would need to be created every time the system is started.

In this case, your best choice would be to change the device entry in the InputDevice section of the configuration file. Here is an automatically generated configuration:

```
Section "InputDevice"
        Identifier  "Mouse0"
        Driver      "mouse"
        Option      "Device"   "/dev/mouse"
EndSection
```

Change the last argument of the Option "Device" entry to the device you wish to use:

```
Option     "Device"  "/dev/input/mice"
```

Almost all mice now use a variation of the PS/2 protocol and can be detected and managed automatically. Some very old mice may need to have the mouse protocol specified; this can be set with an Option "Protocol" entry.

## 3.8  Configuring a Two-Button Mouse

The X Window system supports mice with almost any number of buttons. Most X users prefer mice with three or more buttons, since many X applications permit pasting with the middle mouse button (Section 5.4)—a great timesaver.

If you have a two-button mouse, you can configure the server to interpret the simultaneous press of both buttons as a middle mouse click. To set this up, add the Emulate3Buttons option to the mouse's InputDevice section:

```
Section "InputDevice"
        Identifier  "Mouse0"
        Driver      "mouse"
        Option      "Device" "/dev/input/mice"
        Option      "Emulate3Buttons"  "On"
EndSection
```

Most mice equipped with scrollwheels have a middle button switch attached to the scrollwheel. Simply press the scrollwheel in to click the middle button.

As long as the mouse buttons are pressed within 50 milliseconds (1/20 of a second) of each other, a middle click will be registered instead. If you find it difficult to press them almost simultaneously, you can adjust the time factor with the Emulate3Timeout option:

```
Option     "Emulate3Timeout"  "250"
```

That would set the threshold for detection of simultaneous presses to 250 milliseconds, or one quarter of a second.

If you use one of the *rocker navigation* extensions with Firefox—which lets you navigate through your history by pressing the left and right mouse buttons in rapid succession—you'll probably want to turn Emultate3Buttons off to prevent your rocker gestures from being interpreted as a middle-button click.

## 3.9  Configuring a Mouse with a Scrollwheel

In order to use the scrollwheel with most applications, you will need to configure the X server to translate scrollwheel motion into button clicks on mouse buttons 4 and 5.

This is set up with an entry in the InputDevice section:

```
Option   "ZAxisMapping"   "4 5"
```

If you have two scrollwheels, you can configure the second scrollwheel to generate button clicks on buttons 6 and 7, which some applications interpret as left/right scrolling (or history navigation in a browser):

```
Option   "ZAxisMapping"   "4 5 6 7"
```

You can test your configuration using xev.

> You may also need to specify the IMPS/2 (Intellimouse) protocol to enable the use of a scrollwheel:
> ```
> Option "Protocol" "IMPS/2"
> ```

## 3.10  Configuring a Synaptics TouchPad

Many laptops use a Synaptics TouchPad (or an Alps GlidePoint, which can use the same driver). By default, a TouchPad will emulate a PS/2 mouse, so it should work fine with the default driver; but if you change the Driver entry in the InputDevice section of *xorg.conf* to synaptic, you can use its advanced features. It's also a good idea to turn on the SHMConfig option, which enables you to change the TouchPad options on-the-fly using *synclient*; if your TouchPad has two buttons, enable the Emulate3Buttons option as well:

```
Section "InputDevice"
        Identifier  "Mouse0"
        Driver      "synaptics"
        Option      "Emulate3Buttons"  "on"
        Option      "SHMConfig"         "on"
EndSection
```

Note that the synaptics driver appears to operate fine without a device entry!

When you restart the X server, the synaptics driver's default configuration will permit you to do the following:

- Click the left mouse button by tapping one finger in the middle area or by tapping the upper-left corner.
- Drag with the left mouse button by tapping and then dragging one finger (touch-release-touch, then drag).
- Click the middle mouse button by tapping two fingers in the middle area or by tapping the upper-right corner.
- Click the right mouse button by tapping three fingers in the middle area or by tapping the lower-right corner.

- Scroll up and down by running your finger up and down the right side (if supported by your application).
- Scroll left and right by running your finger across the bottom (if supported by your application). Some web browsers, such as Firefox, use this for history navigation (left for previous page, right for next page).

 Not all of these options are supported by all TouchPad models.

This driver is incredibly customizable; it can be permanently configured through options in the InputDevice section of the configuration file or temporarily configured on-the-fly using the synclient program.

I find that the default options work well for most people. If you find that the vertical and horizontal scrolling features are driving you crazy, you can disable them by setting VertScrollDelta and HorizScrollDelta option values to 0:

```
Section "InputDevice"
        Identifier  "Mouse0"
        Driver      "synaptics"
        Option      "Emulate3Buttons"  "on"
        Option      "SHMConfig"         "on"
        Option      "VertScrollDelta"  "0"
        Option      "HorizScrollDelta" "0"
EndSection
```

 The *Synaptics* driver has been maintained separately from the X.org (and XFree86) servers for some time. Multiple efforts have been made to relicense it in a way that is compatible with the X.org license (BSD-style), and it appears that it may be managed as part of the X.org server project soon. Until that happens, information about the driver is maintained at *http://web.telia.com/~u89404340/touchpad/*.

# 3.11  Enabling DPMS

DPMS is a VESA standard that conserves energy by using the horizontal and vertical sync signals to select one of four power states.

These are the four states defined by VESA, with maximum power levels defined by the EPA's Energy Star program and typical turn-on times:

| State name | H-sync | V-sync | Maximum power used (Energy Star - Tier 2, January 2006) | Typical time to On state |
|---|---|---|---|---|
| On | Active | Active | 28 W per megapixel | --- |
| Standby | Off | Active | Not specified; typically less than 22 W per megapixel | <5 seconds |

| State name | H-sync | V-sync | Maximum power used (Energy Star - Tier 2, January 2006) | Typical time to On state |
|---|---|---|---|---|
| Suspend | Active | Off | Max 2 W | <10 seconds |
| Off | Off | Off | Max 1 W | <30 seconds |

 A few extremely old monitors cannot handle having just one of the sync signals turned off. These monitors could be permanently damaged or pose a fire hazard if used with DPMS. However, almost all monitors in use today support DPMS.

In a CRT-based monitor, energy savings are accomplished by turning off the electron beam, electromagnets, and cathode heater. LCD monitors don't have these energy-hungry components, so most LCD monitors treat all three energy-saving modes in the same way: by turning the display off entirely.

These four states are selected automatically by the X server according to the length of time since the last user input. When the server detects mouse or keyboard activity, the display state is changed to On.

DPMS is enabled on a monitor-by-monitor basis by adding an option to the Monitor section of the config file:

```
Option "DPMS"
```

Once that is done, the length of time before the Standby, Suspend, and Off states are activated is specified in the ServerFlags or ServerLayout sections:

```
Option    "StandbyTime"    "8"
Option    "SuspendTime"    "12"
Option    "OffTime"        "16"
```

The times specified are in minutes. There's also a similar-but-unrelated BlankTime option, which controls when the screensaver will blank the screen, but that doesn't save any energy.

 Unfortunately, the Gnome and KDE environments change these settings at desktop startup to values entered to their control panels, so there is little value in setting these times in the *xorg.conf* file when using these desktops, except that the *xorg.conf* settings may have effect before a user is logged in.

It's possible to change these times on-the-fly or disable DPMS entirely using xset, which is handy during software demonstrations. xset also permits you to immediately enter a particular state, which is mainly useful for testing.

The optimal setting for each of the DPMS timeouts depends on the application. For example, the timeout on a point-of-sale (PoS) terminal could be fairly low, because in normal operation, the user will interact with the display almost continuously.

However the timeout for a lecture hall podium projector should probably be set much higher because the keyboard and mouse might not be touched for significant periods, even though many people could be studying the image.

Ideally, the timeouts should be set so that the screen does not blank during normal use, but does go into a power-saving mode when the display is legitimately unused.

 Selecting very short timeouts for DPMS may actually reduce hardware life, especially for the fluorescent tubes used to illuminate many LCD screens. A *minimum* setting of 8–10 minutes is safe for most hardware. (Some newer LCD screens are illuminated with LEDs, which can be turned on and off without consequence.)

## 3.12  Configuring Video Card Driver Options

Many of the X.org video card drivers are designed to work with a particular video chipset, but different video cards may use a chipset in different ways. For example, a chipset might support a TV-out connection, but a low-end video card based on that chipset may not have TV-out circuitry on the card. Likewise, the amount of video memory and the speed of the DACs may vary considerably.

In most cases, these card-to-card differences can be automatically detected, but most of the video drivers provide configuration options so that their operation can be optimized and so that features can be turned off if a card compatibility issue arises.

A manpage is provided listing the options supported by each video driver, but an easier way to find out what options are supported by a specific driver is to run X -configure and then examine the Device section of the generated file. The options available for the selected driver will be listed, or commented-out. For example, these entries are automatically added to the *xorg.conf* file when the ati driver is selected:

```
### Available Driver options are:-
### Values: <i>: integer, <f>: float, <bool>: "True"/"False",
### <string>: "String", <freq>: "<f> Hz/kHz/MHz"
### [arg]: arg optional
#Option     "accel"                 # [<bool>]
#Option     "crt_display"           # [<bool>]
#Option     "composite_sync"        # [<bool>]
#Option     "hw_cursor"             # [<bool>]
#Option     "linear"                # [<bool>]
#Option     "mmio_cache"            # [<bool>]
#Option     "panel_display"         # [<bool>]
#Option     "probe_clocks"          # [<bool>]
#Option     "reference_clock"       # <freq>
#Option     "shadow_fb"             # [<bool>]
#Option     "sw_cursor"             # [<bool>]
```

The options marked [<bool>] accept an optional boolean value: "true", "1", "on", "yes", or no value to turn the option on; "false", "0", "off", or "no" to turn the option off. You can also turn an option off by prepending no to the option name and omitting the value. Underscores and spaces in the option name are ignored, and option names and values are case-insensitive.

Therefore you could turn the accel option on with any of these entries:

```
Option  "accel"
Option  "Accel"
Option  "accel"  "True"
Option  "accel"  "true"
Option  "ACCEL"  "TRUE"
Option  "accel"  "1"
Option  "accel"  "yes"
Option  "accel"  "on"
```

You could turn off the accel option with any of these entries:

```
Option  "noaccel"
Option  "NoAccel"
Option  "no_accel"
Option  "No Accel"
Option  "accel"  "False"
Option  "accel"  "false"
Option  "accel"  "FALSE"
Option  "accel"  "0"
Option  "accel"  "no"
Option  "accel"  "off"
```

Instead of <bool>, options may be marked as accepting another type of value:

<integer>
This accepts an integer in decimal, hexadecimal, or octal format.

This accepts a floating-point number.

<string>
A group of characters.

<frequency>
A floating-point value or a range or values separated by a dash, suffixed by Hz, k, kHz, M, or MHz. (If omitted, a reasonable unit is assumed based on the context— for example, Hz for vertical refresh rates and kHz for horizontal sync rates.)

Two options are common to most of the video drivers:

accel
Turns on video acceleration using the GPU. If the driver (or chip revision!) has bugs, accelerated drawing my be incorrect—for example, lines may not join together properly or drawing artifacts such as dots, line segments, or improperly filled areas may be visible. Turning off acceleration may fix these problems, but the main CPU is much slower at performing graphics operations than the GPU, so performance will take a significant hit. The default for most drivers is to turn acceleration on.

hw_cursor *or* sw_cursor

> Selects whether the mouse cursor will be handled in hardware or in software. Hardware cursor handling uses the sprite or overlay capabilities of the graphics card to superimpose the image of the mouse cursor on the main image. Software cursor handling requires the server to save the pixels that will be covered by the cursor, and then draw in the cursor. When the cursor is moved, the original pixels are restored, and then the process is repeated at the new cursor location. Obviously, software cursor handling is much slower and may result in cursor flickering, but it may be required for certain buggy chipsets and exotic video modes. hw_cursor and sw_cursor are the opposite of each other, and only one should be enabled.

Fortunately, newer video cards are getting progressively better at reporting their capabilities to software, so the need for driver options is steadily diminishing.

## 3.13 LightSteelBlue and Other Color Names

Video hardware uses varying amounts of red, green, and blue light to generate color. On most video cards, this is specified as *color triplets*—three values representing the amount of each color.

Color triplets are easy for the server to understand, but miserable for humans. It's much easier for us to understand a color name such as orange than a color triplet such as (255,165,0). X provides a mechanism for cross-referencing color names to triplets, enabling you to use color names in command options and configuration files.

The Files section of the server configuration file usually includes an RGBPath entry. This specifies the location of a file that maps color names to color triplets; the file is traditionally named *rgb.txt*, and most distributions place it in */usr/share/X11/*. Some other servers use a compiled version of this database, named *rgb.db*.

Several versions of this file have been in existence, but the current one has been in use for many years. This current *rgb.txt* file contains 752 entries, with 232 duplicate names, yielding 520 unique colors. Here is a sample of some of the 87 blues:

```
240 248 255        AliceBlue
 25  25 112        MidnightBlue
100 149 237        CornflowerBlue
 70 130 180        SteelBlue
176 196 222        LightSteelBlue
173 216 230        LightBlue
176 224 230        PowderBlue
138  43 226        BlueViolet
```

The first three fields in each line are the red, green, and blue components, each expressed as a fraction of 255 (24-bit color)—so 255 255 255 is white, and 0 0 0 is black.

Some colors have numbered variations:

```
135 206 255          SkyBlue1
126 192 238          SkyBlue2
108 166 205          SkyBlue3
 74 112 139          SkyBlue4
202 225 255          LightSteelBlue1
188 210 238          LightSteelBlue2
162 181 205          LightSteelBlue3
110 123 139          LightSteelBlue4
```

And there's also 100 shades of gray (spelled *gray* as well as *grey*) numbered from 0 (black) to 100 (white):

```
  0   0   0          gray0
  0   0   0          grey0
  3   3   3          gray1
  3   3   3          grey1
              ...
252 252 252          gray99
252 252 252          grey99
255 255 255          gray100
255 255 255          grey100
```

You can add colors to this file, but it's not recommended—using custom color names is not portable. However, you're free to use any of these color names anywhere that a color code is needed, such as for a background color for the screen, and you can be confident that the name will be recognized by any X server.

To access the color names through the X server, use the following command:

```
$ showrgb
```

This permits you to view the exact names that have been loaded into the server without knowing the *rgb.txt* file location.

The colors from the *rgb.txt* file have been used in many places. They were even incorporated into the Netscape browser at an early stage—which is why color names such as LightSteelBlue are understood by Mozilla browsers to this day and can be used in HTML and CSS:

```
<head bgcolor="LightSteelBlue">
<div style="color: grey25">
```

# 3.14  Configuring a Monitor's Scan Rates

VESA has defined a probing technology for video monitors called the *Display Data Channel* (DDC). The early versions of this standard enabled the monitor to send data to the video card to describe the monitor's capabilities; later versions of the standard also permit you to control the monitor settings using the computer.

DDC makes monitor configuration automatic. But there are three common situations where it can't be used. These are described next.

- When the monitor is not on or connected when the X server starts up
- When using a monitor that doesn't support DDC (obviously!), which includes some laptop panels and old monitors
- When you're using a device in between the monitor and the video card (such as some KVM switches), video splitters (to drive multiple monitors from one video output), or signal boosters (to connect a monitor at a distance)

For example, when I'm teaching, my computer drives both a monitor and a classroom video projector. Since these devices have different capabilities, the video splitter does not connect the video card's DDC pins to either device.

In these cases, you need to specify the horizontal and vertical sync frequencies that will work with the monitor. This is done by adding two entries to the Monitor section of the configuration file:

```
HorizSync    31.5 - 90.0
VertRefresh  59.0 - 75.0
```

The frequency range specified on the VertRefresh line is in Hz (cycles per second).

Almost all CRT monitors handle a 60-Hz refresh rate, and most modern CRT monitors support refresh rates up 75 Hz, which reduces eyestrain. It's debatable whether pushing the refresh rate over 75 Hz can be perceived as improving the image, and it's almost certain that refresh rates over 85 Hz have no benefit to most users.

Until recently, scan rates on LCD panels didn't make as much difference as the scan rates on CRTs, since the liquid crystal cells were too slow to appreciably change their state between scans, even at 60 Hz. Ever-improving LCD response times mean that scan rate may become as much of an issue as with CRTs; fortunately, most current LCDs support 75-Hz refresh rates.

 To see if the refresh rate is low (~60 Hz) on a CRT, place a mostly white image on the screen. Stand back a meter (3 feet) from the screen and look about 60 cm (2 feet) above the screen. The image on the screen will be in the lower periphery of your vision. You will be able to see visible flicker if the refresh rate is low.

Repeat the experiment with the refresh rate set to 75 Hz, and you'll see why users complain about eyestrain and headaches at the lower speeds.

This experiment will usually fail on an LCD.

The HorizSync range is specified in kHz (thousands of cycles per second).

You should avoid guessing at the HorizSync and VertRefresh values; look them up in the monitor manual or on the manufacturer's web site. As a last resort, perform a general web search to find the values. On some monitors—especially older ones—you can cause serious damage by using the wrong frequency. Once you know the correct values, do yourself a favor and mark it on the back of the monitor.

If you are using a video splitter to connect two monitors, use the intersection of the two monitors' frequency ranges. Pick the higher of the two lower range limits, and the lower of the two upper range limits.

For example, if you are connecting a video monitor and a projector, and the monitor has a HorizSync range of 31.5–90.0 while the projector supports 28.0–84.0, use 31.5–84.0 in your config file.

If you cannot find documentation for your monitor and *must* calculate a frequency range, be conservative! Here is a quick-and-dirty formula that lets you calculate an approximate horizontal frequency, generally within 1 kHz:

```
HorizSync = VertRefresh * (VerticalResolution + 40) / 1000
```

In this formula, *VerticalResolution* is the height of the selected resolution, in pixels. What's the 40 doing in there? Well, it provides some time for the *vertical retrace*, when the CRT beam is repositioned from the bottom to the top of the display.

 This formula does not work for double-scan and interlaced modes.

It's important not to restrict the X server too tightly. If you want to use a VertRefresh rate of exactly 60.0, you may find that no modes are available that exactly match that frequency, and the X server will be unable to start. But, if you relax the range by just 1 Hz to 59.0–61.0, the server is much more likely to find a workable configuration (Section 3.15).

Let's suppose that you have a monitor for which you don't have any documentation—but you're fairly confident that it can support a resolution 1024×768 at a 75 Hz refresh rate, and you want to use it at only that resolution. First, calculate the approximate HorizSync rate:

```
HorizSync = VertRefresh * (VerticalResolution + 40) / 1000
HorizSync = 75        * (768  + 40)              / 1000
HorizSync = 60.68
```

Let's go plus or minus 1 kHz on this HorizSync value, and plus or minus 1 Hz on the VertRefresh value to give the server some wiggle room:

```
HorzSync      59.6 - 61.6
VertRefresh   74.0 - 76.0
```

When we fire up the server and check the log file (Section 3.15), we find that the server has found three VESA standard modes that fits our frequency ranges:

```
(**) NVIDIA(0): Validated modes for display device DFP-0:
(**) NVIDIA(0):     Default mode "1024x768": 78.8 MHz, 60.1 kHz, 75.1 Hz
(**) NVIDIA(0):     Default mode "640x384": 51.5 MHz, 60.2 kHz, 75.0 Hz (D)
(**) NVIDIA(0):     Default mode "512x384": 39.4 MHz, 60.1 kHz, 75.1 Hz (D)
```

The first (selected) default mode is the one that the server will initially use (notice that the refresh rate is 75.1 Hz, so this mode would not have been found if we'd specified a refresh rate of exactly 75 Hz). The two other modes are double-scan modes, as indicated by the (D) at the end of the line, which can be selected using the RANDR extension (Section 5.3).

# 3.15  Reading Server Log Files

At startup, the server will output some diagnostic information to standard output. It will log a more detailed version of that information in */var/log/Xorg.displaynumber.log*. This log is a key source of information when debugging a configuration setup.

The log file includes, in order:

1. Version and build information for the server, so you know which version is in use.

2. OS Kernel version information.

3. A marker legend. Many of the lines in the file are marked with two characters in parenthesis, indicating the source of the information or type of message displayed in that line. These markers are vitally important, since the various sources of information can override one another and interact in unexpected ways. The marker legend explains what these symbols mean:

    *(--) Probed*
    The information was discovered by directly querying the hardware.

    *(\*\*) From config file*
    The information was pulled from entries in the configuration file.

    *(==) Default setting*
    Since no applicable overriding values were found, the compiled-in default setting was used.

    *(++) From command line*
    The value was given as an option value on the X server command line.

    *(!!) (II) Notice or informational*
    No error is indicated—the data is printed only for your information.

    *(WW) Warning*
    Something may be wrong, but the server can continue. The warning lines can be very helpful when tracking down server quirks, such as requested modules not loading or extensions not initializing properly.

    *(EE) Error*
    The server cannot continue, so it aborts.

*(NI) Not implemented*
    A valid configuration references a feature that is not yet implemented.

*(??) Unknown*
    Rarely seen!

4. The filenames of the logfile and configuration file. Check this line to ascertain that the server is using the correct configuration file (or you could waste hours modifying the wrong file!).

5. The server layout hierarchy used. This portion of the log file contains a little ASCII-art diagram of the selected ServerLayout and child sections. In this example, the ServerLayout was selected because it was the only one in the file, as indicated by the (==) marker; if it was selected because it was specified in a -layout command-line option, it would be marked with (++). The other sections were selected due to internal references in the configuration file, as indicated by the (**) markers:

```
(==) ServerLayout "Default Layout"
(**) |-->Screen "Screen0" (0)
(**) |    |-->Monitor "Monitor0"
(**) |    |-->Device "Card0"
(**) |-->Input Device "Mouse0"
(**) |-->Input Device "Keyboard0"
(**) |-->Input Device "Synaptics"
```

6. Any auxilliary files and paths that have been configured, including the RGBPath and FontPath.

7. Any modules loaded. Some of these are specified in the Modules section of the configuration file, some are loaded by other modules, and some are loaded by default.

8. Extension initialization. Note that both built-in and module-based extensions are initialized.

9. InputDevice initialization results.

During device initialization, the video driver will go through all of the possible modes—the built-in VESA modes plus any added by the configuration file—and test them to see whether they can be used with the hardware configuration. Most will be discarded for one reason or another. Here is a log excerpt showing five modes being rejected for various reasons:

```
(II) NVIDIA(0): Not using default mode "2560x1600"
        (bad mode clock/interlace/doublescan)
(II) NVIDIA(0): Not using default mode "1280x800"
        (hsync out of range)
(II) NVIDIA(0): Not using default mode "1920x1440"
        (width too large for virtual size)
(II) NVIDIA(0): Not using default mode "1024x768"
        (vrefresh out of range)
(WW) NVIDIA(0): Not using mode "960x720"
        (height 1440 is larger than EDID-specified maximum 1050)
```

The acronym EDID refers to *Extended Display Identification Data*, which is the formatted data block retrieved from the monitor through DDC probing.

Once the mode list has been narrowed down through this process of elimination, the remaining validated modes are logged:

```
(**) NVIDIA(0): Validated modes for display device DFP-0:
(**) NVIDIA(0):     Default mode "1400x1050": 155.8 MHz, 81.5 kHz, 74.8 Hz
(**) NVIDIA(0):     Default mode "1280x1024": 135.0 MHz, 80.0 kHz, 75.0 Hz
(**) NVIDIA(0):     Default mode "1024x768": 78.8 MHz, 60.1 kHz, 75.1 Hz
(**) NVIDIA(0):     Default mode "800x600": 49.5 MHz, 46.9 kHz, 75.0 Hz
(**) NVIDIA(0):     Default mode "640x480": 31.5 MHz, 37.5 kHz, 75.0 Hz
```

For each validated mode, the log shows the resolution, the *dot clock* (the speed at which pixels are sent to the display), the HorizSync value, and the VertRefresh value. Note that the mode 1024x768 shows up in both the list of rejected modes and the list of validated modes; the rejected entry was at a higher scan rate than the validated entry (unfortunately, the log file does not state the rejected scan rate value).

If any modes are listed in the Modes entry in the Display subsection of a Screen section (Section 3.16), those modes only are used to set up the display. This enables you to select just the modes you want out of all of the valid modes.

At least one validated mode is required for the server to start up successfully. If multiple modes pass the validation, they can be accessed through the RANDR extension (Section 5.3); any modes that are listed in a Display subsection of a Screen section can also be accessed through hotkeys (Section 5.2).

The level of log detail can be adjusted using the -logverbose *level* command-line option, where *level* is a number from 0 to 9. The default is level 3; higher levels introduce a bit more detail, notably the actual contents of the EDID decoded into readable strings.

# 3.16  Configuring the Default Depth of a Screen

Many video drivers will default to an 8-bit color depth, but most video hardware supports (and users want) a 24-bit depth.

The desired depth is specified in the Screen section of the configuration file:

```
DefaultDepth    24
```

You can override this by specifying a different value on the command line using the -depth option.

The color depth affects the available visuals (Section 9.2). These are the most commonly used depths:

*4-bit*
    16 colors using a StaticColor visual.

*8-bit*

> 256 colors using a PsudeoColor visual.

*16-bit*

> 65,536 colors using a TrueColor visual. Sixteen-bit values fit nicely into 2 bytes, but there are 3 colors channels (red, green, and blue), and 16 doesn't divide evenly by 3. The red and blue channels are usually assigned 5 bits and the green channel is assigned 6, because the human eye seems to be slightly more sensitive to variations in green than in red or blue. Some hardware will actually assign 5 bits per channel (32,768 colors).

*24-bit*

> Just over 16 million colors using a TrueColor visual. Since most modern processors perform 32-bit writes, the 24 bit values will usually be contained in a 32-bit word.

*48-bit*

> About 28 trillion colors using a TrueColor visual. This requires specialized and expensive hardware, and you won't notice the extra colors on a desktop monitor—but 48-bit color is used for film production (such as in Hollywood).

Current display hardware is optimized for 24-bit processing; some GPUs will also accelerate 16-bit operations.

However, 24-bit data (stored into 32-bit words) can be managed more easily than 16-bit data on 32-bit hardware. Changing one 24-bit pixel requires a single write; but changing one 16-bit pixel (where 2 pixels are stored in each 32-bit word) requires a read of the current pixel value, an AND operation to clear out the old value of the affected pixel while keeping the value of the unaffected pixel, an OR operation to insert the new pixel value, and then a write to memory. And that's the best case scenario—a 16-bit left-rotation may be required if the target pixel is stored in the high-order bits of the 32-bit word.

# 3.17 Configuring the Resolution of a Screen

Although you can usually set the screen resolution using *xrandr*, you can also directly specify it by creating a subsection in the Screen section of the configuration file:

```
SubSection "Display"
    Depth 24
    Modes "1280x1024" "800x600"
EndSubSection
```

There can be one section for each possible color depth.

The first mode listed in the Modes entry that will work with the screen's hardware will be the default resolution for the display. The user can change resolution using hotkeys (Section 5.2).

When the user changes resolution, only the displayed resolution changes, not the size of the screen image. If the screen is configured with a resolution of 1280×1024 and the user switches to a display resolution of 800×600, only about one-third of the desktop will be visible on the display. You can scroll the display around this virtual desktop using the mouse; when you touch the edge of the screen, it will scroll automatically.

This can be useful if you want to temporarily zoom in on part of the screen. It is also the preferred configuration of some vision-impaired users, who need a low display resolution but like a large desktop size.

By default, the virtual screen size is the largest size specified in the Modes entry, which works with the hardware. The virtual screen size is reported in the log file (Section 3.15).

Note that a Modes entry does not have to list the highest resolution as the first (default) entry. The virtual screen size will be set to resolution of the largest valid mode.

Alternately, you can specify a specific virtual screen size in the Display subsection:

```
Virtual  2048  1536
Viewport 0     0
```

The Virtual entry specifies the size of the virtual screen in pixels. In this example, we're configuring a huge 3-megapixel virtual screen. Any display modes larger than the specified size will be disabled (unlikely in this case!).

The Viewport entry specifies the starting point of the upper-left corner of the physical screen within the virtual screen; the value of 0 0 given here will position the physical screen in the upper-left corner of the virtual screen. The default is to show the center of the virtual screen, but that's not always the best choice, since desktop menus and panels are usually displayed on the edge of the screen so the initial display may look deceptively empty.

# 4

# Advanced X.org Configuration

## 4.1   Multi-Screen Configuration

Some people just can't get enough—at least when it applies to screen space. Many users can productively benefit from more screen space than a single monitor can provide.

It's fairly easy to configure the X.org server to support multiple screens on one display, if you have the hardware. In fact, if you get the X server to configure itself, it will do a reasonable job of setting up a *multi-screen* configuration if it detects multiple video cards and monitors.

To configure or tune a multi-screen setup by hand, take the following steps:

1. Create two (or more) normal Screen sections and the corresponding Device and Monitor sections in the *xorg.conf* file. Ensure that each screen has a unique identifier; in the following example, I've used the identifiers *ScreenA*, *ScreenB*, and *ScreenC*.

2. Add both screen sections to the ServerLayout section, numbering the screens starting at 0:

```
Section "ServerLayout"
        Identifier      "Multiscreen layout"
        Screen      0   "ScreenA" 0 0
        Screen      1   "ScreenB" Below      "ScreenA"
        Screen      2   "ScreenC" RightOf    "ScreenA"
        InputDevice     "Mouse0"             "CorePointer"
        InputDevice     "Keyboard0"          "CoreKeyboard"
EndSection
```

Notice that Screen0 is positioned to 0 0, but Screen1 and Screen2 are positioned relative to Screen0. The positioning keywords available are Above, Below, RightOf, and LeftOf; the keyword is followed by the quoted name of one of the other screens. (There are also other ways of positioning screens; see Section 4.4.)

When you start the X server, you will be able to move the mouse pointer between screens according to the layout given. In this example, the mouse pointer will start in the middle of screen 0. Moving it to the right will cause it to appear on screen 2; moving it back to the left will return it to screen 0, and moving it further to the left will make it appear on screen 1.

In this type of multi-screen configuration, a window can appear only on one screen and cannot be moved from screen to screen. These limitations can be overcome using a Xinerama configuration (Section 4.2) instead of a multi-screen configuration.

One advantage of multi-screen mode is that, since the screen number can be specified in a displayspec, you can easily cause new clients to appear on a particular screen. If the screen number is not specified for a new window, it will appear on screen 0.

If the preceding configuration was used on the host `blue.example.com` display `:0`, you could specify that a window should open on the righthand screen by using the displayspec:

```
blue.example.com:0.1
```

Or, for local clients:

```
:0.1
```

## 4.2   Xinerama Configuration

Xinerama mode is similar to multi-screen mode, but it merges several video cards and monitors into one big screen. This permits you to move windows between monitors and even span monitors. Xinerama is the most common multiple-monitor configuration and the most useful for many applications.

The X.org server won't configure Xinerama automatically, but it's fairly easy to convert a working multi-screen configuration:

1. Ensure that all of the screens have the same color depth. Each `Screen` section of the configuration file should contain a `DefaultDepth` entry with the same depth value (typically 24 bits per pixel):

   ```
   DefaultDepth 24
   ```

2. Add this line to the `ServerFlags` or `ServerLayout` sections of the configuration file:

   ```
   Option    "Xinerama"
   ```

You can configure any number of screens into a Xinerama display, as long as you can physically fit the video cards into the system (without shorting them out, overloading the power supply, or overheating). If you want to configure a display that has more screens than you have video card slots, you can use *DMX* to combine displays on multiple computers into a single, virtual Xinerama display.

Thin-bezel LCD screens, which have a minimal border surrounding the active LCD area, are ideal for creating monitor arrays for use with Xinerama. They can be physically positioned close together, and their light weight, low-power consumption, and low-heat output make dense placement easier.

For a graphics artist who may prefer a CRT display, it may be better to use a large flat-screen CRT for image preview and editing flanked by LCDs or smaller CRTs for menus, tool palettes, and office productivity software such as email.

 The meaning of *screen* becomes a bit cloudy when dealing with Xinerama. Each monitor and video card is a called a screen in the configuration file, but the merged image area that spans all of the monitors is called a screen in the displayspec and the X protocol. Wherever there might be confusion, I'll use the term *hardware screen* to denote a monitor and video card, and the term *Xinerama screen* to mean the merged image area.

# 4.3  Differences Between Multi-Screen and Xinerama Modes

There are advantages and disadvantages to both Xinerama and multi-screen modes.

When using a multi-screen configuration, each screen stands on its own, and the only relationship between the screens is that one window manager, mouse, and keyboard is used with all three. But when using Xinerama, the hardware screens are merged into one logical Xinerama screen; a single, rectangular Xinerama screen is created that is large enough to contain all of the areas displayed the hardware screens.

If the monitors are different sizes, then there will be portions of this rectangle that are inaccessible—part of the Xinerama screen, but not part of any hardware screen, as shown in Figure 4-1.

Since these areas will not be displayed on any monitor, it is possible to temporarily lose your mouse pointer (or entire windows) in them. You can't do that on a multi-screen configuration, because multi-screen mode doesn't have inaccessible areas—the mouse pointer position is warped so that it's always visible on one of the screens.

The behavior of window managers and desktops also varies significantly between the Xinerama and multi-screen modes, as shown in Table 4-1.

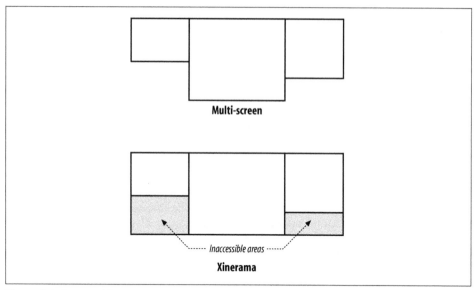

Figure 4-1. Inaccessible areas in a Xinerama screen

Table 4-1. Differences in desktop and window manager behavior between Xinerama and multi-screen modes

| Desktop or window manager | Xinerama mode | Multi-screen mode |
| --- | --- | --- |
| Gnome (using Metacity) | Xinerama-aware: maximizing a window causes it to fill one monitor only, and dialogs are centered on the monitor. Wallpapers can be scaled or tiled to fill the whole screen (across all of the monitors). One menu and panel bar appears, on screen 0. | Panel bars appear on screen 0 only. Wallpaper images are repeated on all screens. |
| KDE (using kwm) | Ximerama-aware, same as Gnome. | Panel bars and K-menus repeated on each screen. Wallpaper images appear on screen 0 only; selected background colors or gradients appear on other screens. |
| MWM (Lesstif version) | Unaware that the screen is not physically one large display. Maximizing a window causes it to span all monitors, and centered dialogs are centered in the whole Xinerama screen (which may cause them to span monitors or even appear in an inaccessible area), instead of being centered on a monitor. | Client windows opened using the root menus open in the correct screen. Maximizing a window causes it to fill one screen only. |
| twm | Manages whole screen as though it were one physical display. | Manages only screen 0. |

So when is each mode useful?

Xinerama is probably the best bet if you're using multiple screens just to get more real estate—for example, if you have multiple monitors side-by-side on a desk or arranged with monitor arms or frames in a rectangular array.

Multi-screen operation is a good choice when the screens serve different purposes, such as when one screen is connected to a projector and the other is used for display management, or one screen is used for a customer-facing point-of-sale display and the other is used for a staff-facing display.

# 4.4   Positioning Screens

If you have two or more monitors, you can place them one above the other, side by side, or diagonally. Even a simple side-by-side arrangement can take different forms, especially when the monitors are different sizes: do the tops of the monitors line up, or the bottoms? Or is the side of the smaller monitor centered at the side of the larger monitor?

Figure 4-2 illustrates a few of the many possibilities for two monitors of different sizes.

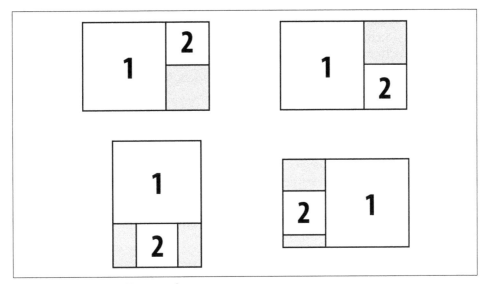

*Figure 4-2. Two-screen Xinerama layouts*

You can use three different methods to describe position information in Screen entries within a ServerLayout section:

- You can use an absolute X-Y pixel position within the Xinerama screen. Increasing X values go to the right, and increasing Y values go down.

```
# Three 1024x768 video projectors. ProjectorA is at the top, ProjectorB
# is below that, and ProjectorC is at the bottom. Each projector
# and is aligned on the left side. Note that the Absolute keyword
# is optional (and not supported by old versions of the server).
Screen 0 "ProjectorA" 0 0
Screen 1 "ProjectorB" Absolute 0 768
Screen 2 "ProjectorC" Absolute 0 1536
```

- You can use the Above, Below, LeftOf, or RightOf keywords. This will cause the top or left side of the screens to be aligned. For example:

```
# ProjectorB is to the right of ProjectorA. The tops of all
# projectors are aligned. Note that we don't need to know the
# resolution of the projectors - the the positions are
# calculated by the X server.
Screen 0 "ProjectorA" 0 0
Screen 1 "ProjectorB" RightOf "ProjectorA"
Screen 2 "ProjectorC" LeftOf  "ProjectorA"
```

- You can use the Relative keyword and specify a position relative to the upper-left corner of another screen using X-Y pixel coordinates:

```
# ProjectorB is directly above ProjectorC on the left.
# ProjectorA is centered between them on the right.
Screen 0 "ProjectorA" 0 0
Screen 1 "ProjectorB" Relative "ProjectorA" -1024 -384
Screen 2 "ProjectorC" Relative "ProjectorA" -1024  384
```

When using Xinerama, screen position affects how windows that span screens will be presented, where inaccessible areas are located, and where the cursor appears when you move from one screen to another.

When using a multi-screen configuration, screen position affects only how the mouse cursor moves from screen to screen.

## 4.5   Overlapping Xinerama

Hardware screens in a Xinerama configuration are usually set up to be adjacent—but they don't have to be. The screens can overlap, as shown in Figure 4-3.

One of the simplest uses of overlapping layouts is to drive two monitors with the same image without using a video splitter. The ServerLayout for this configuration looks like this:

```
Section "ServerLayout"
        Identifier      "layout0"
        Screen       0  "Screen0" 0 0
        Screen       1  "Screen1" 0 0 # Same origin as screen 0
        InputDevice     "Mouse0" "CorePointer"
        InputDevice     "Keyboard0" "CoreKeyboard"
        Option          "SingleCard" "true"
EndSection
```

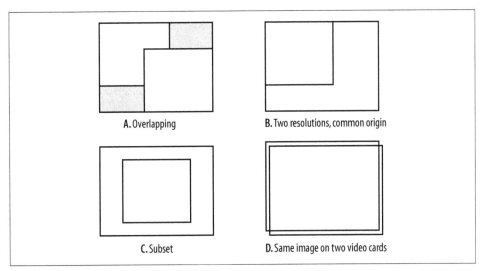

A. Overlapping  B. Two resolutions, common origin

C. Subset  D. Same image on two video cards

*Figure 4-3. Overlapping Xinerama layouts*

Overlapping layouts can also be used to creatively solve some tricky display problems. For example, the presentation program OpenOffice.org Impress does not have a dual-screen display feature (as of version 2.0). This missing feature is vital for certain live presentations, because it permits an operator to preview and select the next slide to appear using a control screen that is not visible to the audience. This is used in churches to handle unexpected changes in the flow of the service—such as a songleader deciding to repeat a chorus—and it is used in business meetings to jump directly to appropriate slides during Q&A sessions.

Until this feature is added to Impress, overlapping Xinerama windows provide a partial solution. When operating with the default user interface layout, Impress provides a display with three panes: a slide preview, an enlarged image of the current slide, and a task plane with layouts that can be applied to slides.

By configuring the X server to display the control screen at high resolution (such as 1440×1050 or 1280×1024) and the projector screen at a lower resolution (800× 600), with the projector screen positioned as a subset of the control screen, it is possible to simulate two-screen operation. Figure 4-4 shows the contents of the control screen, and Figure 4-5 shows the contents of the projector screen using this configuration. The presentation operator can preview the next slide to be displayed using the Impress slide pane without disturbing the projected image.

To configure this operation, set the resolution of the two screens, and then offset the projector within the control screen. In this ServerLayout section, I placed the projector screen 200 pixels below and to the right of the upper-left corner of the control screen:

```
Section "ServerLayout"
        Identifier     "layout0"
```

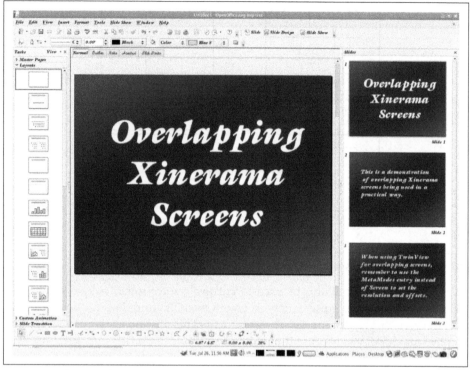

*Figure 4-4. The control screen at 1400×1050*

```
Screen      0  "Screen0"   0 0
# Screen 1 is 200 pixels down and to the right
Screen      1  "Screen1"   200 200
InputDevice    "Mouse0"       "CorePointer"
InputDevice    "Keyboard0" "CoreKeyboard"
EndSection
```

This configuration assumes multiple video cards. However, some video cards with multiple outputs—including laptops—can be configured for Xinerama operation using driver-specific options.

 It's possible to configure multi-screen mode with overlapping screens, but I don't know of any situation where this would be useful.

## 4.6   Scrolling Virtual Screens and Xinerama

The virtual screen facility permits a screen to exceed the size of a physical display, which results in a physical display that scrolls around the virtual screen. It is possible to combine this with Xinerama, but the results are pretty strange.

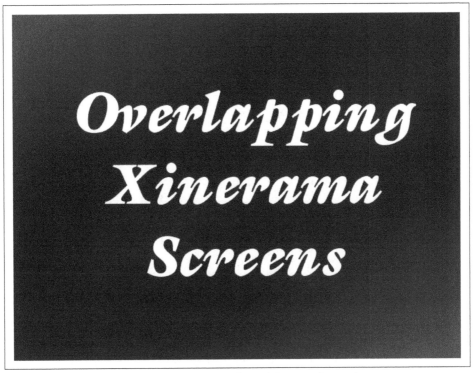

*Figure 4-5. The projected screen (an 800×600 subset of the control screen)*

Figure 4-6 shows the relationship between virtual screens, physical screens, and the Xinerama screen. In this example, the virtual size of screen 0 is the same as the physical size of screen 1, but the resolution of the physical screen 0 is lower.

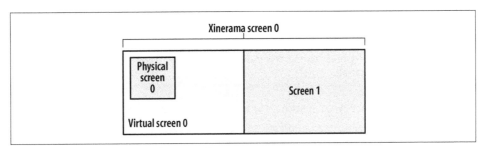

*Figure 4-6. Xinerama and scrolling virtual screens*

The mouse pointer will still cause the screen 0 to scroll until the right edge of the virtual screen is encountered, at which point the mouse will move onto the adjacent screen 1.

I find the visual effect disorienting, and it's even worse if more than one screen is configured to scroll. I can't think of a good use for this configuration!

However, it might be useful to configure two Xinerama screens of the same size, where one screen is completely displayed on a monitor and the other screen is a virtual screen with a smaller physical screen, as shown in Figure 4-7.

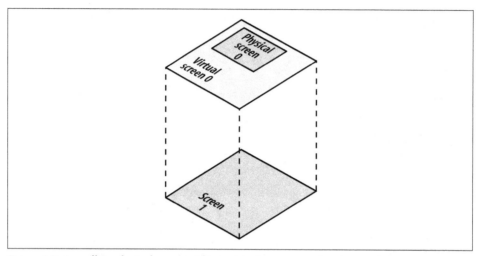

*Figure 4-7. A scrolling physical screen within a virtual screen, overlapping another screen*

In this configuration, the monitor on screen 1 will show the entire screen, while the monitor on screen 0 will show a scrolling enlargement of one portion of the display—potentially useful for people with visual impairment. Unfortunately, Xinerama will only display the mouse cursor on one monitor at a time, and unless the cursor is on the scrolling screen, there is no way to scroll it. Since the mouse cursor will appear on the lowest-numbered screen, the scrolling screen must be configured as screen 0.

 Some of the drivers that permit the simultaneous use of two video outputs from one video card (Section 4.7) enable the mouse pointer to appear on both monitors simultaneously when using an overlapping configuration.

The Screen and ServerLayout sections for this configuration look like this:

```
Section "ServerLayout"
        Identifier      "XFree86 Configured"
        Screen       0  "Screen0" 0 0
        Screen       1  "Screen1" 0 0
        InputDevice     "Mouse0" "CorePointer"
        InputDevice     "Keyboard0" "CoreKeyboard"
        Option          "Xinerama"
EndSection

Section "Screen"               # Scrolling, magnified display
        Identifier "Screen1"
```

```
        Device      "Card1"
        Monitor     "Monitor1"
        DefaultDepth    24
        SubSection "Display"
                Depth     24
                Virtual 1280 1024       # Virtual size to scroll around
                # Do not specify a viewport -- center around the cursor
                Modes   "640x480"
        EndSubSection
EndSection

Section "Screen"              # Full-screen display
        Identifier "Screen0"
        Device      "Card0"
        Monitor     "Monitor0"
        DefaultDepth    24
        SubSection "Display"
                Depth     24
                Modes   "1280x1024"
        EndSubSection
EndSection
```

# 4.7   Using Multiple Outputs from One Video Card

Many current video cards support multiple video outputs: dual VGA, DVI and VGA, VGA and TV-out, and laptop panel and VGA are all common combinations. Some of the X.org drivers support the simultaneous use of both outputs; this works by allocating a large framebuffer and then positioning the rectangles that will be output to each video connection within that framebuffer.

This sounds a lot like Xinerama, because it is! However, there are a few differences between using multiple outputs on one card and using multiple video cards, as outlined in Table 4-2.

*Table 4-2. Differences between using multiple outputs from one video card and using Xinerama mode on multiple cards*

|  | Multiple outputs on one video card | Xinerama with multiple video cards |
| --- | --- | --- |
| Mouse cursor | Appears on both monitors if overlapping | Appears on one monitor at a time |
| Configuration file | One `Screen` section (with driver-specific options in the `Device` section) | Two `Screen` sections |
| 3D capabilities | Available on both monitors (if supported at all) | Dependent on the combination of cards and drivers; many configurations will not support all features on all cards. |

This capability is available in a number of drivers: the NVIDIA closed-source driver *NVIDIA*, the ATI open source driver *radeon*, and the ATI closed-source driver *fglrx*. All of these drivers have some limitations; for example, the NVIDIA driver, when used on a laptop, will always configure an external monitor as primary (screen 0), and the ATI drivers permit only general monitor positioning (you can specify that one monitor is to the right of another, but you can't indicate a difference in their vertical alignment).

 *xrandr 1.2* can reconfigure and add outputs on-the-fly, enabling full Xinerama configuration while the server is running. This feature is not yet supported by many of the drivers or desktop environments, but it promises incredible flexibility—for example, new monitors could automatically work as soon as they are plugged in. You can experiment with this dynamic reconfiguration capability using the *xrandr* utility.

Although the configuration process is similar for each card, the option names vary. Here is a description the process for the options that you will need in the Device section:

1. Enable the driver:

| | |
|---|---|
| **NVIDIA** | Option "TwinView" |
| **radeon** | Option "MergedFB" |
| **fglrx** | Option "DesktopSetup" "0x00000200" if connector 1 is connected to the monitor on the left, or Option "DesktopSetup" "0x00000201" if connector 1 is connected to the monitor on the right |

2. Set the second monitor's horizontal synchronization and vertical refresh rates (the first monitor's rates are set with the normal HSync and VRefresh entries):

| | |
|---|---|
| **NVIDIA** | Option "SecondMonitorHorizSync" "*range*" |
| | Option "SecondMonitorVertRefresh" "*range*" |
| **radeon** | Option "CRT2HSync" "*range*" |
| | Option "CRT2VRefresh" "*range*" |
| **fglrx** | Option "HSync2" "*range*" |
| | Option "VRefresh2" "*range*" |

3. Set the relative CRT positions:

| | |
|---|---|
| **NVIDIA** | Option "TwinViewOrientation" "*position*" where *position* is Above, Below, LeftOf, or RightOf; or use the MetaModes option (see step 4) |
| **radeon** | Option "CRT2Position" "*position*" where *position* is Above, Below, LeftOf, or RightOf |
| **fglrx** | Controlled by the DesktopSetup option |

4. Set the CRT modes to be used on each monitor:

| | |
|---|---|
| **NVIDIA** | `Option "MetaModes" "`*`modes`*`"`, where *modes* are pairs of values separated by commas. For example, `"800×600,1024×768"` would configure 800×600 resolution on the first monitor and 1280×1024 resolution on the second monitor. You can indicate the absolute monitor position within the screen by specifying the X and Y coordinates in the form *+X+Y* after the resolution; `"800x600+150+200,1280x1024+0+0"` would specify that the first monitor displayed an 800×600 subset of the image on the second monitor, starting at the screen coordinate (150,200). To enable the user to switch between metamodes using the server's zoom keys, separate multiple configurations with a semicolon: `"800x600,1024x768;640x480,1024x768"`. |
| **radeon** | `Option "MetaModes" "`*`modes`*`"`, where *modes* are pairs of values separated by dashes. "800x600-1024x768" configures 800×600 on the first monitor and 1280×1024 on the second monitor. To enable the user to switch between metamodes using the server's *zoom keys*, separate multiple configurations with a space: `"800x600-1024x768 640x480-1024x768"`. |
| **fglrx** | Configured by the driver based on available modes. |

5. Choose whether or not to enable hints through the Xinerama extension.

If hints are enabled, clients can get information about the monitors from the X server, which will in most cases result in more intelligent operation of the window managers—for example, maximized windows will fill one monitor instead of both, and dialogs will be centered in one monitor instead of being centered in the virtual screen (which may cause them to span monitors, or—in rare cases—end up in an inaccessible area). You should not enable both this option and the X server's normal Xinerama handling at the same time.

| | |
|---|---|
| **NVIDIA** | `Option "TwinViewXineramaInfo" "bool"` where `bool` is `On` or `Off`. This option is enabled by default. |
| **radeon** | `Option "MergedXinerama" "`*`bool`*`"` where *`bool`* is `On` or `Off`. This option is enabled by default. |
| **fglrx** | Xinerama extensions are not available. |

 The second monitor does not require a `Monitor` section in the configuration file.

You can find specific configuration information for the *radeon* driver from `man radeon`, and for the *NVIDIA* closed-source driver from */usr/share/doc/NVIDIA_GLX-1.0/README.txt*.

# 4.8 Parallel Pointing Devices

It's often convenient to have multiple pointing devices that work in parallel—such as a TouchPad and a mouse. This gives the user the flexibility to use whichever device is

---

most convenient for the task at hand; perhaps input is easier with a keyboard-mounted TouchPad, but surfing is easier with a mouse.

If youre using Linux, there is a very simple way to configure multiple mice: simply specify */dev/input/mice* as the pointer input device. This will merge input from the PS/2 and all USB mice.

However, if you're not using Linux, have serial mice, or wish to configure each device separately (for example, to enable the special features of a Synaptics Touch-Pad), you will need to create multiple InputDevice sections, then reference each of them through an InputDevice entry in the ServerLayout.

The first, primary InputDevice entry must have the argument CorePointer. Other devices must have the argument SendCoreEvents (or the synonym, AlwaysCore):

```
Section "ServerLayout"
        Identifier      "XFree86 Configured"
        Screen      0  "Screen0" 0 0
        InputDevice     "Mouse0"      "CorePointer"         # Main pointer
        InputDevice     "Synaptics" "SendCoreEvents"        # Secondary pointer
        InputDevice     "Keyboard0" "CoreKeyboard"
EndSection
Section "InputDevice"
        Identifier  "Mouse0"
        Driver      "mouse"
        Option      "Device" "/dev/input/mouse0"
EndSection
Section "InputDevice"
        Identifier  "Synaptics"
        Driver      "synaptics"
        # Device will be discovered automatically
EndSection
```

Alternately, the CorePointer and SendCoreEvents values can be moved from the ServerLayout section to the InputDevice section; this syntax is used in configuration files generated by the automatic configuration tools on Debian systems:

```
Section "ServerLayout"
        Identifier      "XFree86 Configured"
        Screen      0  "Screen0" 0 0
        InputDevice     "Mouse0"
        InputDevice     "Synaptics"
        InputDevice     "Keyboard0" "CoreKeyboard"
EndSection
Section "InputDevice"
        Identifier  "Mouse0"
        Driver      "mouse"
        Option      "Device" "/dev/input/mouse0"
        Option      "CorePointer"                           # Main pointer
EndSection
Section "InputDevice"
```

```
        Identifier  "Synaptics"
        Driver      "synaptics"
        Option      "SendCoreEvents"           # Secondary pointer
        # Device will be discovered automatically
    EndSection
```

The X server will fail if no pointer device can be opened. You can override this behavior with an `AllowMouseOpenFail` option entry in the `ServerFlags` (or `ServerLayout`) section:

```
Section "ServerFlags"
    Option "AllowMouseOpenFail" "Yes"
EndSection
```

You can also specify the option `-allowMouseOpenFail` on the X server command line.

 It's also possible to merge the input from two or more mice using *GPM* or *MOUSED* (Section 4.10).

# 4.9   Parallel Keyboards

The X server normally gets keyboard input from the VT on which it is running. On some systems, including Linux and some versions of Solaris, the input from multiple keyboard devices is merged by the kernel (with help from the hotplug subsystem). Therefore, no configuration is required to set up additional parallel keyboards.

Instead of relying on this default behavior, you can specify a specific device in the keyboard `InputDevice` section. This is potentially useful if you want input from only one of several attached keyboards, if you wish to use different layouts for different keyboards, or if you're using a system that does not merge keyboard input. However, the keyboard device interfaces don't present data in the same form as the VT interfaces, so they can't be used with the X server's normal keyboard driver.

The solution? Use the endev keyboard driver.

To use a keyboard with this patch, you need to identify the keyboard either by name or by physical connection. You can get the name and physical connection values for current devices by examining */proc/bus/input/devices*. The keyboard entries in this file will look like this:

```
I: Bus=0011 Vendor=0001 Product=0001 Version=ab41
N: Name="AT Translated Set 2 keyboard"
P: Phys=isa0060/serio0/input0
H: Handlers=kbd event0
B: EV=120013
B: KEY=4 2000000 3802078 f840d001 f2ffffdf ffefffff ffffffff fffffffe
B: MSC=10
B: LED=7

I: Bus=0003 Vendor=0566 Product=2802 Version=0211
```

```
N: Name="MONTEREY USB K/B WITH ACPI"
P: Phys=usb-0000:00:1d.1-1/input0
H: Handlers=kbd event4
B: EV=12000b
B: KEY=ff 10000 7 ff87207a c14057ff febeffdf ffefffff ffffffff fffffffe
B: ABS=100 0
B: LED=7

I: Bus=0003 Vendor=0566 Product=2802 Version=0211
N: Name="MONTEREY USB K/B WITH ACPI"
P: Phys=usb-0000:00:1d.1-1/input1
H: Handlers=kbd event5
B: EV=3
B: KEY=1f0000 0 0 c000 100000 0 0 0
```

This system has a standard PS/2 keyboard attached, as shown in the first block, plus a USB keyboard, shown in the last two blocks. The USB keyboard is shown twice because it presents two keyboard interfaces to the system: the first one for standard keys, and the second one for additional multimedia keys, such as volume control, mute, scroll, and dedicated application buttons.

In each case, the device name is specified on the N: line, after Name=, and the physical connection is specified on the P: line, after Phys=.

The physical connection of a USB device will change every time the USB arrangement is disturbed—for example, when the keyboard is unplugged and moved to a different USB port, or a hub is added between the keyboard and the system. If you have just one keyboard of a particular type, it's best to identify it by device name, so that it can be found regardless of which port you plug it into. However, if you need to specify one keyboard out of several identical ones, you have no choice but to use the physical connection name.

Here is an InputDevice section configured to accept input only from a USB keyboard (taken from the */proc/bus/input/devices* output above), specifying the evdev protocol and using the DevPhys option to specify the physical connection:

```
Section "InputDevice"
    Identifier    "USB Keyboard"
    Driver        "kbd"
    Option        "Protocol"    "evdev"
    Option        "DevPhys"     "usb-0000:00:1d.1-1/input0"
EndSection
```

To specify a keyboard by name, use the DevName option:

```
Section "InputDevice"
    Identifier    "USB Keyboard"
    Driver        "kbd"
    Option        "Protocol"    "evdev"
    Option        "DevName"     "MONETEREY USB K/B WITH ACPI"
EndSection
```

Both the DevName and DevPhys options accept wildcards:

\*     Matches zero or more characters

?     Matches any one character

This permits you to specify device names such as \*KEYBOARD\* or physical connections such as usb-\*/input0 for maximum flexibility with hot-plugged devices.

Once you have the InputDevice sections set up, you can include references to them in the ServerLayout section. Similar to parallel mice (Section 4.8), the primary keyboard must be identified as a CoreKeyboard in the ServerLayout or InputDevice sections; secondary keyboards must have the SendCoreEvents option:

```
Section "ServerLayout"
        Identifier     "XFree86 Configured"
        Screen      0  "Screen0" 0 0
        InputDevice    "Mouse0"
        InputDevice    "Synaptics"
        InputDevice    "AT Keyboard"     "CoreKeyboard"
        InputDevice    "USB Keyboard0"    "SendCoreEvents"
EndSection
```

The X server will fail if no keyboard can be found.

# 4.10  Using X with GPM or MOUSED

Both Linux and FreeBSD provide daemons that permit a mouse to be used on text consoles. The X server mouse configuration may need to be changed if you are using these daemons.

## GPM Under Linux

The *General Purpose Mouse (GPM)* daemon on Linux automatically detects the mode of current VT; when it is in a graphic mode, it stops processing mouse events. When the VT returns to text mode, *GPM* resumes processing.

For serial, PS/2, and USB mice, this works well. A few very old mice use a separate adapter, either on a standalone ISA/PCI card or built into the video card. The kernel drivers for these *bus mice* cannot be opened by more than one program at a time, so if *GPM* is in use, the X server won't be able to get input from the mouse.

*GPM* provides a solution: for these types of mice, it can repeat all of the mouse data on a different device interface whenever the VT is in graphic mode. This permits the X server to get the mouse input without opening the mouse device a second time.

To use *GPM* in this mode, configure the X server to use the mouse device */dev/ gpmdata* in the pointer InputDevice section:

```
Section "InputDevice"
        Identifier  "Mouse0"
        Driver      "mouse"
        Option      "Device" "/dev/gpmdata"
EndSection
```

You must ensure that the gpm command is invoked with the -R (repeat) option:

```
$ gpm -R
```

If *GPM* is started at boot time by your system's init scripts, you may be able to add this option by editing a configuration file. For example, on Fedora systems, you can add the -R to the OPTIONS setting in */etc/sysconfig/mouse*; on older Red Hat systems, adjust the OPTIONS setting in */etc/sysconfig/gpm*; and on SUSE systems, edit the GPM_ PARAM setting in */etc/sysconfig/mouse*.

Only one copy of *GPM* should be run at a time. To use *GPM* with multiple mice, use the -M option. If you use -M and -R together, *GPM* will repeat the data from both mice on */dev/gpmdata*, so you do not need to mention the second mouse in the X server configuration file.

## MOUSED Under FreeBSD

The FreeBSD *MOUSED* daemon provides mouse capabilities for text-mode VTs. It always reads the mouse device, regardless of whether the VT is in text mode or graphic mode, and it repeats the mouse data on */dev/sysmouse*.

To use *MOUSED* with X, configure the pointer InputDevice section of the X configuration file to read from */dev/sysmouse*:

```
Section "InputDevice"
        Identifier  "Mouse0"
        Driver      "mouse"
        Option      "Device" "/dev/sysmouse"
EndSection
```

The *sysmouse* data protocol is automatically detected by the X mouse driver and does not need to be specified.

To use multiple mice on FreeBSD, start multiple instances of the *MOUSED* daemon, one for each mouse you wish to use; the data from all of the daemons will be merged and presented on */dev/sysmouse*.

# 5

# Using the X Server

## 5.1  Interacting with the X Server

When you use an X-based GUI, almost all of your interaction is with client programs and not with the X server itself. However, there are a few keystroke combinations that are directly recognized by the server, and there are some features of the X server—such as the clipboard—that are accessible from a number of clients. This chapter covers the use of these features.

## 5.2  Changing Resolution On-the-Fly

The X.org and XFree86 X servers permit you to change between selected resolutions dynamically. The virtual screen size does not change, so any resolution that is lower than the virtual resolution will result in a scrolling screen:

- To go forward in the list of resolutions, press Ctrl-Alt-Plus (on the keypad).
- To go backward in the list of resolutions, press Ctrl-Alt-Minus (on the keypad).

The resolutions are taken from the Modes entry in the X server configuration (Screen section, Display subsection), or the modes reported by your monitor during probing. For example, your Modes entry might look like this:

```
Modes "1280x1024" "1024x768" "800x600" "640x480"
```

In this case, Ctrl-Alt-Plus will reduce the resolution in steps to 640×480, then cause it to jump to 1280×1024; Ctrl-Alt-Minus will increase it in steps to 1280×1024, then jump to 640×480.

This feature, called *zooming*, is useful for temporarily magnifying one part of the screen to inspect fine details in the user interface or to read small text. It can be disabled with a ServerLayout entry:

```
Option "DontZoom"
```

Zooming does not inform clients that the resolution has changed, so nothing is redrawn on the screen. However, the scrolling effect caused by having a virtual resolution higher than the physical resolution can be really annoying.

# 5.3 Changing the Resolution and the Screen Size Dynamically

Although zooming (Section 5.2) has its place, it's often more useful to change both the screen resolution and the virtual screen size simultaneously to eliminate scrolling. Besides the resolution, it can be desirable to change the orientation between landscape and portrait modes (useful on PDAs, tablet PCs, and pivoted monitors) and to change the refresh rate (handy when switching monitors on-the-fly).

The Rotate and Resize (RANDR) extension (Section 1.15) provides these capabilities. When instructed, the server will change the resolution, orientation, and refresh rate of the screen. Clients can use the RANDR extension to request notification of changes in the screen geometry, and then take appropriate action when such notification is received; for example, the desktop environment will change the position and size of panel bars and desktop icons, and the window manager will resize maximized windows and reposition other windows so that they stay on the screen.

To signal the server to change resolution, a special client is required. A command-line client called xrandr is provided with most X distributions.

To see the available modes, simply execute the command xrandr (a --query or -q argument is optional):

```
$ xrandr
SZ:    Pixels        Physical       Refresh
*0   1400 x 1050  ( 301mm x 232mm )  *75   70   60
 1   1280 x 1024  ( 301mm x 232mm )   75   60
 2   1280 x 960   ( 301mm x 232mm )   60
 3   1280 x 800   ( 301mm x 232mm )   75   70   60
 4   1152 x 864   ( 301mm x 232mm )   75   70   60
 5   1280 x 768   ( 301mm x 232mm )   75   70   60
...(lines deleted)...
22    424 x 240   ( 301mm x 232mm )   75   70
23    320 x 240   ( 301mm x 232mm )   75   73   60
Current rotation - normal
Current reflection - none
Rotations possible - normal left inverted right
Reflections possible - none
```

The resolution and refresh rate currently in use are marked with an asterisk.

To change the resolution, use the -s option and provide one of the size codes (the first column of output shown in the preceding code) or the resolution. For example, to change to 1280 × 800 resolution, enter either of these commands:

```
$ xrandr -s 3
$ xrandr -s 1280x800
```

To change the orientation, use the -o option:

```
$ xrandr -o orientation
```

where *orientation* is normal, left, inverted, or right, or the corresponding number 0, 1, 2, or 3.

To change the refresh rate, use the -r option with the refresh rate in Hz (only certain values are permitted at each resolution; see the output of xrandr -q earlier). To select a 70 Hz refresh rate:

```
$ xrandr -r 70
```

Some displays permit *reflection*—mirroring the image left-to-right or top-to-bottom. This can be useful for rear projection applications. The -x and -y options control vertical and horizontal reflection: if they are present, then the image will be reflected.

Most drivers do not provide reflection capability. Some provide rotation only when enabled in the X server configuration file; for example, the closed-source NVIDIA driver requires the entry Option "RandRRotation" to be added to the Device section of the configuration file to enable rotation using RANDR.

KDE provides an applet, *krandr*, which can be added to your panel bar. Clicking on the *krandr* icon will present a list of available resolutions, rotations, reflections, and refresh rates; simply click on the value you wish to use. A similar program named *gnome-display-properties* is included in Gnome.

## 5.4   Using the Middle Mouse Button

The Mac GUI was designed to work optimally with a one-button mouse; Microsoft Windows was designed for two buttons; and the X Window System works best with at least three buttons.

By convention, the middle mouse button pastes currently selected text; this works in almost all X applications. Selected text is text that you've highlighted by holding the primary mouse button while dragging your mouse.

Copying text is therefore a matter of highlighting it, then clicking the middle button wherever you want to paste it. In many cases, this is far more convenient and productive than using the clipboard (which is also available; see Section 5.5). This technique can be used to paste information from a web page into an email message, from a terminal window into a word processor (which is how many of the examples got into the text of this book), or from part of a web form to another part of the same form.

The middle-button behavior is exploited by most X-based web browsers to offer users certain conveniences:

- Middle-clicking on a blank or text portion of a web page (not over a link) will paste selected text as a URI, and the browser will go to that location. Therefore, to go to a URI mentioned in a README file, just highlight the URI and then middle-click in your browser.

- Since many browsers will automatically perform a search if plain words are entered where a URI is expected, you can search by simply highlighting any words (anywhere!) and then middle-clicking in your browser.

- When a link is clicked with the middle mouse button, most X-based browsers will open the link target in a new window or tab instead of replacing the current page; this can be configured in the browser's preference settings.

If you have a scrollwheel, your middle mouse button is probably connected to it; pressing the scrollwheel will click the middle mouse button. If you're using a two-button mouse, you can configure it so that simultaneously pressing the left and right mouse buttons results in a middle mouse click (Section 3.8).

## 5.5   Using the Clipboard

Most modern GUIs, both X-based and non-X-based, have a clipboard mechanism, allowing you to copy or cut data from one document and paste it into another. Table 5-1 outlines the standard clipboard operations.

*Table 5-1. Standard clipboard operations in X-based GUIs*

| Operation | Keyboard shortcut | Memory aid | Description |
|---|---|---|---|
| Copy | Ctrl-C | C for Copy | Copies the current selection to the clipboard. |
| Cut | Ctrl-X | X looks like Scissors | Removes the current selection from the document or file being edited and places it on the clipboard. |
| Paste | Ctrl-V | V looks like an arrow (indicating paste location) | Places the current clipboard data into the document or file being edited. If there is a current selection, the selection is overwritten with the clipboard data. |

Cut, copy, and paste operations may also be invoked from most programs' edit or context menus.

Because X is networked-based, the program placing data onto the clipboard and the program receiving the data from the clipboard may not be on the same computer—in fact, they may not be in the country. They may also have different capabilities as far as the types of data which they understand.

So where is the actual clipboard? There isn't one!

Data is kept by the client that performed the cut or copy operation, and the clipboard contents and available formats are advertised to other clients through the X server. For example, the Firefox web browser may advertise that clipboard data is available in both *text/plain* and *text/html* formats.

When a program is ready to receive clipboard data, usually in response to a paste operation invoked by the user, it requests it from the other client through the X server. The data is formatted into the requested data type and then sent to the requesting client.

If you're pasting from Firefox into OpenOffice, for example, text attributes such as bold, italic, and color can be determined from the HTML markup and preserved; but if you're pasting into the programmer's editor Nedit, the *text/plain* format is used instead, and the HTML tags are not included in the pasted text.

The design of this mechanism has several implications:

- The pasting speed is limited by network performance (practically speaking, this has an impact only for very large amounts of data or slow network connections).
- You can't paste from the clipboard after the program that placed data on the clipboard exits (for example, if you use the Copy function in Mozilla, and then exit Mozilla, you won't be able to paste into another application. The data will be lost.)
- Data that is placed on the clipboard but not pasted is never transferred over the network.
- Data is pasted in the best format that both programs can handle.
- Only one item may be on the clipboard at a time.

A *clipboard manager* is a client that accumulates clipboard selections. This serves two purposes: it lets the user preview and select from several selections, and it keeps the clipboard data around after the *source client*—the program that placed the data on the clipboard—terminates.

Both of these features are valuable, but unfortunately, using a clipboard manager also has two disadvantages: all data placed on the clipboard is copied over the network, regardless of whether it is ever used, and data stored by the clipboard manager is converted into a single format (usually the lower common denominator—the most basic format for a particular type of data).

Three clipboard managers are available:

*xclipboard*
: The clipboard manager traditionally distributed with X. xclipboard handles plain text only.

*Klipper*

> The KDE clipboard manager. Installed by default with KDE, klipper does not interfere with the more recent clipboard action as long as the source client (the one supplying the data) stays running, which lets you do an immediate cut/copy and paste with content negotiation. All other paste operations are in one format only (e.g., when pasting text, formatting and attributes will be lost).

*Gnome-clipboard-manager*

> The Gnome equivalent of klipper. This project was discontinued in 2004 but the software is still available

Various projects on freedesktop.org are focused in improving the clipboard system.

Although the clipboard mechanism can be used with all types of data—including images, sound, and video—very few applications support data types other than text. For a simple example of pasting an image, you can copy an image from Firefox and paste it into OpenOffice.

> Pasting with the clipboard and pasting using a middle mouse click (Section 5.4) work in an almost identical manner: the X server facilitates the data transfer directly from the source client (select/cut/copy) to the destination client (paste). The only real difference is that when the data is advertised through the X server, selected data—used for middle mouse paste—is tagged as being the PRIMARY selection, while data that has been cut or copied to the clipboard is tagged as being the CLIPBOARD selection. (Yes, there is also a SECONDARY selection, but it's almost never used.)

## 5.6   Keyboard Focus

Most modern GUIs (whether X-based or not) use a *click-to-focus* policy: to connect the keyboard to a window, click on it. The window that currently has focus is indicated by a different titlebar or window border.

But as with everything else, X provides mechanism but not policy. In this case, the policy is enforced by the window manager.

The alternative to click-to-focus is *focus-follows-pointer*: whichever window is under the pointer receives focus. This policy is the default for twm and is a configurable option under many window managers. It's also the default when no window manager is active, so if you're experimenting with running clients directly on a raw X server (Section 2.3), you'll need to keep one eye on the mouse cursor when typing.

## 5.7   Keyboard and Mouse Grabs

Instead of using focus to get data from the keyboard, an application can *grab* the keyboard, receiving all keystrokes that are typed. It's also possible for a client to grab the mouse. This is used far more often than may first be apparent; for example, drop-down menus involve a mouse grab, making everything except the menu insensitive to mouse clicks. If you click outside of the menu, the menu code will release the grab and remove the menu. Mouse grabs are also used for modal dialogs that grab the entire screen (but not for modal dialogs that do not interfere with other applications); for example, when logging out of KDE or GNOME, a confirmation dialog is presented to the user, which takes precedence over all other activity—all keystrokes and mouse activity is processed by the confirmation dialog. This forces the user to deal with the confirmation dialog before performing any other task.

Keyboard grabbing presents a security risk, because an application could use a grab to receive keystrokes it otherwise wouldn't. This is potentially a concern when entering passwords or PIN numbers into applications.

The *xterm* terminal program (Section 7.4) provides a *Secure Keyboard* feature that can be used to defend against this type of attack. It ensures that you are typing into the *xterm* window and that no other application can access your keystrokes. It works by grabbing the keyboard itself; the foreground and background colors in the *xterm* window are reversed as long as the keyboard grab is active.

To enable Secure Keyboard mode, hold the Ctrl key and press and hold mouse button 1 (generally the left mouse button, but this is configurable). A pop-up menu will appear, as shown in Figure 5-1; the first option enables the Secure Keyboard mode.

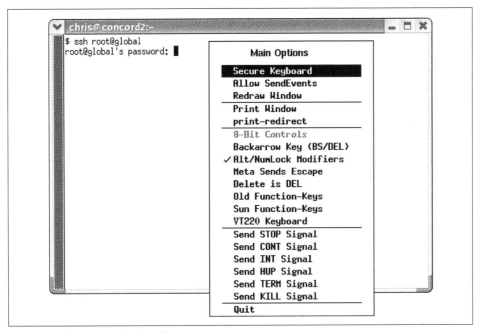

*Figure 5-1. The Secure Keyboard menu option in xterm*

While Secure Keyboard mode is active, you won't be able to type into any other window, regardless of focus. The menu option acts like a toggle; select it again to release the keyboard grab.

Another problem with keyboard and mouse grabs is that a buggy or malicious client application can hang after grabbing these resources, thus making it impossible to end the grab or use other clients. X provides an escape hatch so you don't have to kill the X server. You can configure the X.org server to provide a key combination that releases keyboard and mouse grabs, and another key combination that kills the client performing a keyboard or mouse grab. To enable this feature, add these entries to your X server configuration file's `ServerFlags` or `ServerLayout` section:

```
Option "AllowDeactivateGrabs"
Option "AllowClosedownGrabs"
Option "HandleSpecialKeys" "Always"
```

`AllowDeactivateGrabs` enables the Ctrl-Alt-Keypad Divide key combination, which releases all keyboard and mouse grabs. `AllowClosedownGrabs` enables Ctrl-Alt-Keypad Multiply, which terminates any clients with keyboard or mouse grabs. The `HandleSpecialKeys` entry ensures that these keys will be processed by the server regardless of the keyboard map currently installed.

You can easily check that these key combinations are working by starting an *xterm* and placing it in Secure Keyboard mode. Ctrl-Alt-Keypad Divide should cause the *xterm* to come out of reverse video mode and permit you to type into other applications. On the other hand, pressing Ctrl-Alt-Keypad Multiply terminates the xterm.

There is one situation where keyboard grabs shouldn't be overridden: when a locking screensaver is in use. If the screensaver's keyboard grab can be released, a user could then change VTs; if the X session was started from a shell prompt using the startx command, it could be terminated with Ctrl-C, and the user would then have access to a full shell prompt. An API has been written to guard against this, but it doesn't work with xscreensaver (Section 6.13) because of permission issues, and it won't work with older screensavers at all.

Therefore, a locking screensaver used in an X session started from a command prompt allows a sophisticated user to bypass password protection if the `AllowDeactivateGrabs` or `AllowClosedownGrabs` features are enabled.

# Part II

# X Clients

# 6

# X Utility Programs

## 6.1   The Unused Toolbox

The standard X distribution contains a number of command-line utilities to configure and administer the X server. These tools have been collected over many years, and some have a very old look and feel to them. Indeed, many have been superseded by tools built into modern desktop environments. Nonetheless, they continue to be extremely useful for system administrators. The articles in this chapter will introduce you to the more useful tools in this toolbox.

In addition to the tools discussed in this chapter, the utilities available from X.org include:

*xev (Section 15.4)*
> For testing input events

*xkbsetmap (Section 12.7) and xmodmap (Section 15.4)*
> For setting the keymap

*xlsfonts (Section 10.4), xfontsel (Section 10.4), mkfontdir (Section 10.5), and mkfontscale (Section 10.5)*
> For dealing with old-style fonts

*x11perf, x11perfcomp, and xmark*
> For testing and benchmarking a X server

*xsm (Section 8.2)*
> For session management

*glxinfo, xtrapinfo, and xvinfo*
> For getting information about specific extensions

# 6.2 Determine the Display Configuration

*xdpyinfo* is an X client that gathers information about the display and outputs it to standard output. This very simple program is invaluable when debugging an X server setup.

*xpyinfo* must be run from a terminal program (Section 7.4) or have its output redirected to be useful. It is used like this:

```
$ xdpyinfo
name of display:     :0.0
version number:    11.0
vendor string:    The X.Org Foundation
vendor release number:    60802000
X.Org version: 6.8.2
maximum request size:  16777212 bytes
motion buffer size:  256
bitmap unit, bit order, padding:    32, LSBFirst, 32
image byte order:    LSBFirst
number of supported pixmap formats:    7
supported pixmap formats:
    depth 1, bits_per_pixel 1, scanline_pad 32
    depth 4, bits_per_pixel 8, scanline_pad 32
    depth 8, bits_per_pixel 8, scanline_pad 32
    depth 15, bits_per_pixel 16, scanline_pad 32
    depth 16, bits_per_pixel 16, scanline_pad 32
    depth 24, bits_per_pixel 32, scanline_pad 32
    depth 32, bits_per_pixel 32, scanline_pad 32
keycode range:    minimum 8, maximum 255
focus:  window 0x2a0001c, revert to Parent
number of extensions:    34
    BIG-REQUESTS
    DAMAGE
...snipped...
    XKEYBOARD
    XTEST
    XVideo
    XVideo-MotionCompensation
default screen number:    0
number of screens:    1

screen #0:
    dimensions:    1400x1050 pixels (301x232 millimeters)
    resolution:    118x115 dots per inch
    depths (7):    24, 1, 4, 8, 15, 16, 32
    root window id:    0x113
    depth of root window:    24 planes
    number of colormaps:    minimum 1, maximum 1
    default colormap:    0x20
    default number of colormap cells:    256
    preallocated pixels:    black 0, white 16777215
    options:    backing-store NO, save-unders NO
    largest cursor:    64x64
```

```
current input event mask:     0xfa2033
  KeyPressMask                KeyReleaseMask           EnterWindowMask
  LeaveWindowMask             ButtonMotionMask         StructureNotifyMask
  SubstructureNotifyMask      SubstructureRedirectMask FocusChangeMask
  PropertyChangeMask          ColormapChangeMask
number of visuals:     80
default visual id:  0x21
visual:
  visual id:     0x21
  class:     TrueColor
  depth:     24 planes
  available colormap entries:     256 per subfield
  red, green, blue masks:     0xff0000, 0xff00, 0xff
  significant bits in color specification:     8 bits
visual:
  visual id:     0x22
  class:     DirectColor
  depth:     24 planes
  available colormap entries:     256 per subfield
  red, green, blue masks:     0xff0000, 0xff00, 0xff
  significant bits in color specification:     8 bits
...snipped...
```

I've highlighted the most useful general information in this output: the X server version number, the list of available extensions, and the root information for each screen (including the monitor size, resolution, dots per inch, and color depth).

This information can be used to confirm that your X server configuration file is being processed properly. It can also be used to quickly examine the configuration of a display without digging into the server configuration file—and it works with all X servers, regardless of the vendor.

# 6.3   Getting Window Information

X provides a utility named *xwininfo* for obtaining basic information about a window, including its size, location, visibility, color depth, ID, and name.

When run without arguments, *xwininfo* permits you to interactively select the window to be used:

```
$ xwininfo

xwininfo: Please select the window about which you
          would like information by clicking the
          mouse in that window.
...User selects a window with the mouse...
xwininfo: Window id: 0x363809e "chris@concord2:~"

  Absolute upper-left X:   464
  Absolute upper-left Y:   20
  Relative upper-left X:   6
  Relative upper-left Y:   20
```

```
Width: 737
Height: 898
Depth: 24
Visual Class: TrueColor
Border width: 0
Class: InputOutput
Colormap: 0x20 (installed)
Bit Gravity State: NorthWestGravity
Window Gravity State: NorthWestGravity
Backing Store State: NotUseful
Save Under State: no
Map State: IsViewable
Override Redirect State: no
Corners:  +464+20  -79+20  -79-106  +464-106
-geometry 80x58-73+0
```

I've highlighted the most useful information in the output. Window id, on the first line, can be used as an argument for other commands, such as *xwd* (Section 6.11). Map State indicates whether the window is currently visible or not, and the last line shows the geometry argument (Section 7.4) that could be used on a command line to open the window with the same size and position.

Instead of interactively selecting the window for which you wish to display information, you can select a window by ID (using the -id option). However, this is not often useful, because you usually won't know the ID until you've used *xwininfo*.

Somewhat more useful is the -root option, which tells you about the root window of a screen:

```
$ xwininfo -root
xwininfo: Window id: 0x93 (the root window) (has no name)
   Absolute upper-left X:  0
   Absolute upper-left Y:  0
   Relative upper-left X:  0
   Relative upper-left Y:  0
   Width: 1280
   Height: 1024
   Depth: 24
   Visual Class: TrueColor
   Border width: 0
   Class: InputOutput
   Colormap: 0x20 (installed)
   Bit Gravity State: NorthWestGravity
   Window Gravity State: NorthWestGravity
   Backing Store State: NotUseful
   Save Under State: no
   Map State: IsViewable
   Override Redirect State: no
   Corners:  +0+0  -0+0  -0-0  +0-0
   -geometry 1280x1024+0+0
```

The -children option displays information about the child windows, and the -tree option recursively displays information about child windows and all of their descendants. Since X treats all windows as part of a hierarchy, using -root and -tree together displays information about all of the windows on the screen:

```
$ xwininfo -root -tree
xwininfo: Window id: 0x93 (the root window) (has no name)

  Root window id: 0x93 (the root window) (has no name)
  Parent window id: 0x0 (none)
     311 children:
     0x9ff528 (has no name): ()  749x414+492+0  +492+0
        1 child:
     0x3620ec2 "chris@concord2:~": ("gnome-terminal" "Gnome-terminal")
           737x388+6+20  +498+20
           5 children:
           0x3620eea (has no name): ()  15x362+722+26  +1220+46
           0x3620ece (has no name): ()  722x362+0+26  +498+46
           0x3620ee3 (has no name): ()  737x26+0+0  +498+20
              6 children:
              0x3620ee9 (has no name): ()  40x24+240+1  +738+21
              0x3620ee8 (has no name): ()  31x24+203+1  +701+21
              0x3620ee7 (has no name): ()  64x24+133+1  +631+21
              0x3620ee6 (has no name): ()  42x24+85+1  +583+21
              0x3620ee5 (has no name): ()  37x24+42+1  +540+21
              0x3620ee4 (has no name): ()  35x24+1+1  +499+21
           0x3620ecd (has no name): ()  10x10+0+0  +498+20
           0x3620ec3 (has no name): ()  1x1+-1+-1  +497+19
     0x5600006 "screensaver": ("xscreensaver" "XScreenSaver")
           1280x1024+0+0  +0+0
...lines skipped...
```

The output tells us that the *gnome-terminal* program has 11 child windows; these are not necessarily full-blown application windows, but they may include user interface elements such as pop-up dialogs and menus. Not all of the child windows will be mapped (visible onscreen) at the same time.

The screensaver window is an example of an unmapped window. At 1280×1024, it's large enough to cover the entire screen; *xscreensaver* simply maps this window—making it visible—when the screensaver activates and unmaps it when the screensaver deactivates.

The information displayed for each window includes the window ID, the window name, the application name, and the window geometry.

*xwininfo* also provides options to display other information about the selected window; many of the options are primarily of use to the application developer.

*xwininfo* reveals interesting details about how window managers differ in the way that they implement virtual desktops. Some leave the windows in their original position but unmap (hide) them; others leave them mapped but position them off the screen. This difference explains why some window managers—such as *fvwm2*—permit you to position your viewable desktop so that it arbitrarily spans virtual desktops, but others—such as *Metacity*—require the viewable and virtual desktops to be aligned.

# 6.4   Viewing Server Settings

There are a number of X server configuration settings that can be changed on-the-fly. The *xset* utility enables you to view and change these settings.

To find the current settings, run *xset* with the q (query) option:

```
$ xset q
Keyboard Control:
  auto repeat:  on    key click percent:  0    LED mask:  00000002
  auto repeat delay:  500    repeat rate:  30
  auto repeating keys:  00ffffffdffffbbf
                        fadfffffffdfe5ff
                        ffffffffffffffff
                        ffffffffffffffff
  bell percent:  50    bell pitch:  400    bell duration:  100
Pointer Control:
  acceleration:  3/1    threshold:  3
Screen Saver:
  prefer blanking:  yes    allow exposures:  yes
  timeout:  0    cycle:  0
Colors:
  default colormap:  0x20    BlackPixel:  0    WhitePixel:  16777215
Font Path:
  /home/chris/.gnome2/share/cursor-fonts,unix/:7100,
  /home/chris/.gnome2/share/fonts
Bug Mode: compatibility mode is disabled
DPMS (Energy Star):
  Standby: 600    Suspend: 600    Off: 1200
  DPMS is Enabled
  Monitor is On
Font cache:
  hi-mark (KB): 5120  low-mark (KB): 3840  balance (%): 70
File paths:
  Config file:  /etc/X11/xorg.conf
  Modules path: /usr/lib/xorg/modules/extensions/nvidia,/usr/lib/xorg/modules
  Log file:     /var/log/Xorg.0.log
```

The main difference between *xdpyinfo* and *xset* is that, for the most part, *xdpyinfo* displays unchangeable server information, while the settings displayed by *xset* can be adjusted while the server is running.

The *xset* command holds the key to a number of runtime adjustments to the X server. Here are some of them:

- Changing the X bell (Section 6.5)
- Setting the keyboard repeat options (Section 6.6)
- Accelerating the mouse (Section 6.7)
- Keeping the screen from blanking (Section 6.12)
- Adjusting the font path (Section 10.2)

## 6.5   Control That Bell!

X includes a very basic bell facility—actually, more of a beep than a bell. The term *bell* comes from old teletype terminals, which (in the fashion of typewriters before them) actually contained a bell that could be triggered remotely.

The *xset* command allows you to change the pitch, volume, and duration of the X bell. Any application can trigger the bell, and most terminal programs (Section 7.4) do so when an ASCII *BEL* character (code 7) is received.

On PC hardware, the bell is usually implemented through the system speaker instead of a sound card, since almost every PC has a speaker installed. On some newer laptops (and desktops), the speaker output is routed through the sound card mixer and is sent to the main audio outputs, but many machines still use a separate built-in speaker for the bell.

Your desktop, therefore, might have a 15 cent speaker in the system unit under the desk, packed full of dust and competing with multiple system fans to be heard. There's no way to really control the bell volume, because the PC's speaker circuit simply clocks out a 5-volt square wave of adjustable frequency.

To set the bell, use the b subcommand provided by *xset*:

```
$ xset b volume pitch duration
```

Where *volume* is the volume level from 0–100%, *pitch* is in Hertz, and *duration* is in milliseconds. The X.org server will actually shorten the duration based on the volume setting, in a feeble attempt to make up for the lack of hardware volume control.

The default bell settings in the X.org server are 50% volume, 400 Hz, and 100 ms, which are reasonable for most purposes. If you can't hear the bell, try 100%, 1,200 Hz, and 100 ms:

```
$ xset b 100 1200 100
```

If you don't like the result, just experiment; given the cheap speaker, you'll probably want to stay in the 100 Hz–14,000 Hz range.

You can leave out any of the numeric arguments to xset b starting at the end; if you leave them all out, the settings reset to the defaults. To turn off the bell entirely, use the following:

```
$ xset b off
```

The X bell mechanism provides a trivial way to give audio feedback in a script; this can be useful for various quick-and-dirty applications.

For example, it can be difficult to position Wi-Fi antennas optimally. Here is a simple Linux shell script that, when run in a terminal window, gives audible feedback on Wi-Fi link quality using the X bell. This lets you know what effect your antenna adjustments are having without looking at the screen, which is particularly helpful when you are adjusting an access point in one room to improve reception in another room—just turn up the volume on your laptop to maximum and listen as you fiddle:

```
#!/bin/bash
#
# iwbeep :: beep with a pitch that corresponds to the current
#           link quality reported by iwconfig

while true    # Loop forever
do
    # Get the current link quality from iwconfig
    q=$(/usr/sbin/iwconfig 2>&1|sed -n "s/^.*Link Quality:\([0-9]\+\).*$/\1/p")

    # Calculate a tone based on the quality. Experiment!
    ((b= (q * 3 / 2) ** 2 + 100))

    # Set the bell tone, display the quality, then sound the bell.
    xset b 100 $b
    echo -e "$q\a"
done
```

Warning: this script sounds like a deranged electronic bagpipe player!

It should also be possible to enable a keyclick sound through the PC speaker using the c subcommand of *xset*, but this does not appear to be implemented in X.org.

# 6.6   Adjusting the Keyboard Repeat Rate

Keyboard repeat is a useful option; it lets you enter a row of dashes, or repeatedly move the cursor, simply by holding a key down. But if the keyboard repeats too easily or too quickly, it can be very annoying. The X server permits keyboard repeat to be individually enabled on a key-by-key basis, and the delay before keys start repeating as well as the rate at which they repeat can be adjusted. These parameters are adjusted using *xset*.

---

You can turn keyboard repeat off with the -r or r off options:

```
$ xset r off
$ xset -r
```

Likewise, you can turn it on with r or r on:

```
$ xset r on
$ xset r
```

To enable repeat for a specific key, find the keycode value using *xev* and use that as an argument:

```
$ xset r  65          # spacebar will repeat
$ xset -r 65          # spacebar will not repeat
```

To adjust the repeat rate, the XKB extension must be loaded (which is the default for most X servers). Execute xset with the r subcommand followed by the word rate, the length of time in milliseconds that the key must be held down before it starts repeating, and finally the repeat rate in Hz (with a maximum of 255).

For example, to repeat keys at the rate of 10 characters per second, starting 1 second after a key is held down, enter the following code:

```
$ xset r rate 1000 10
```

To reset the repeat rate to the default settings:

```
$ xset r rate
```

The default settings are a 660 ms delay and a 25 Hz repeat rate.

 Setting the repeat delay too low and the repeat rate too high may make it impossible to type!

# 6.7   Adjusting the Mouse Acceleration

It's important to be able to finely control the pointer position, but it's also important to be able to move the pointer quickly. Mouse acceleration multiplies pointer motion when a preset rate threshold is exceeded; this permits the pointer position to be finely controlled when moving the mouse slowly, but to be moved large distances when the mouse is moved quickly.

The two parameters used to adjust the mouse acceleration are the *acceleration factor*—the number by which the pointer motion is multiplied—and the *threshold*, which must be exceeded before acceleration is applied. The acceleration factor is a straight integer or a fraction (*integer/integer*); the threshold is expressed as the minimum number of pixels the mouse must move in one sample period.

The default acceleration factor is 2, and the default threshold is 4, so moving more than 4 pixels in a sample period will cause the movement to be doubled. This may seem heavy or sluggish to some people; most users seem to prefer acceleration factors in the range of 2–6 but can easily adjust to values up to 10 or higher.

To change the acceleration parameters, use the m subcommand of xset; for example, to set an acceleration factor of 5 and a threshold of 4:

```
$ xset m 5 4
```

To reset to the default values:

```
$ xset m
```

KDE and GNOME each provide their own tools for setting the mouse acceleration, which adjust the same two parameters.

## 6.8 Playing with the Lights

Most keyboards have LEDs indicating NumLock, CapsLock, and ScrollLock status. This is useful information, but most users leave NumLock on and CapsLock off, and never do anything with ScrollLock, so may be more useful to use the LEDs to display other information.

In order to use the keyboard LEDs for other information when using the X.org server and the XKB extension, you will need to enable control of the LEDs from clients. Include this entry in the keyboard InputDevice section of the server configuration file, specifying the list of LEDs you wish to control in the last argument:

```
Options    "Xleds"    "1 2 3"
```

Recent versions of the X.org server do not permit control of LEDs 1 and 2 (NumLock and CapsLock). Only LED 3 (ScrollLock) can be altered.

The LEDs are turned on or off using the led subcommand of xset:

```
$ xset led          # all controllable LEDs on
$ xset -led         # all controllable LEDs off
$ xset led 3         # LED 3 on (ScrollLock)
$ xset -led 3        # LED 3 off
```

Here is a simple script to light the ScrollLock LED whenever you have email:

```
#!/bin/bash
#
# mailled :: light the scroll lock LED when we have mail
#
while sleep 1
do
```

```
        if [ -s $MAIL ]
        then
            xset led 3
        else
            xset -led 3
        fi
    done
```

This script can be executed in the background by a line in your shell profile:

```
    mailed &
```

## 6.9    Killing a Rogue Client

The *xkill* utility enables you to kill an X client by clicking on it. Actually, it doesn't kill the client process, but it does kill the connection between the X server and the client. In most cases, that's enough to cause the client to terminate; in any case, it gets it off the screen.

*xkill* is usually run without any arguments:

```
    $ xkill
```

The mouse cursor will change to a skull-and-crossbones or a type of crosshair, depending on the version of *xkill* installed. Click on the offending window to kill it; middle-click to abort *xkill*.

 KDE will invoke an internal version of xkill when you press Ctrl-Alt-ESC, turning the cursor into a skull-and-crossbones. Pressing Ctrl-Alt-ESC again will turn off xkill mode.

## 6.10  Examining Part of the Display in Detail

*xmag* is a simple utility that magnifies part of the display and displays the color code of selected pixels. Start it without any arguments:

```
    $ xmag
```

The cursor will change into an upper-left frame (⌐). Click on the upper-left corner of the area you wish to magnify. A magnification window will appear, as shown in Figure 6-1.

Click on any pixel to see its color code and screen coordinates. The color codes are reported in 64-bit hexadecimal format, so white is reported as (ffff, ffff, ffff). To convert to 24-bit format, just take the first 2 hexadecimal digits from each group of 4 digits; for example, if the reported color is (3e3e, 4444, a9a9), then the 24-bit X color code is #3e44a9.

You can increase or decrease the magnification by changing the *xmag* window size.

*Figure 6-1. An xmag window*

The buttons at the top of the window perform some useful operations:

*close*
Closes this window.

*replace*
Enables you to select a new region for magnification.

*new*
Opens another window.

*select*
Selects the magnified area (just like highlighting a portion of text in a text editor); a middle mouse click in another program, such as OpenOffice.org, will paste the image. There is no way to place the image on the clipboard (except by pasting into another program and then copying onto the clipboard from that program).

*paste*
Pastes the current selection (*not* the current clipboard contents) into the image display portion of the *xmag* window.

*xmag* is perfect for finding out the color code for a mystery color in a photograph or a web page, for examining fine details of a user interface rendering, or for examining anti-aliased character displays.

# 6.11 Script a Screen Dump

It's often useful to make a *screen dump* (or screen shot), which is a copy of what is on the screen. KDE, GNOME, and the Gimp all provide facilities for doing this, but some applications require a classic tool that is distributed with X itself.

The *X window dump* (*xwd*) tool takes a snapshot of the current screen, a manually selected window or a window designated by its numeric ID, and outputs the image to standard output or to a file. What I find useful about *xwd* is that it can be used in a shell script.

By default, *xwd* will present a crosshair cursor for you to manually select a window:

```
$ xwd >file
```

You can select the entire root window (the whole screen) with the -root option:

```
$ xwd -root >file
```

This works well for getting screenshots of Compiz special effects in action.

You can also specify a particular window by ID. You can obtain the ID from the *xwininfo* command:

```
$ xwd -id IdNumber >file
```

The image format used by *xwd* is unique. A utility named *xwud* (for *X window un-dump*) is provided to display window dump files:

```
$ xwud <file
```

The *xwd* image format can also be opened by the Gimp, ImageMagick (*convert* and *display* programs), and the NetPBM utilities (*xwdtopnm*).

Several of these tools can be combined to automate the process of creating periodic screen dumps:

```
#!/bin/bash
# Produce a screen dump periodically and save as a JPEG

DELAY=5         # seconds between screen dumps
DIR=/tmp/screen # directory to hold screen dumps
I=0             # current image number

mkdir -p ${DIR}

while sleep $DELAY
do
        xwd -root | xwdtopnm | cjpeg >${DIR}/screendump.${I}.jpg
        ((I++))
done
```

Variations on this script could easily update a web page or create an animation demonstrating how to do a task.

 *xwd* clearly demonstrates that an X client can access on-screen data displayed by another client. This poses a serious security risk, which can be somewhat reduced by the use of the SECURITY extension; see Section 13.10 (and, of course, you should never open your X server up to unrestricted network access!).

## 6.12 Preventing the Screen from Blanking During Presentations

DPMS (Section 3.11) is a great tool for saving energy and heat. However, having the screen blank at an inopportune moment—the middle of a presentation, or the most exciting point in a movie—can be very frustrating!

Some applications that may be used for long periods without keyboard or mouse activity, such as *mplayer*, automatically disable the screensaver and DPMS, but many presentation and media player applications do not (surprisingly, this includes some widely used applications such as OpenOffice.org Impress, MagicPoint, and Xine).

*xset* can adjust screensaver and DPMS settings. The `dpms` subcommand can turn DPMS on or off:

```
$ xset +dpms      # dpms on
$ xset -dpms      # dpms off
```

You can also immediately go to one of the four DPMS states:

```
$ xset dpms force state
```

Where *state* is on, standby, suspend, or off.

To set the DPMS times, supply three numeric arguments, representing the number of seconds of inactivity before the standby, suspend, and off states are entered. For example, to set the server to switch to DPMS standby mode after 10 minutes of inactivity, suspend after 15 minutes, and off after 20 minutes, enter the following:

```
$ xset dpms 600 900 1200
```

 The dpms timeouts are configured in minutes in the *xorg.conf* file, but in seconds when using the *xset* command.

*xset* can likewise turn the X server's built-in screensaver on or off using the s subcommand (this is separate from the *xscreensaver* program; see Section 6.13):

```
$ xset s on       # screensaver on
$ xset s off       # screensaver off
```

```
$ xset s default     # screensaver back to default rules
$ xset s time chg    # screensaver times
```

The screensaver time arguments, *time* and *chg*, set the time before the screensaver kicks in and the time before the screensaver image changes, respectively.

It's very easy to write a script to turn off DPMS before starting an application and to turn it on again afterward. This script also checks to see whether *xscreensaver* (Section 6.13) is running, and if it is, exits *xscreensaver* for the duration of the application:

```
#!/bin/bash
xset -dpms s off        # disable dpms and X server screensaver

# determine if xscreensaver is running
if killall -signal 0 xscreensaver >/dev/null 2>&1
then
    xscreensaver-command -exit    # exit current xscreensaver
    xscreensaver="yes"            # remember it was running
fi

"$@"                # run the application specified on the command line

# re-start xscreensaver if necessary
if [ "$xscreensaver" ]
then
    xscreensaver -nosplash &
fi

xset +dpms s default    # dpms and screensaver re-enabled
```

If this script is saved in the file *noblank*, you could use it with xine to show a movie uninterrupted:

```
$ noblank xine MovieFile
```

## 6.13  Eye Candy: xscreensaver

Most security applications rate poorly for fun and overall coolness. *xscreensaver*, on the other hand, is all about fun—in the form of eye candy—and it can help tighten up security, too.

Will a screensaver actually save your screen? Not really; to reduce wear and tear on your monitor, you're probably better off shutting it down using DPMS (Section 3.11). But *xscreensaver* can express your personality, create a bit of pizzaz, and as a bonus, lock your workstation when it's left idle.

The *xscreensaver* package is made up of four programs:

*xscreensaver*
> The server process, which runs in the background waiting until a set amount of time has passed since the last keyboard or mouse input was received.

*xscreensaver-command*
> A command-oriented client for the server.

*xscreensaver-demo*
> An interactive client for the server, which lets you preview the screensaver.

*graphics demos or hacks*
> Programs that provide the interesting visual effects for the screensaver; these exist as individual files in */usr/share/xscreensaver*.

To begin using *xscreensaver*, start the server in the background—this can be done in a startup script file, such as *~/.xinitrc*:

```
$ xscreensaver &
```

The configuration will be retrieved from *~/.xscreensaver*. You can change the configuration using *xscreensaver-demo*:

```
$ xscreensaver-demo
```

You can also control the *xscreensaver* server using *xscreensaver-command* followed by options indicating the action you wish the server to perform. These are the most common and useful options:

*-exit*
> Terminates the server.

*-restart*
> Restarts the server with the same options used when it was initially invoked. This reloads the configuration file and is useful when you have changed the *~/.xscreensaver* file manually (or copied one from another account).

*-activate*
*-deactivate*
> Immediately enables or disables the screen saver, respectively.

*-watch*
> Prints screensaver events to the screen as they happen; useful for logging and to trigger other events that should take place when the screensaver is activated (such as causing a kiosk to revert to its initial state; see Section 15.8).

For example, this command will cause *xscreensaver* to start immediately, as though the display had been left idle for a long period of time:

```
$ xscreensaver-command -activate
```

Note that *xscreensaver* will set the server's DPMS timeouts to the values contained in *~/.xscreensaver* when started. This will override the DPMS settings in the X server configuration file (Section 3.11) or previously set with *xset* (Section 6.12).

To help secure the display when it's idle, you can configure *xscreensaver* to lock the display; the login password is required to unlock it. But beware: this provides little protection if the X server was started from a character-mode VT (Section 2.9). The user can disable keyboard grabs (Section 5.7), and then switch VTs using the keyboard (Section 2.2).

If you're using X in a customer-accessible setting—perhaps at the point of sale or on a receptionist's computer—a screensaver can reduce the risk that a customer will view private or sensitive information. You may as well use the opportunity to convey a message; several of the graphics hacks, such as *fontglide*, enable you used to present text in an interesting manner. Hiding sensitive information on idle displays may be required in regulated industries such as healthcare in some jurisdictions.

Current versions of GNOME and KDE, by default, do not use *xscreensaver*. Instead, they provide their own screensaver utilities.

## 6.14 Redrawing the Screen

Once in a while, a bug in a client program (or, in rare cases, a buggy video card driver) will cause it to leave *artifacts* in its windows—dots, lines, or partial images that shouldn't be there. If you encounter such a misbehaving application, you can clean up the screen image by running *xrefresh*, which causes every client to redraw itself:

```
$ xrefresh
```

xrefresh has no effect on composited displays.

# 7

# Running X Clients

## 7.1 Running X Clients

Running an X client is generally a fairly simple proposition, but it is different from running a character application. This chapter covers:

- Running clients in the background (Section 7.2)
- Requesting a certain window size and position (Section 7.3)
- Running nongraphical programs on an X display (Section 7.4)

Displayspecs (Section 1.12) are a closely related topic.

## 7.2 Background Operation

Most X applications don't need to interact with the user through the standard input and output; therefore, when starting them from a shell prompt, you may as well put them into the background. Simply add an ampersand to the end of the command name:

```
$ kcalc &
```

If you close the terminal from which you started the client, the client will (in almost all cases) be terminated. To avoid this, use the *nohup* command:

```
$ nohup kcalc &
```

 Some error messages may be sent to standard error, which may not be visible when the client is run in the background. When debugging the operation of a client, it may be necessary to redirect *stdout* and *stderr* to a file:

```
$ nohup kcalc >kcalc.log 2>&1 &
```

# 7.3  Geometry

In X Window parlance, *geometry* refers to the size and position of windows. Clients may request a particular geometry when placing a new window, but the window manager can override the request and force another geometry.

The units used for window size vary by application. Terminal windows, for example, are usually sized in text rows and columns (for example, $80 \times 24$ or $132 \times 44$); many applications, such as Firefox, are sized in pixels; and others, such as the *Gimp*, use arbitrary units of the programmer's choosing.

The *xwininfo* command (Section 6.3) will display information about a window's current geometry:

```
$ xwininfo
xwininfo: Please select the window about which you
          would like information by clicking the
          mouse in that window.
...User clicks on a terminal window...
xwininfo: Window id: 0x36059c4 "chris@concord2:~"

  Absolute upper-left X:  485
  Absolute upper-left Y:  59
  Relative upper-left X:  6
  Relative upper-left Y:  20
  Width: 710
  Height: 538
  Depth: 24
  Visual Class: TrueColor
  Border width: 0
  Class: InputOutput
  Colormap: 0x20 (installed)
  Bit Gravity State: NorthWestGravity
  Window Gravity State: NorthWestGravity
  Backing Store State: NotUseful
  Save Under State: no
  Map State: IsViewable
  Override Redirect State: no
  Corners:  +485+59  -85+59  -85-427  +485-427
  -geometry 77x34-79+39
```

Note that the *geometry specification* (or simply, *geometry*) is 77x34-79+39, but the width is 710 pixels and the height is 538 pixels!

The geometry specification is in this form:

```
WIDTHxHEIGHT XPOSITION YPOSITION
```

where the following definitions are true:

*WIDTH*
    The window width in the increments used by the application.

*HEIGHT*

The vertical height of the window in the increments used by the application.

*XPOSITION*
*YPOSITION*

The horizontal and vertical coordinates of the upper-left corner of the window frame, including any window border, title bar, or other ornamentation added by the window manager. If these numbers start with a plus sign (+), then they are relative to the upper-left corner of the screen; if they start with a minus sign (-), then they are relative to the lower-right corner of the screen.

Therefore, the geometry shown in the earlier example, 77x34-79+39, is interpreted as meaning that the window should be 77 units high and 34 units wide, and the upper-left corner of the window should be 79 pixels left from the right side of the screen and 39 pixels down from the top of the screen.

You can use both + and - on the same geometry positioning expression. The first sign indicates the starting corner (upper-left or lower-right), and the second is used to indicate the sign of the value. Therefore, a geometry specification of 200x200+-100+50 specifies a window size of 200×200, and a window starting off the screen 100 pixels to the left of the screen's left edge and 50 pixels from the top.

But what is the unit of measure for the size? We can determine that by giving *xwininfo* the -size option:

```
$ xwininfo -size

xwininfo: Please select the window about which you
          would like information by clicking the
          mouse in that window.
...User selects the window...
xwininfo: Window id: 0x36059c4 "chris@concord2:~"

   Normal window size hints:
       Program supplied minimum size: 53 by 58
       Program supplied base size: 17 by 28
       Program supplied x resize increment: 9
       Program supplied y resize increment: 15
       Program supplied minimum size in resize increments: 5 by 3
       Program supplied base size in resize increments:  1 by 1
       Program supplied window gravity: NorthWestGravity
   No zoom window size hints defined
```

Here we can clearly see that the window has set the size increment to 9 pixels horizontally and 15 pixels vertically. Therefore the width of the window is 77*9=693 pixels, and the height is 34*15=510 pixels. We can also see that the minimum window size is 5*9=45 pixels, and the minimum height is 3*15=45 pixels.

Many applications allow you to specify the geometry on the command line. The option is -geometry for applications that use Xt-based toolkits (Athena and Motif), or it's --geometry for GTK+ and Qt-based applications.

These commands all open up a 25-line, 80-character-wide terminal window, located 100 pixels below the top of the screen and 50 pixels to the right of the left edge of the screen:

```
$ gnome-terminal --geometry 80x25+50+100     # GTK+
$ konsole -geometry 660x475+50+100           # Qt
$ xterm -geometry 80x25+50+100               # Xt
```

Notice that the *konsole* size is specified in pixels, which the *xterm* and *gnome-terminal* sizes are specified in characters.

# 7.4   Split Personality: Running Nongraphical Applications

From before X was released up to a few years ago, character terminals were in widespread use. These devices had a character-only display, typically 80 columns wide by 24 or 25 rows high, and a keyboard. Each model of terminal varied in its display capabilities—some had color, some offered varying font sizes for 132- and 40-column display modes, and some could draw underlined and bold text—and in its keyboard layout. These terminals were typically connected to the host computer through a serial cable, which required as little as 3 wires and could be over 100 meters long (300 foot). Modems, designed to work with serial interfaces, could be used to extend this distance over the dial-up telephone network.

Many applications have been written with a character-based interface intended for use with a terminal. Standard utilities such as cp, mv, and ls, and server programs such as Apache just write plain text to standard output and standard error; other programs—including many editors (vi, Emacs, Joe, and Pico) and applications such as Midnight Commander and Pine—take over the full terminal screen, sending sequences of control characters to position text and control the display attributes.

These full-screen programs use a *curses* library, which looks up the terminal type in a database to determine its capabilities, the codes used to control those capabilities, and the special codes that may be received from the keyboard (for example, when a function key is pressed). The terminal type is retrieved from the environment variable TERM.

In addition to controlling the terminal using *curses*, character applications also control the characteristics of the serial line connected to the terminal, such as whether characters that are typed are echoed back to the display (which is the case when using a shell) or not (when entering a password). These attributes are configured using the operating system's *termios* interface.

X by itself is incompatible with all character-based applications. The X server does not provide a *termios* interface and cannot be configured to understand the types of control codes emitted by *curses*.

In order to bridge this gulf and use character-based programs with X, it is necessary to use a two-sided application that presents a *termios* interface on one side and is a client to an X server on the other side. This application must translate incoming X events: keypress events are translated into ASCII sequences, window closure is translated into a modem hangup signal (SIGHUP), and so forth. Likewise, it must emulate *termios* operations such as echo management and translate *curses* code sequences into the appropriate X protocol commands.

These applications are known as *terminal emulators*. The granddaddy of them all is *xterm*, which has been distributed with X11 since it was first released. Various terminal emulators have been developed to extend or improve on *xterm*, including *rxvt*, *wterm*, and *eterm*. Each of the major desktop environments also includes a terminal emulator: GNOME has *gnome-terminal* and KDE has *konsole*.

Most of the Unix/Linux terminal emulators used with X understand the same codes as the original *xterm* program, and therefore are usually used with the TERM environment variable set to *xterm* (since the *xterm* codes are based on those used by the DEC VT102 terminal, which were later standardized in ANSI X3.64, the value vt102 or ansi is sometimes used).

In addition to the ASCII-based terminal emulators discussed here, most X installations also include *x3270*, which is an IBM EBCDIC-based terminal emulator that is used with mainframes. Another common emulation is IBM 5250, which is also EBCDIC-based and is used with IBM i-Series systems (formerly AS/400s).

As shown in Table 7-1, *xterm*, *konsole*, and *gnome-terminal* have similar command-line options to set the terminal window name, the TERM variable value, and the program to be executed on the terminal-interface side (the default is the $SHELL). These programs may be extensively customized using resources (in the case of *xterm*) or named settings profiles (in the case of *gnome-terminal* and *konsole*).

*Table 7-1. Basic command-line options for common terminal emulators*

| Description | xterm | gnome-terminal | konsole |
|---|---|---|---|
| Program to be executed | -e | -e | -e |
| Window title | -T | -t | -T |
| TERM environment variable value | -tn *value* | (TERM value is always xterm) | --tn *value* |

These three commands all run *vi* in a terminal window with the title set to Vi Editor:

```
$ xterm  -T "Vi Editor" -e vi
$ gnome-terminal -t "Vi Editor" -e vi
$ konsole -T "Vi Editor" -e vi
```

Note that the window title can be changed by emitting a control code sequence. The sequence is:

```
ESC ] 0 ; text BEL
```

where ESC and BEL are the corresponding ASCII codes (27 and 7 in decimal, 033 and 007 in octal, 0x21 and 0x7 in hexadecimal), and *text* is the text that should be presented in the title bar. Therefore, to set the title to **My Window**, you could execute the following:

```
$ echo -e "\033]0;My Window\007\c"
```

When using *bash*, you can set the PROMPT_COMMAND environment variable to a command that should be executed before each prompt is printed. This is often set to show useful information, such as the current directory, using a command such as this:

```
$ export PROMPT_COMMAND='echo -e "\033]0;${PWD}\007\c"'
```

You can also set the title bar in the prompt:

```
$ export PS1="\e]0;\$USER@\$HOST: \$PWD\a$ "
```

If you're using *csh*, the cwdcmd, precmd, and postcmd aliases enable you to execute a command after each directory change, before each prompt is printed, or after each command is entered, respectively. To update the window title to the current directory after each directory change:

```
% alias cwdcmd 'echo -n "^[]0;$cwd^G"'
```

To enter the ^[ in this line, press Ctrl-V, ESC; to enter ^G, press Ctrl-V, Ctrl-G. Or, if you're using *tcsh* and have echo_style set to both, you can type \e in place of ^[ and \a in place of ^G.

# 8

# Session Managers, Desktop Environments, and Window Managers

## 8.1    X and Desktop Environments

When the X Window System was first released, no desktop environment was available. Even when Motif was released in 1989, it did not include a desktop environment; although a few proprietary desktops were available, none of them gained widespread acceptance.

If you look back at X screen dumps taken in the late 1980s or early 1990s, you will find that in most cases there were no panel bars, application launching menus, or window lists. Instead, applications were launched from file-management windows containing icons or from root menus invoked by clicking on the root (background) window, and icons representing minimized programs sat directly on the root window or in icon boxes. This was possible because most of the window managers evolved (out of necessity) basic root-menu and icon-box capabilities.

By the mid-1990s, system vendors recognized the need for a desktop manager, and in 1995, the *Open Software Foundation* (OSF) introduced the Motif-based *Common Desktop Environment* (CDE), based upon HP's *Vue* environment.

Today the dominant desktop environments are GNOME and KDE. CDE continues to be the default desktop on AIX and HP/UX systems, though IBM offers both GNOME and KDE for AIX. Sun Solaris 10 includes both CDE and GNOME.

As an alternative to GNOME or KDE, Xfce provides a GTK+-based desktop environment that uses only about one-third the memory of GNOME. Xfce's window manager, *xfwm*, was the first to include a compositing manager, which made it the first production-quality desktop with integrated support for drop shadows and transparent windows when used with the COMPOSITE extension.

All of the modern desktop environments are actually program suites, which include programs to manage the panel(s), desktop background, files, and program-launching menus; a session manager and a window manager; and a selection of panel applets and utilities including calculators, clocks, and monitors. In order to ensure that these programs function well together, inter-process communications servers, notification agents, object request brokers, and other tools get drawn into the mix. It's not uncommon for KDE or GNOME to consume over 60 MB of memory just to start up.

On the other hand, some window managers have been extended to include program-launching and panel-management features and can serve as minimalist desktop environments. The main difference is that with window managers, most of the heavy lifting is done by a single program.

In this chapter, we'll look at session managers (Section 8.2) and virtual desktops (Section 8.3)—both standard features in today's desktops—and then examine the startup sequences for the following:

- GNOME (Section 8.4)
- KDE (Section 8.5)
- Xfce (Section 8.6)

In each case we'll look at how the window manager can be changed and at additional applications that start when the user logs in.

We'll also examine how a system can be set up to use only a window manager without a full desktop environment (Section 8.7).

# 8.2  Session Managers

An X *session* is roughly equivalent to a character-mode login. A *session manager* (SM) is responsible for saving and restoring the session state; this allows the user to log out and later log in, and to find—more or less—the same programs running. The state information can include the window position, open files, cursor position, and so forth. If the session manager finds that no previous session has been saved, a default session can be started.

Session managers use the *X Session Management Protocol* (XSMP), which is built on top of the *Inter-Client Exchange* (ICE) protocol. This is distinct from the X11 protocol and uses different (and variable) ports.

At the beginning of a session, the SM starts clients that have a saved state. To enable communication with the session manager, clients are passed a connection string in the SESSION_MANAGER environment variable. This takes one of two forms, depending on whether TCP/IP or Unix domain sockets are used:

```
tcp/hostname:port
local/hostname:path
```

Where *hostname* is a suitable hostname (usually a *fully qualified domain name* (FQDN), but possibly a hostname within the local domain, an IP address, or an alias such as localhost), *port* is a TCP/IP port number, and *path* is the pathname of a Unix domain socket.

When an XSMP-aware client starts, it connects to the SM and introduces itself. The SM assigns a unique ID number, and the client informs the SM of the command line that will start it with the same ID number. It's also possible for clients to ask to be restarted if they terminate unexpectedly, or to save their state and ask to be restarted in the next session even if they are not running at the end of the current session. Clients may also provide a command line that will discard the current session information, so that (for example) disk space used to store the session state will free up if the user doesn't want to restore the session.

When a user logs out of her session (and indicates that she wants to save the session, if given the option), the SM sends a message to all registered clients to tell them to save their state. The clients can optionally communicate with the user at this point, which permits the client to ask the user for the filename under which data should be saved. When the next session starts, the SM uses the command that was specified by the client to restart it with the same ID.

Note that the session manager does not save the actual state of the client (other than the ID number). It's up to the client to save its state. This is typically done with hidden files in the user's home directory, but the programmer can choose another method. It's up to the application programmer to decide how much state information is saved; some programs may save only the name of the currently open file, while others may save many details such as the window size and position, cursor position, and undo history.

KDE and GNOME each provide session managers. The standard X distribution also provides a session manager, known as *xsm*, but it is perhaps more of a proof-of-concept than a workable session manager for daily use.

 XSMP was released as part of X11R6. X11R5 used a simpler session management mechanism, which is now regarded as broken.

# 8.3   Virtual Desktops

Many of the current window managers provide *virtual desktop* or *workspace* capability—the ability to access a desktop space that is a multiple of the screen size. For example, a window manager configured with four virtual desktops would permit you to move with the mouse or keyboard from one of the four desktops to another.

Virtual desktops provide a simple, easily understood mechanism for organizing large numbers of windows. It's not uncommon to see users group related applications on different desktops—email and messaging on one, web browsing on another, photo management or writing on a third—and then jump between them.

Most window managers or desktop environments that provide virtual desktops also provide a *pager* (or *workspace switcher*, or *desktop switcher*), which permits the user

---

to see the size and position of windows on each desktop and to switch desktops by clicking on one. Some pagers also permit you to drag windows from one virtual desktop to another.

The GNOME desktop switcher, shown in Figure 8-1, shows the typical appearance of most pagers; when this example was taken, there were 22 windows on 6 virtual desktops (some are hidden under other windows).

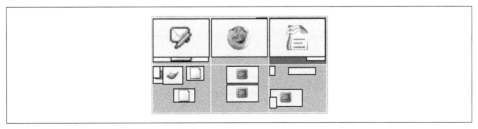

*Figure 8-1. The GNOME desktop switcher*

Resource-wise, virtual desktops are a freebie. This is because they are an illusion created by the window manager.

Studying the output of *xwininfo* gives the secret away. There are two different ways to create virtual desktops:

*mapping*
>   Windows are mapped (made visible) or unmapped (hidden) according to whether the desktop they are "on" is the current desktop.

*positioning*
>   Windows are positioned relative to the current desktop; if they are on a desktop to the right of the current desktop, then they are positioned to the right of the visible screen area, off the screen.

Figure 8-2 shows three virtual desktops as imagined by the user and as displayed in a pager. There are three separate application windows shown on the three desktops: *kcalc*, Firefox, and OpenOffice.org.

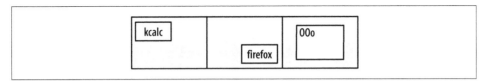

*Figure 8-2. User's view of three virtual desktops*

If the user makes the center desktop current, and the window manager is using mapping to create the virtual desktop illusion, then the actual window placement will be as shown in Figure 8-3. Any window not on the current desktop is unmapped (hidden), as shown here with a dotted outline.

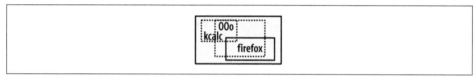

*Figure 8-3. Actual window positions (dotted outlines represent unmapped windows)*

If the window manager is instead using window positioning to create the virtual desktop illusion, the window positions will be as shown in Figure 8-4. Windows that are not on the current desktop are still mapped, but are positioned off-screen.

*Figure 8-4. Actual window position created by positioning windows off-screen*

When the virtual desktop illusion is created by window positions, it is possible to have the current desktop positioned between virtual desktops, so that parts of two or more virtual desktops are visible simultaneously (however, this precludes easily setting different backgrounds on each virtual desktop). It's also possible to have windows span virtual desktops. A window manager in this system has to update the position of *all* of the windows when changing desktops. The *fvwm2* window manager uses this approach.

If the virtual desktop illusion is created by mapping and unmapping windows, less information needs to be updated when switching desktops, and it becomes possible to set the desktop background on a per-desktop basis. This approach is used by the KDE (*kwin*) and GNOME (*Metacity*) window managers; *kwin* allows the use of per-desktop background images.

Windows managed on multiple virtual desktops do not take significantly more resources than windows managed on a single desktop (unless you're using multiple background images), but virtual desktops may encourage users to keep more applications open at one time.

 Virtual desktops may be combined with Xinerama (Section 4.2) and scrolling virtual screens (Section 4.6)—but since each of these techniques alters the user's perception of the display space, using them together may overload the user's mental model of the display and may leave him disoriented and unproductive.

# 8.4   Starting GNOME

GNOME is started through its session manager, *gnome-session*, which may be directly called from the command line if the `DISPLAY` variable has been set to point to a running X server:

```
$ gnome-session
```

When started, *gnome-session* will look up the current session name in the *~/.gnome2/session-options file*, and then look for that session in *~/.gnome2/session*. If that file can't be found, *gnome-session* uses the default session in */usr/share/gnome/default.session* as a system-wide default session definition.

A standard GNOME session includes these standard GNOME clients:

- The window manager (*gnome-wm*)
- The panel manager (*gnome-panel*)
- The *Nautilus* file manager, which also manages desktop icons
- *gnome-volume-manager*, which monitors the desktop bus (DBUS) for new devices and media and performs specific actions when they are found (for example, mounting a device, starting a media player, or loading images from a camera)

Other applications may also be started.

GNOME is usually used with the Metacity window manager, but it can be used with others. In order to provide some flexibility, *gnome-wm* is a script that can be customized to use a different window manager. You can select a specific window manager by placing its name in the `WINDOW_MANAGER` environment variable, or you can place line setting that variable near the top of the *gnome-wm* script:

```
WINDOW_MANAGER=mwm
```

Using a window manager other than Metacity or Compiz sometimes results in a much longer startup time for GNOME.

To start an X server and the GNOME desktop by hand:

```
$ export DISPLAY=:1
$ X $DISPLAY &
$ gnome-session
```

You can specify a specific session name by using the `--choose-session` option:

```
$ gnome-session --choose-session SessionName
```

Alternately, you can also specify that the *default.session* file be used by specifying the `--failsafe` option.

When the user exits from the GNOME desktop, he is presented with a dialog as shown in Figure 8-5; this dialog may have options for reboot, shutdown, or hibernation in some cases. The checkbox labeled Save Current Settings controls whether the session is saved—if that box is checked, and the user clicks the OK button, then the current clients are queried using XSMP, and the session information is written to ~/.gnome2/session using the session name supplied with the --choose-session option (or default, if no name was specified). Otherwise, the contents of ~/.gnome2/session are not disturbed.

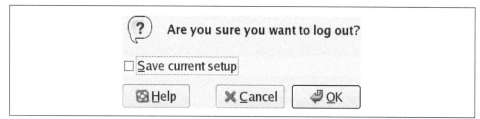

*Figure 8-5. The gnome-session logout dialog*

You can edit the default session definition (*/usr/share/gnome/default.session*) using a standard text editor. Here is the Fedora version of *default.session*:

```
# This is the default session that is launched if the user doesn't
# already have a session.
# The RestartCommand specifies the command to run from the $PATH.
# The Priority determines the order in which the commands are started
# (with Priority = 0 first) and defaults to 50.
# The id provides a name that is unique within this file and passed to the
# app as the client id which it must use to register with gnome-session.
# The clients must be numbered from 0 to the value of num_clients - 1.

[Default]
num_clients=5
0,id=default0
0,Priority=60
0,RestartCommand=pam-panel-icon --sm-client-id default0
1,id=default1
1,Priority=10
1,RestartCommand=gnome-wm --default-wm gnome-wm --sm-client-id default1
2,id=default2
2,Priority=40
2,RestartCommand=gnome-panel --sm-client-id default2
3,id=default3
3,Priority=40
3,RestartCommand=nautilus --no-default-window --sm-client-id default3
4,id=default4
4,Priority=40
4,RestartCommand=gnome-volume-manager --sm-client-id default4
```

Notice that there are five clients in this session, as indicated by the *num_clients* entry. These clients are numbered from 0 to 4, and the client number appears as the first comma-delimited field on each line.

The clients are started in order based on the *Priority* entry for each client, with lower-numbered clients going first. If the Priority is omitted, it defaults to 50. These priority values are used to ensure that, for example, the window manager starts before the panel client, so that the virtual desktop switcher applet in the panel (which talks to the window manager) can initialize without any errors.

The client ID value (`defaultN`) is a placeholder and will be updated by the SM when the client registers with it. The `id` line informs *gnome-session* about the client ID in use; the options in the `RestartCommand` entry pass the same information to the client. Once the client connects to the SM, the `id` value is changed to a concatenation of the IP address, current time, process ID, and a sequence number. This is (in almost all cases) a globally unique identifier.

The actual command used to start each client is listed in the `RestartCommand` entry. It's called the `RestartCommand` because the session manager is trying to restore a saved session by restarting clients that were running in a previous session.

You can easily add entries. For example, to set a system-wide default of starting Evolution when the GNOME desktop starts, append these lines to the end of the file:

```
5,id=default7
5,Priority=60
5,RestartCommand=evolution --sm-client-id default7
```

You would also need to change the `num_clients` entry:

```
num_clients=6
```

In order to successfully start GNOME using *gnome-session* when another session manager is running—for example, to start GNOME when KDE is already active (not all that useful, but interesting for testing!)—you will need to remove the `SESSION_MANAGER` variable first:

```
$ unset SESSION_MANAGER
$ gnome-session
```

 Some systems start *gnome-smproxy* to handle session management for X11R5 clients (which used a protocol that predates XSMP). This has been reported to be a source of problems, and it may be a good idea to disable it—the worst thing that will happen is that X11R5 applications may not be subject to session management. X11R5 applications that actually recognize and preserve session information are few and far between.

# 8.5   Starting KDE

KDE uses a very different approach to initialization. Although KDE does have a session manager, it does not start many of the KDE components. Instead, most of the startup sequence is initiated by a script named *startkde* (imagine that, a KDE program that doesn't start with *k*!):

```
$ startkde
```

Since *startkde* is a script, you can simply open it in a text editor to read or modify it.

*startkde* runs through a number of sanity checks, verifying that there is sufficient temporary disk space available, the home directory is writable, and so forth. Finally, it starts *kdeinit*, which starts a number of processes; some of these are normal binary programs, and some are *KDE loadable modules* (KLMs). KLMs may load faster than traditional binaries and are typically found in */usr/lib/kde3*.

These are some of the key processes:

*kwin*
> The KDE window manager.

*dcopserver*
> The desktop communication server, which facilitates interprocess communication between the the various KDE components.

*ksmserver*
> The KDE session manager.

*klauncher*
> The KDE service initializer. This does not start desktop applications, but starts background services on request.

*kcminit*
> The desktop service launcher. Programs started by *kcminit* are generally used to load users' hardware preferences.

Many of these background processes are like daemons, but are executed once per active display per logged-in user. In other words, if four users are logged into KDE desktops, and one of those users is logged in on two displays, then five copies of these background programs will be executed.

The *startkde* script will use a different window manager if one is defined in the KDEWM environment variable. This is useful if you're starting KDE using *startx* (Section 2.9)—for example:

```
$ KDEWM=mwm startx
```

You can also set this variable near the top of the *startkde* script itself. This line would specify *mwm* as the window manager in place of *kwin*:

```
KDEWM=mwm
```

---

Note that both KDE and GNOME use a full-screen window on top of the normal root window, and some window managers (such as *mwm*) will re-parent that window and add a normal window border, a title bar, and controls to it. Visually, this is very confusing!

The *ksmserver* process in turn starts the desktop session, using three sources of information:

- The files */usr/share/autostart/*.desktop*, which follow the format for *.desktop* files. The execution of the programs identified in these files may be sequenced using X-KDE-autostart-after. A program can be started conditionally, based on preference settings, using a X-KDE-autostart-condition entry.
- The per-user session files in *~/.kde/share/config/session/*.
- The information in *~/.kde/share/config/ksmserverrc*, which includes traditional session management data such as client IDs and the command lines used to restart clients. This information is cross-referenced by client ID into *~/.kde/share/config/session/kwin_*\**.

The */usr/share/autostart/*.desktop* files are started regardless of the per-user session configuration, and these files in turn launch the foundational KDE applications including *kdesktop* and the KDE panel manager *kicker*, as well as less-critical applications such as *ktip* (the tip-of-the-day program).

To add an additional program to the standard, system-wide startup sequence, create an additional desktop file in */usr/share/autostart/*. For example, here is a minimal desktop file to start the Evolution PIM client (yes, Evolution is a GNOME application—mix 'n' match is one of the joys of X); this file should be saved as */usr/share/autostart/evolution.desktop*:

```
[Desktop Entry]
Encoding=UTF-8              # Character set used in this file
Name=Evolution             # Program name
GenericName=Evolution PIM  # Description
Exec=evolution             # Command to be executed
Icon=evolution             # Icon name
Type=Application           # This is an application program
Terminal=false             # Don't start in a terminal
```

If you want this client to start only for a particular user instead of for all users, then place the file in *~/.kde/Autostart/* instead of */usr/share/autostart*, and *kdeinit* will start it instead of *ksmserver*.

Like GNOME, KDE will save the state of the session when the user logs out; however, the user is not given the option to avoid saving the session (unless she aborts the session, perhaps by zapping the server; see Section 2.13).

# 8.6  Starting Xfce

Xfce is a lightweight desktop environment based on GTK+; it is particularly well suited to systems with limited resources and to remote access (for example, through VNC; see Section 14.1). Xfce was originally built on top of the XForms toolkit (not the web specification!), which was the source of its name.

Xfce is started using the *startxfce4* script. Unlike *gnome-session* or *startkde*, the *startxfce4* script will attempt to start an X server—via *xinit*—if one isn't already running (which it assumes is the case if the DISPLAY environment variable is unset):

```
$ startxfce4
```

*startxfce4* does some sanity checks and basic setup, and then starts the session manager *xfce4-session*.

The user's session information is taken from *~/.cache/sessions/* if it exists; otherwise, it's taken from the [Failsafe Session] section of */etc/xdg/xfce4-session/xfce4-session.rc*.

Here is the default *xfce4-session.rc* file with the [Failsafe Session] section highlighted:

```
# $Id$: xfce4-session.rc 4690 2004-10-06 14:03:11z benny $
#
# Default xfce4-session configuration file.
#
# Copyright (c) 2003-2004 Benedikt Meurer <benny@xfce.org>
# All rights reserved.
#
# This program is free software; you can redistribute it and/or modify
# it under the terms of the GNU General Public License as published by
# the Free Software Foundation; either version 2, or (at your option)
# any later version.
...(comment lines lines snipped)...

[General]
SessionName=Default
SessionName[de]=Standard

# Disable management of remote clients by default. The user
# has to explicitly enable this for security reasons.
DisableTcp=True

# This the default session launched by xfce4-session if the
# user hasn't saved any session yet or creates a new session.
[Failsafe Session]
Count=4
Client0_Command=xfwm4
Client0_PerScreen=False
Client1_Command=xfce4-panel
Client1_PerScreen=True
Client2_Command=xftaskbar4
```

```
Client2_PerScreen=True
Client3_Command=xfdesktop
Client3_PerScreen=False

# Default splash screen selection.
[Splash Screen]
Engine=mice
```

The Count entry specifies the number of clients in the session, and each client has two lines: ClientN_Command, which specifies the command line used to start the client, and ClientN_PerScreen, which specifies whether the command should be run on each screen in the display.

To change the default window manager, simply edit the *Client0_Command* line:

```
Client0_Command=mwm
```

To add additional clients to the default session, add additional *Client* lines:

```
Client4_Command=evolution
Client4_PerScreen=False
```

Then change the *Count* line to reflect the new total:

```
Count=5
```

If the user has already saved session information, you can clear it out to force a fail-safe session to be used at next login:

```
# rm ~user/.cache/sessions/*
```

Xfce gives the user the option of saving the session when the logout icon on the panel is clicked, as shown in Figure 8-6. This updates the *~/.cache/session* directory.

*Figure 8-6. Xfce Session logout dialog*

# 8.7    Using a Window Manager Alone

Sometimes a full-blown desktop environment can be overkill, particularly on a machine with limited memory or CPU resources, or when the user will be limited to a small range of tasks (such as certain kiosk [Section 15.1] designs).

Although there are dozens of window managers available, the granddaddy of them all is *twm*, which has been distributed with X since Release 4. *twm* was the first of the re-parenting window managers, which wrap each window in a larger window to add a border and title bar, and its code formed the foundation for many other window managers.

*twm* is still distributed with X. Most OS distributions also include additional window managers; Table 8-1 lists some common ones that are not part of a desktop environment. Remember that window managers included with desktop environments, such as *kwin* and Metacity, can also be used independently of those environments.

*Table 8-1. Common window managers*

| Window manager (binary) | Name | Virtual desktop capability | Themes | Notes |
|---|---|---|---|---|
| *enlightenment* | Enlightenment | Y | Y | Image-intensive window manager, evolving into a desktop environment. |
| *fvwm* (fvwm2) | F Virtual Window Manager | Y | N | No one remembers what the F stands for (perhaps "Favorite"?). |
| *icewm* | IceWM | Y | Y | Designed to be lightweight and fast. |
| *mwm* | Motif Window Manager | N | N | Available as part of Motif, OpenMotif, or Lesstif. |
| *twm* | Tab Window Manager | N | N | Original re-parenting manager. Default operation is significantly different from most other WMs. |
| *vtwm* | Virtual Tab Window Manager | Y | N | Enhanced version of *twm* with virtual desktop capability. |
| *wmaker* | WindowMaker | Y | Y | Look and feel similar to NextStep. |

When using a window manager by itself, you need to ensure that one or more clients are automatically started for the user, or that the window manager is configured with a program-launching menu. Here is a very simple script that will start an X server along with a window manager and selected clients:

```
#!/bin/sh
# Start an X server with specific clients

# === CONFIGURATION VARIABLES
```

```
# Display number
NEWDISPLAY=":8"

# X server command line (can use Xnest for testing)
# Warning!: -ac disables access control
XSERVER="Xnest -terminate -ac"

# Window manager binary name (twm, mwm, etc).
WM=mwm

# Clients to be started, space-separated
CLIENTS="/usr/bin/evolution /usr/local/bin/firefox"

# === END OF CONFIGURATION VARIABLES

unset SESSION_MANAGER

# Start X server
$XSERVER $NEWDISPLAY &

# This is performed after server is started in
# case we're using Xnest

export DISPLAY="$NEWDISPLAY"

# Wait for ports to be opened
sleep 2

# Start window manager
$WM&

# Start clients
for NAME in $CLIENTS
do
     $NAME&
done
```

Note that this script has been configured to use Xnest for testing purposes; change the XSERVER environment variable to make it start a normal hardware-driving X server:

```
XSERVER="X -terminate"
```

Note that the X server won't terminate until the last client dies—and the last client is usually the window manager. The default root menu for *mwm*, for example, includes an option to exit, which must be selected to exit the X server. If you're building a kiosk, you can use a more robust solution (Section 15.10).

You can modify the script above to work as an *~/.xinitrc* script, for use with *startx* (Section 2.9), if you remove the X server startup:

```
#!/bin/sh
# Start an X server with specific clients
```

```
# === CONFIGURATION VARIABLES

# Window manager binary name (twm, mwm, etc).
WM=mwm

# Clients to be started, space-separated
CLIENTS="/usr/bin/evolution /usr/local/bin/firefox"

# === END OF CONFIGURATION VARIABLES

# Start clients
for NAME in $CLIENTS
do
    $NAME&
done

# Start window manager - server will be terminated
# when the window manager exits
$WM
```

Since *xinit/startx* will shut down the X server when the *~/.xinitrc* script terminates, the last client—in this case, the window manager—should be run in the foreground (that is, without an ampersand), preventing the script from ending until you exit from the window manager.

You can test this *.xinitrc* using Xnest through *startx* (using display :8 in this example):

```
$ startx -- /usr/bin/Xnest -ac :8
```

To start those clients on a regular X server, leave out the server binary:

```
$ startx -- :8
```

# Part III

# Colors, Fonts, and Keyboards

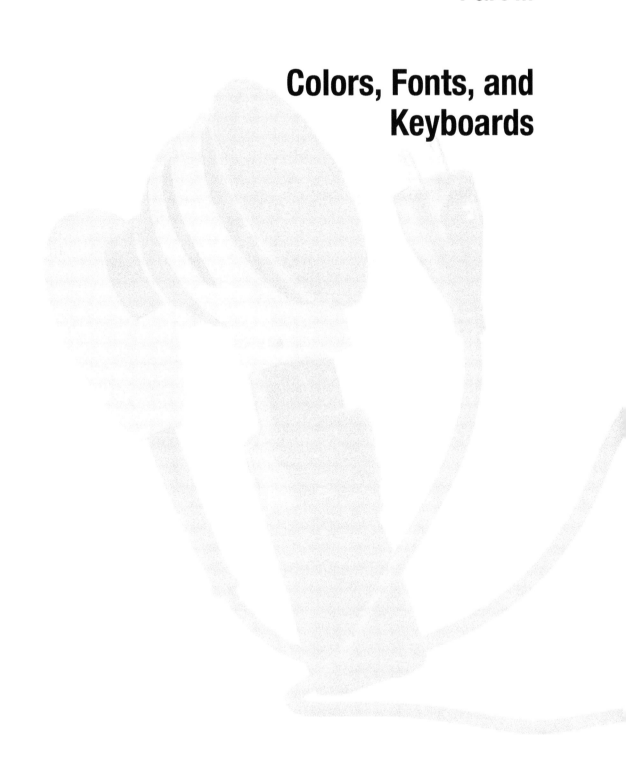

# Color

## 9.1 RGB and Other Color Systems

Almost all modern color computer displays display colors by combining varying amount of red, green, and blue (RGB) light. These three colors stimulate the eye's color receptors and approximate the sensation of viewing various colors; for example, orange light with a wavelength of about 600 nm cannot be produced by a computer screen, but emitting a modest amount of green light, a large amount of red light, and no blue light will provoke a sensation in the eyes of most viewers that will be indistinguishable from the sensation of viewing orange light.

Throughout X, *color* is spelled without a *u*, reflecting the American origins of the system. However, for those of us raised in Canada, the U.K., or any of the other commonwealth countries, that *u* is a hard habit to break, and it can lead to all sorts of mischief including syntax errors—so check your *u* at the door!

Since the perceived colors are created by the addition of three different wavelengths of light, this RGB color is considered to be an *additive color system*. The red, green, and blue colors used are called *additive primaries*.

Computer printers, on the other hand, use a *subtractive color system*. The white paper reflects all visible wavelengths almost evenly; the dyes or pigments deposited on the paper absorb certain colors, effectively subtracting undesired wavelengths from the light reflected by the paper. The colors used (*subtractive primaries*) are the complements of red, green, and blue: cyan, magenta, and yellow. To make it easier (and cheaper) to modulate the intensity of light, black is usually also used; since the color code for black is K, this color system is usually called CMYK (cyan, magenta, yellow, black).

*Color spaces* are the mathematical models that allow colors to be represented using a particular color system. For example, sRGB is a standardized RGB color space created in 1995 by HP and Microsoft and endorsed by many companies and organizations for use on consumer computer electronics such as monitors, digital cameras, and printers. The W3C has endorsed the sRGB standard for use on the Web. (*http://www.w3.org/Graphics/Color/sRGB* is referenced in specifications such as the HTML 4.01 at *http://www.w3.org/TR/html4/*.)

There are many other ways of describing color in addition to the RGB and CYMK schemes; the *International Commission on Illumination*, or *Commission Internationale de l'Eclairage* (CIE), is the international authority on these matters and has defined several very precise color spaces.

The range of colors that can be represented by a particular color space is called its *gamut*. Disparity between the gamuts of sRGB and CMYK color spaces is a source of continual frustration to graphic designers and computer artists, because printed images can never perfectly match screen images.

It's important to keep in mind that we're dealing with the *perception* of color, since there are few absolutes when dealing with the human eye. Consider a projection screen: when first unrolled, most people will tell you that the screen is white. But if you use a video projector to project a presentation slide with a few bright words onto the screen and ask the viewers what color the background is, those same people will tell you that the background is black, despite the fact that it is just as brightly lit as when they said it was white!

# 9.2 Visuals

When you use *xdpyinfo* to view the properties of an X server, you will see a number of *visuals* listed:

```
number of visuals:     80
default visual id:  0x21
visual:
  visual id:     0x21
  class:     TrueColor
  depth:     24 planes
  available colormap entries:     256 per subfield
  red, green, blue masks:     0xff0000, 0xff00, 0xff
  significant bits in color specification:     8 bits
visual:
  visual id:     0x22
  class:     DirectColor
  depth:     24 planes
  available colormap entries:     256 per subfield
  red, green, blue masks:     0xff0000, 0xff00, 0xff
  significant bits in color specification:     8 bits
...Lines snipped...
```

These visuals are methods of managing pixel color on the display. There are seven types of visuals available, as shown in Table 9-1; the number after each visual class

---

name is the visual class number used by the X protocol. The output from *xdpyinfo* shows the visual class along with information about the size of the colormaps, the order of the RGB color information within the pixel color (controlled by the mask), and the size of each color component (significant bits).

*Table 9-1. X visuals*

| Monochrome visual class | Color visual class | Colormap details | Typical number of panes | Notes |
| --- | --- | --- | --- | --- |
| StaticGray (0) | StaticColor (2) | Nonwritable | 1-16 | |
| GrayScale (1) | PseudoColor (3) | Writable | 4-16 | |
| — | TrueColor (4) | Separate map for each RGB channel; nonwritable (linear ramp) | 24 | Most commonly used visual on modern displays |
| — | DirectColor (5) | Separate map for each RGB channel; writable | 24 | |
| — | ARGB (6) | Same as True-Color | 32 | Alpha channel enables variable transparency; used with COMPOSITE extension |

A *colormap* (or palette) is a numbered list of colors; a good analogy is that of a paint-by-number kit, where the number given for each area in the image is looked up in the colormap to determine the color to paint. In a similar way, the StaticColor and PseudoColor visuals interpret each pixel's value in the video framebuffer as a color number which is looked up in the colormap; the color specified by the red, green, and blue values in the colormap is drawn on the screen. A StaticColor visual uses preset colors (such as the 16 VGA colors) while a PseudoColor visual allows the colors to be adjusted.

Changing a PseudoColor colormap entry will cause all pixels that are displayed in that color to immediately change. This feature is sometimes used by older games to produce fade-out and flashing effects.

TrueColor and DirectColor visuals store an actual RGB value in the video framebuffer. The individual red, green, and blue components are looked up in separate colormaps, or *color lookup tables* (CLUT), to determine the value of the signal to send to the monitor on the screen. TrueColor uses nonwritable colormaps to ensure linear intensity changes, while DirectColor uses a writable colormap to provide color-correction capabilities.

Most current desktop and notebook systems use a 24-bit RGB visual (DirectColor/TrueColor), but small-form-factor devices such as phones, PDAs, and tablets may use a more restrictive visual due to memory and power constraints.

When using 24-bit RGB values on a 32-bit system, multiple (sometimes partial) pixels occupy each memory word. This slows write speed by a factor of 75 to 90% and is so inefficient that many 24-bit systems actually devote 32 bits of framebuffer memory to each pixel; this wastes 8 bits per pixel (25% of the memory) but significantly speeds up write operations.

ARGB visuals use that extra 8 bits of data to represent transparency. This information is used by the COMPOSITE extension when building the screen image from the component images.

The default visual class—the class of the root window—is usually determined by the X server based on the number of bits per pixel, but it can be requested on the X server command line using the -cc option and a visual class number from Table 10-1:

```
$ X -cc 3 -depth 24
```

In many cases, the X server will ignore the -cc option (or, as the Xserver manpage politely notes, this option is "Not obeyed by all servers").

 Your X sever may have an astounding number of TrueColor or DirectColor visuals defined; these are intended for use as OpenGL contexts.

## 9.3 Gamma

Cathode ray tubes, which were the first video output devices available and the earliest form of computer display monitor, have a nonlinear response to input. Output luminance is approximately equal to the input value (in the range 0–1) raised to a power of 2.2 (of course, the monitor's brightness and contrast controls will also come into play, offsetting and amplifying this value). The exponent in this transfer function is called the *gamma* value.

Non-CRT monitors such as LCD panels, plasma displays, and projectors all process the input to produce roughly the same gamma curve as a CRT. In order to compensate for the this curve, video cameras are designed with a gamma of approximately 0.4; most digital images (such as those from digital cameras) are also adjusted to assume a nonlinear output curve.

sRGB assumes an effective monitor gamma of 2.2. If your monitor's gamma value is incorrect, images will not be displayed as accurately as possible; *gamma correction* can be applied to the X server's output to compensate.

The XFREE86-VIDMODE Extension enables the dynamic adjustment of the gamma correction settings. As the name implies, this is an extension that originated with XFree86 and has been inherited by the X.org project; since this is an extension to the X11 protocol, not all servers will be equipped with it.

---

A basic client program for displaying and adjusting the X server's gamma value is
*xgamma*. Used by itself, it will display the current gamma correction factors:

```
$ xgamma
-> Red  1.000, Green  1.000, Blue  1.000
```

To set the correction factors, use the -gamma option to set the same value for all channels, or use -rgamma, -ggamma, or -bgamma to adjust just one channel:

```
$ xgamma -gamma 1.5152
-> Red  2.000, Green  1.000, Blue  1.000
<- Red  1.515, Green  1.515, Blue  1.515
$ xgamma -rgamma 2
-> Red  1.000, Green  1.000, Blue  1.000
<- Red  2.000, Green  1.000, Blue  1.000
```

The values marked -> show the previous gamma settings; the values marked <- are
the new settings.

Note that the gamma values are passed to the server with three decimal places.

For systems with multiple displays, you can apply a specific gamma correction to a
single display by running *xgamma* with the -display option. When you're using a
Xinerama display, you may need to set the gamma for just one monitor, but you
can't specify the screen in the displayspec (because Xinerama counts all of the physical screens as part of one logical screen). The -screen option lets you specify the
physical screen to be queried or adjusted:

```
$ xgamma -display :0.0 -screen 2 -gamma 1.3
-> Red  1.000, Green  1.000, Blue  1.000
<- Red  1.300, Green  1.300, Blue  1.300
```

Values set with *xgamma* are temporary—they will be reset when the X server is reset
or restarted. To permanently set the gamma correction factors when using the X.org
server, use a Gamma entry in the Monitor section of the *xorg.conf* file:

```
Section "Monitor"
        Identifier    "Monitor0"
        VendorName    "Samsung"
        ModelName     "205BW"
        HorizSync     28.0 - 55.0
        VertRefresh   55.0 - 70.0
        Option        "DPMS"
        Gamma         1.21 1.30 1.22
    EndSection
```

The arguments to the Gamma entry are separate red, green, and blue gamma values;
you can instead write a single value that will be applied equally to all channels.

But what values should you set? That's a difficult question, because the answer
depends on that material being displayed, the monitor hardware, and lighting condi-
tions. In most cases, you'll want your display's effective gamma to be around 2.2 (as
defined in the sRGB specification), but it's hard to know what correction factor will
give that to you.

To answer this question, Norman Koren has produced a set of web-based charts that let you test and adjust your monitor's gamma by eye. These charts are available at *http://www.normankoren.com/makingfineprints1A.html*.

The GAMMApage software available from Paul Sherman at *http://www.pcbypaul.com/software/GAMMApage.html* uses Norman Koren's charts to provide an interactive tool for gamma adjustment.

## 9.4  Color Management Systems

For most purposes, the color accuracy provided by modern computer systems and peripherals as shipped from the manufacturer is sufficient. But higher-accuracy color reproduction is critical for certain types of work, including professional photography, graphic design, and fashion. A *color management system* (CMS) uses a numeric model of an output device to accurately map between a color space and that device. The device model is called a *profile*; the *International Color Consortium* (ICC) manages and promotes specifications for vendor-neutral, cross-platform color profiles.

In X11R5, the *X Color Management System* (Xcms) was introduced, based on technology provided by Tektronics. Xcms was primarily concerned with loading display color correction tables into the root window properties, and then using these properties within client programs to adjust the colors drawn on the screen—but Xcms was poorly documented and never really caught on, and it did not use ICC profiles.

Two open source projects now provide color management capability for X:

*Argyll (http://www.argyllcms.com/)*
> A set of command-line tools for calibrating displays, printers, and scanners, and for setting the CLUT for displays, as well as client-side libraries for color space conversion.

*LittleCMS (http://www.littlecms.com/)*
> A very compact color management library designed for use by applications. It supports color management for displays, printers, and scanners using color profile files, but it does not include tools for generating those profiles.

LittleCMS is used by many open source applications (including *CinePaint* [Hollywood's version of the *Gimp*], the *Gimp* version 2.3 and higher, *Scribus*, *XSane*, and *digiKam*), and it is becoming the de facto standard for client-side color management.

In most applications that use LittleCMS, color management will be disabled by default. You will need to enable color management in each application and select the correct profiles for your devices.

Profiles for LittleCMS may be supplied by the manufacturer, loaded from a tool used in another operating system, or created with Lprof (*http://lprof.sourceforge.net/*), which is an open source profile editor that can produce rough monitor profiles using subjective tests.

To produce very accurate color profiles, you will need a color target (for input calibration—such as scanners and cameras) or a colorimeter (for output calibration—such as printers and monitors). Color targets are fairly readily available, but colorimeters that work with X11-based systems are quite rare. (And, colorimeters are generally expensive, often costing as much as the monitor or printer being calibrated.)

# 10

# Core Fonts: Fonts the Old Way

## 10.1  Old Fonts Versus New Fonts

Once of the main differences between *Old X* and *New X* (Section 1.3) is the way that fonts are handled. The old font system is often called *Core Fonts*, because it manages fonts using requests defined in the X core protocols (as opposed to extensions; see Section 1.15). Fonts are managed by the server, and clients instruct the server when and where to draw each *glyph* (character image). The actual font information can come from files accessible to the server or from a *font server*, and they may be in any of several different formats.

The problem with core fonts is that they are *monochrome* only, meaning they are one color. This produces a staircase effect on diagonal lines called *aliasing*. The effect is very visible in the enlarged font sample shown in Figure 10-1, despite the fact that this font has been designed to minimize diagonal lines (note the use of vertical lines in the lowercase *y* character). The effect is particularly pronounced on small fonts or low-resolution displays.

Figure 10-1. Enlargement of a monochrome font showing aliasing; note the staircase effect on diagonal lines.

The solution to aliasing is to use intermediate colors—grays if rendering the font black-on-white—to smooth out the staircase effect, as shown in Figure 10-2.

The new font system, discussed in Chapter 11, enables the display of antialiased fonts. Although most modern applications use the new system, there are many legacy applications that use the old font system, and it will be a long time before we're in a position to scrap the old in favor of the new.

*Figure 10-2. Enlargement of an antialiased font. Note the gray pixels smoothing out the image.*

This chapter discusses the configuration and installation of core fonts, including:

- Using a font server (Section 10.3)
- Specifying a font by name or by qualities (Section 10.4)
- Installing and removing fonts (Section 10.5)

Adjusting font paths is discussed in Section 11.1.

## 10.2  Configuring the Font Path

Core fonts are managed by the X server. A *font path* is used to specify the locations that should be searched for a particular font. These locations can include locally accessible directories—either on local storage or mounted across the network—or *font servers* on the network (Section 10.3).

If you're using an X.org server, the initial font path is taken from `FontPath` entries in the `Files` section of the configuration file. Here is an example:

```
Section "Files"
    ModulePath    "/usr/lib/xorg/modules"
    FontPath    "unix/:7100"
    FontPath    "/usr/share/X11lib/fonts/misc"
    FontPath    "/usr/share/X11lib/fonts/TTF"
    FontPath    "/usr/share/X11lib/fonts/Type1"
    FontPath    "/usr/share/X11lib/fonts/CID"
    FontPath    "/usr/share/X11lib/fonts/75dpi"
    FontPath    "/usr/share/X11lib/fonts/100dpi"
EndSection
```

The first entry specifies a font server. The format for font server entries is:

```
protocol/[host]:port[/catalog]
```

`protocol` is the network protocol: `unix` for Unix domain sockets (local connections) or `tcp` for TCP/IP network connections; `host` is the hostname (blank for Unix domain sockets); `port` is the port number (usually 7100); and `catalog` is the list of font catalogs or collections to be used, separated by + symbols (the default is to use all available font catalogs on the font server).

The earlier example, `unix/:7100`, specifies a font server on port 7100 on the local computer. The Unix domain socket is */tmp/.font-unix/fs7100*. To specify a font server on the host *red*, using the standard port number and accessing two catalogs of fonts named *drafting* and *design*, the font server specification would be:

```
tcp/red:7100/drafting+design
```

The most commonly used font server, *xfs*, supports only one catalog named *all*.

The other *FontPath* entries in the earlier configuration file specify directory names on the local filesystem. The directories shown in the example are some of the traditional ones, used to separate fonts into groups according to type:

*75dpi, 100dpi*
    Bitmapped fonts designed for use with 75-dpi and 100-dpi screens.

*TTF or TrueType*
    Scalable fonts in the Microsoft/Apple TrueType format.

*Type1, CID*
    Scalable fonts in the Adobe Type 1 or Character Identifier (CID) formats. CID is an enhanced version of Type 1, which is well suited to large character sets.

*misc*
    Various bitmapped fonts, most with character cell spacing (for use with terminal programs) or symbol character sets.

*Bitmapped* fonts describe each glyph as a pattern of pixels in a particular size, and cannot be smoothly scaled to other sizes. *Scalable* fonts describe each glyph as a pattern of lines and arcs (curves) that can be scaled to any desired size and rendered into a bitmap.

Instead of specifying the font path in the server configuration file, you can specify it on the X server command line using the -fp option:

```
$ X -fp tcp/purple:7100
```

To view the font path on a running server, use the *xset* command with the -q (query) option:

```
$ xset -q
...(Output snipped)...
Font Path:
  /home/chris/.gnome2/share/cursor-fonts,
  unix/:7100,/home/chris/.gnome2/share/fonts,
  /usr/share/X11/fonts/75dpi
...(Output snipped)...
```

To remove an entry from the font path, use the -fp argument:

```
$ xset -fp /usr/share/X11/fonts/75dpi/
```

To add an entry, use +fp (add at the front of the font path—search first) or fp+ (add at the end of the font path—search last). Some examples are as follows:

```
$ xset +fp unix/:7100
$ xset fp+ /usr/share/X11/fonts/localfonts/
```

To ignore the current font path and set a new value, use the fp= argument (note the space after fp= and the comma between elements):

```
$ xset fp= unix/:7100,/usr/share/X11/fonts/TT/
```

# 10.3  Using a Font Server

Font server technology was added to X so that catalogs of fonts could easily be made available to large numbers of desktop systems. Large font catalogs can be gigabytes in size, and centralized font storage can result in significant storage savings over replicated local font storage. The use of a font server for scalable fonts also reduces the size of the X server, and enables fonts to be rendered in parallel with X server tasks on a multi-processor system.

Although several font servers have been written, the *xfs* font server distributed with X is the one most commonly used. Some operating systems and distributions set up *xfs* by default, while others prefer local font directories; for example, Fedora uses *xfs*, while SUSE and Debian/Ubuntu install with a file-based configuration.

*xfs* has a configuration file, usually located at */etc/X11/fs/config*. Here is the Fedora version:

```
#
# xfs font server configuration file
#

# allow a max of 10 clients to connect to this font server
client-limit = 10

# when a font server reaches its limit, start up a new one
clone-self = on

# alternate font servers for clients to use
#alternate-servers = foo:7101,bar:7102

# where to look for fonts
catalogue = /usr/share/X11/fonts/misc:unscaled,
        /usr/share/X11/fonts/75dpi:unscaled,
        /usr/share/X11/fonts/100dpi:unscaled,
        /usr/share/X11/fonts/Type1,
        /usr/share/X11/fonts/TTF,
        /usr/share/fonts/default/Type1,

# in 12 points, decipoints
default-point-size = 120

# 75 x 75 and 100 x 100
default-resolutions = 75,75,100,100

# use lazy loading on 16 bit fonts
deferglyphs = 16
```

```
# Log errors via syslog.
use-syslog = on

# For security, don't listen to TCP ports by default.
no-listen = tcp
```

The most important settings are catalogue, which lists the directories searched by the font server, and no-listen, which disables a network protocol. In this example, the font server is configured so that it will not listen to TCP/IP, so only local connections (through Unix domain sockets) are enabled.

To start *xfs* by hand, simply run it in the background (root privilege is not required):

```
$ xfs &
```

If you are going to use *xfs* in your standard configuration, it is best to enable the *xfs* init script, at least for runlevel 5 (and for runlevel 3 if you plan to start X by hand).

 The font *fixed* must be found in order for the X server to start up successfully (though recent builds of the X.org server have this font compiled in to the server binary). If you specified the font server as the only source of fonts for the X server, *xfs* must be started before the X server in the boot sequence so that the *fixed* font can be found.

# 10.4  Font Names

Core fonts are named and selected using the *X Logical Font Description* (XLFD) syntax. This is a set of 14 fields starting with a dash and separated by dashes; the fields and their meaning are listed in Table 10-1.

*Table 10-1. XLFD font name fields*

| Field | Name | Description | Example |
|---|---|---|---|
| 1 | FOUNDRY | The name of the organization supplying the font (some fonts are available in slightly different form from multiple vendors). | adobe, bitsteam, xfree86 |
| 2 | FAMILY_NAME | The basic font face name. | courier, helvetica |
| 3 | WEIGHT_NAME | A subjective description of the font weight. | bold, demibold, normal |
| 4 | SLANT | A slant code; most commonly i for italic, r for roman (no slant), or o for oblique. | i, r, o |
| 5 | SETWIDTH_NAME | A subjective description of the font width. | semicondensed, normal, wide |
| 6 | ADD_STYLE_NAME | Additional subjective font description text. | sans, ja |

*Table 10-1. XLFD font name fields (continued)*

| Field | Name | Description | Example |
|---|---|---|---|
| 7 | PIXEL_SIZE | Body height of the font in pixels, or 0 for scalable fonts. | 0, 20, 46 |
| 8 | POINT_SIZE | Body height of the font in decipoints (1 decipoint equals 1/722.7" or 0.035 mm). | 120, 180, 240 |
| 9 | RESOLUTION_X | Integer indicating the horizontal screen resolution for which the font was designed in dots per inch, or 0 for scalable fonts. | 0, 75, 100 |
| 10 | RESOLUTION_Y | Integer indicating the vertical screen resolution for which the font was designed in dots per inch, or 0 for scalable fonts. | 0, 75, 100 |
| 11 | SPACING | P for proportional, M for monospaced, or C for character-cell (typewriter-style). | P, C |
| 12 | AVERAGE_WIDTH | Average (mean) width of all of the glyphs in the font, in units of 0.1 pixels. | 95, 240 |
| 13 | CHARSET_REGISTRY | The entity or standard that defines the character set encoding. | iso8859, microsoft |
| 14 | CHARSET_ENCODING | A specific character encoding specified by the entity or standard in CHARSET_REGISTRY. For example, if CHARSET_REGISTRY is iso9959 and CHARSET_ENCODING is 15, then the font is encoded with ISO 8859-15 (also called *Latin-9*—used for Western European languages, including the Euro symbol). | 1, 2, 15, cp1252 |

You can see the font name for all installed fonts using the *xlsfonts* command:

```
$ xlsfonts
-adobe-courier-bold-o-normal--0-0-100-100-m-0-iso10646-1
-adobe-courier-bold-o-normal--0-0-100-100-m-0-iso8859-1
-adobe-courier-bold-o-normal--0-0-100-100-m-0-iso8859-14
...(lines snipped)...
-b&h-luxi serif-medium-r-normal--0-0-0-0-p-0-iso8859-9
-b&h-luxi serif-medium-r-normal--0-0-0-0-p-0-microsoft-cp1252
-bitstream-bitstream charter-bold-i-normal--0-0-0-0-p-0-adobe-standard
-bitstream-bitstream charter-bold-i-normal-0-0-0-0-p-0-iso10646-1
...(lines snipped)...
-sony-fixed-medium-r-normal--24-170-100-100-c-120-jisx0201.1976-0
-sony-fixed-medium-r-normal--24-230-75-75-c-120-iso8859-1
-sony-fixed-medium-r-normal--24-230-75-75-c-120-jisx0201.1976-0
-sun-open look cursor-----0-0-75-75-p-0-sunolcursor-1
-sun-open look cursor-----12-120-75-75-p-160-sunolcursor-1
```

```
-sun-open look glyph-----0-0-75-75-p-0-sunolglyph-1
...(lines snipped)...
-taipei-ming-medium-r-normal--20-200-75-75-c-200-big5-0
-taipei-ming-medium-r-normal--24-240-75-75-c-240-big5-0
-vga-fixed-medium-r-normal--24-230-75-75-c-120-iso8859-1
-xfree86-cursor-medium-r-normal--0-0-0-0-p-0-adobe-fontspecific
```

To select a font, create a name that has the desired values in each field; use an asterisk for any field you don't care about. Some examples are shown in Table 10-2.

*Table 10-2. Examples of font name patterns*

| Description | XLFD value |
| --- | --- |
| *Charter* font, medium weight, no slant, 18 point | `-*-charter-medium-r-*-*-180-*-*-*-*-*` |
| *Helvetica* font, bold, oblique (slanted), 24 point | `-*-helvetica-bold-o-*-*-240-*-*-*-*-*` |
| Any 14-pixel-tall font with character-cell spacing (suitable for use with a terminal) | `-*-*-*-*-*-*-14-*-*-*-c-*-*-*` |
| Any medium-weight, unslanted, sans-serif font, 12 points tall with proportional spacing and iso8859-15 encoding | `-*-*-medium-r-*-sans-*-120-*-*-p-*-iso8859-15` |
| *Luxi sans* font, medium weight, unslanted, scalable, Windows1252 encoding | `-*-luxi sans-medium-r-*-*-*-0-*-*-*-*-microsoft-cp1252` |

The easiest way to come up with a font name is to do it interactively using the *xfontsel* command:

```
$ xfontsel
```

This will display a font selection window as shown in Figure 10-3. Each of the 14 XLFD fields is represented by a pull-down menu containing possible values. As you select values, incompatible options in other fields are disabled. For example, if you select bitstream for the foundry, any font families supplied by other foundries—such as Adobe's Helvetica and B&H's Luxi—are disabled (grayed out) in the font family menu. Clicking on the Select button will make the current font name the PRIMARY selection so that it can be pasted into another application with the middle mouse button (Section 5.4).

To use a font by name with an application that uses core fonts, use the application's command-line options:

```
$ xterm -font -bitstream-terminal-medium-*-*-*-18-*-*-100-c-*-iso8859-*
```

You can also specify the font for Xt-based applications as a resource.

# 10.5  Installing and Removing Fonts

Both *xfs* and the X server expect a font directory file named *fonts.dir* to be present in each directory of fonts. This font directory is a text file that cross-references font names to filenames.

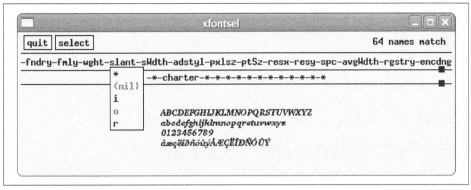

*Figure 10-3. xfontsel core font selection program*

A *fonts.dir* file for nonscalable fonts can be made directly by the *mkfontdir* program; simply run it in a directory containing fonts:

```
# cd /usr/share/X11/fonts/100dpi
# mkfontdir
```

For scalable fonts, it's necessary to run *mkfontscale* first, which creates the *fonts.scale* file. This file can be checked for accuracy and corrected if necessary (since some scalable font files may not contain sufficient information to build an accurate XLFD name) before *mkfontdir* is run:

```
# cd /usr/share/X11/fonts/
# mkfontscale
# mkfontdir
```

Adding core fonts is simply a matter of copying the font files to a directory, running *mkfontscale* (if required), then running *mkfontdir*.

If the directory is not already in the font path and you're using a font server, adjust the configuration file */etc/X11/fs/config* and restart the font server; otherwise, add to the font path through the X server configuration file or *xset* command:

```
$ xset fp+ /newfontdirectory
```

Removing fonts is also straightforward: just delete the unwanted fonts and then run *mkfontscale* and *mkfontdir*.

# 11

# Pango, Xft, Fontconfig, and Render: Fonts the New Way

## 11.1  Client-Side Fonts

Since 2000, font handling has moved from the server to the client, where it is powered by three components:

*RENDER*
> An X server extension that enables rapid rendering of anti-aliased glyphs (character pictures)

*Fontconfig*
> A library (and two utilities) for font configuration and matching

*Xft or Pango*
> Libraries that provide high-quality client-side font rendering

Note that *fontconfig* and *Xft/Pango* both run on the client side; the server-side piece of the puzzle, *RENDER*, simply improves performance—if it is not present, *Xft/Pango* will draw text using core protocol requests (which is slower than using *RENDER* and also slower than using core fonts, but still fast enough on modern hardware to provide good user interface response).

Qt3 uses Xft, and GTK+-2 uses Pango for text display; most older toolkits use core fonts (Section 10.1). A modern desktop system, running a mix of GNOME and KDE applications, a Mozilla-based browser, and OpenOffice.org will be using the new rendering libraries almost exclusively for text display.

## 11.2  Adding and Removing Fonts Manually

In most configurations, *fontconfig* scans */usr/share/fonts*, one or more of the font directories in */usr/share/X11/fonts/* and *~/.font* when it is initialized at the time an application starts. Any changes to the fonts contained in those directories are detected automatically, so adding fonts is simply a matter of placing files into those directories, and removing fonts is simply a matter of deleting them.

For example, if you have a compressed tar file named */tmp/newfonts.tgz* containing TrueType fonts, and you wish to install these fonts for your own private use, you could use these commands:

```
$ cd ~/.fonts
$ tar xvzf /tmp/newfonts.tgz "*.ttf" "*.TTF"
```

Or, to install those fonts so that they are accessible system-wide:

```
# cd /usr/share/fonts
# mkdir newfonts
# cd newfonts
# tar xvzf /tmp/newfonts.tgz "*.ttf" "*.TTF"
```

To delete all of your personal fonts:

```
$ rm -rf ~/.fonts/*
```

To delete the system-wide fonts just installed:

```
# rm -rf /user/share/fonts/newfonts
```

Changes will take effect the next time the affected application is started.

## 11.3  Adding and Removing Fonts Using GNOME

GNOME's *Nautilus* file manager has a special URI for viewing and managing fonts. To access it:

1. Start Nautilus—use the My Computer or Home desktop icons or panel bar icons, or any folder on the Places menu.
2. Select Open Location... from the File menu in Nautilus, or press Ctrl-L. An Open Location dialog will appear.
3. Enter the URI fonts:/ and press Enter.

You can also access this window by running this command:
$ **nautilus fonts:/**

The Nautilus font display is shown in Figure 11-1. The appearance will vary depending on the currently selected view.

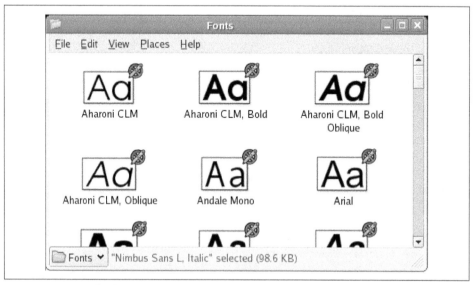

*Figure 11-1. Fonts display in GNOME's Nautilus file manager*

The lower- and uppercase letter A of each font are displayed, if the font has those characters; double-clicking on a font (or right-clicking and selecting Open with Gnome Font Viewer) will display some basic information about the font—including the license, file size, and font style—along with an extended font sample (Figure 11-2).

To install fonts into your personal font directory (*~/.fonts*), simply drag and drop them into the Nautilus font display. The fonts may not show up immediately in the display, but they will be installed.

A personal font can be deleted in the same way that a file is deleted using Nautilus: drag it from the Nautilus window to the trashcan, or right-click on it and select "Move to Trash."

 Nautilus does not permit you to install or delete system-wide fonts. However, Konqueror does (Section 11.4), and it is possible to run Konqueror within a GNOME session.

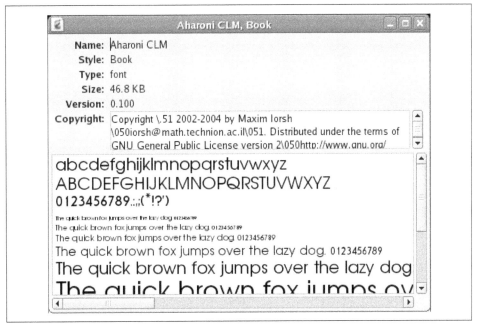

Figure 11-2. GNOME *font viewer*

# 11.4 Adding and Removing Fonts Using KDE

KDE's Konqueror file and web browser enables you to view, install, and delete fonts from both the system-wide font directories and your personal font directory. To access this mode:

1. Start Konqueror, using the Home or Web Browser panel icons, or the K Menu.

2. Enter **fonts:/** into the location field.

> You can also access the Konqueror font display by running this command:
>
> ```
> $ konqueror fonts:/
> ```

The window will show icons labeled Personal and System; double-click on the group you wish to see, and the display shown in Figure 11-3 will appear. The appearance may vary depending on the Konqueror display options you have selected.

Double-clicking on a font presents the KFontView window shown in Figure 11-4, showing an extended font sample. Clicking on the T icon enables you to change the sample sentence; the default sentence is a *pangram* that contains each of the 26 letters in the Latin alphabet.

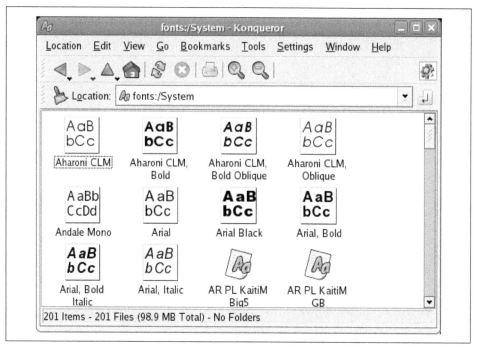

*Figure 11-3. Konqueror system font display*

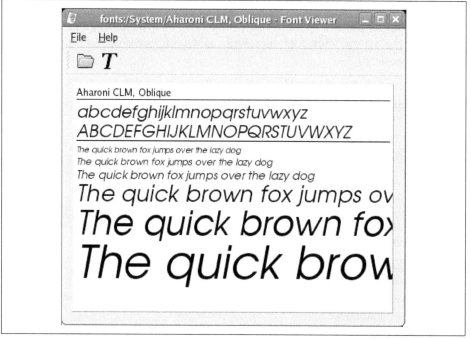

*Figure 11-4. KFontView window*

To add fonts, simply drag-and-drop them into the font window. If you drop them into the system font window, you will be prompted to enter the root password.

To delete a font, treat it like a file: drag-and-drop it onto the trashcan or right-click and select Delete. As with installation, you will be prompted for the root password if the font is from the system font window.

 You can also install and remove fonts through the KDE Control Panel.

## 11.5  Fontconfig Font Names

*Fontconfig* uses a font-naming scheme which is more user friendly than XLFD font names (Section 11.4). Font names consist of a font family; optionally, you can have a font size separated from the font family by a dash; and optionally, you can have a list of additional name and value pairs specifying additional properties, linked by equal signs and separated by colons.

For matching purposes, you can specify multiple values for the font name or size, separated by commas; the first matching value will be selected.

Table 11-1 lists some font names expressed using this notation.

*Table 11-1. Fontconfig font names*

| Font name | Meaning |
| --- | --- |
| Courier-12 | Courier face, 12-point size |
| Utopia:style=italic | Utopia face in Italics |
| Helvetica,Arial,Swiss-12 | Helvetica, Arial, or Swiss face (preferred in that order); 12 point size |
| Fixed-12,16,10 | Fixed face in 12-, 16-, or 10-point size (preferred in that order) |

For a complete list of font properties that can be used in font names, see the documentation on the Fontconfig web site at *http://fontconfig.org*. Note that many of the properties mentioned in the documentation are not used; on most systems, style is the only property specified for most of the fonts.

Recent versions of *xterm* have support for client-side font rendering and can be used to test a Fontconfig font name. The command-line option to use is -fa (it stands for *font face*):

```
$ xterm -fa utopia:style=italic
$ xterm -fa Helvetica,Arial,Swiss-18
```

If the selected font does not use character-cell spacing, *xterm* will add considerable spacing between characters.

## 11.6  Fontconfig Utilities

Since Fontconfig is a library, users don't directly interact with it. However, there are two helpful little utilities provided with the library: *fc-list* and *fc-cache*.

*fc-list* lists the fonts available through Fontconfig. Executed without any arguments, it lists all of the fonts to standard output:

```
$ fc-list
KacstTitle:style=KacstTitle
KacstTitleL:style=KacstTitleL
KacstArt:style=KacstArt
...(Lines snipped)...
Frank Ruehl CLM:style=Bold Oblique
URW Bookman L:style=Demi Bold Italic
Yehuda CLM:style=Light
fxd:style=Bold Italic
```

Sorting the lines will group them by face:

```
$ fc-list|sort
Aharoni CLM:style=Bold
Aharoni CLM:style=Bold Oblique
Aharoni CLM:style=Book
Aharoni CLM:style=Book Oblique
...(Lines snipped)...
Yehuda CLM:style=Bold
Yehuda CLM:style=Light
```

When a font name is provided as an argument, only matching fonts are displayed:

```
$ fc-list utopia
Utopia:style=Bold Italic
Utopia:style=Bold
Utopia:style=Italic
Utopia:style=Regular
```

The other utility provided is *fc-cache*, which generates (or updates) cache files in each font directory. These files are named *fonts.cache* and speed the startup of applications that use Fontconfig. Run this command as root to generate font cache files for system fonts, or as a user to generate them for the fonts in *~/.fonts*:

```
# fc-cache
$ fc-cache
```

## 11.7  Installing the Microsoft Fonts

Web pages and documents created on Microsoft systems often use fonts that are distributed with Windows. For a time, Microsoft made these fonts available free of charge on its web site; although they are no longer available directly from Microsoft, you can get them from Fontconfig.org under Microsoft's fairly simple licensing terms. So, if your distribution does not include these fonts, you can easily add them.

Installing these fonts makes it possible to view Word and Excel documents and web pages created under Windows as they were originally designed. Mozilla, Firefox, OpenOffice, and other applications can all use these.

Before installing these fonts, you need to review and agree to the terms of the license agreement at *http://fontconfig.org/webfonts/Licen.TXT*, and you also need to obtain a copy of the *cabextract* program to extract the fonts from archives created in Microsoft's proprietary CAB format. *cabextract* can be found in many repositories, or it can be obtained directly from the project web page: *http://www.kyz.uklinux.net/ cabextract.php*.

Once you've agreed to the license terms and installed *cabextract*, download and install the fonts:

```
# wget http://fontconfig.org/webfonts/webfonts.tar.gz
# tar xvzf webfonts.tar.gz
# cd msfonts
# cabextract *.exe
# mkdir /usr/share/fonts/microsoft
# cp *.[tT]* /usr/share/fonts/microsoft
# cd ..
# rm -rf msfonts
# fc-cache
```

## 11.8  Rendering Options

Font rendering can be tuned to adjust the amount of CPU time used and to suit user preferences and the display hardware in use. Although Fontconfig permits configuration of rendering using */etc/fonts/local.conf*, rendering is usually configured through GNOME or KDE.

The GNOME configuration window is accessed from the menu entry Desktop → Preferences → Font and is shown in Figure 11-5. The KDE rendering configuration panel is accessed through the KDE Control Panel under Appearance & Themes → Fonts and is shown in Figure 11-6.

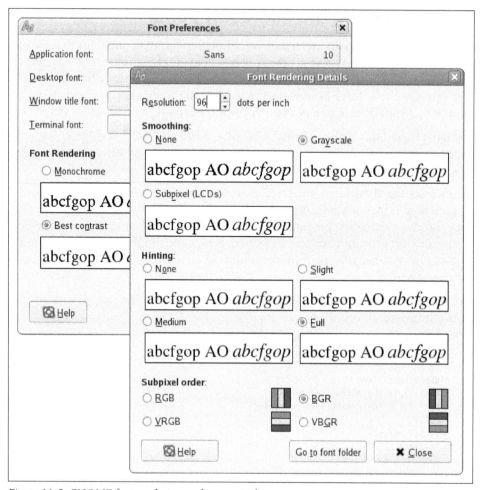

*Figure 11-5. GNOME font rendering preferences tool*

In both cases, you can enable or disable antialiasing, adjust the level of antialiasing hinting, and set subpixel order.

On an older system with a slow CPU and/or low memory resources, turning off anti-aliasing can make enough of a performance difference to turn an unbearably slow system into one that performs reasonably.

When antialiasing is enabled, the hinting level can be set according to user preference.

Subpixel hinting is, by and large, useful only on LCDs. It involves treating each of the RGB color elements in a pixel as a partial pixel. Figure 11-7 shows an enlarged diagonal line border between black and white regions on an LCD screen, rendered using subpixel hinting.

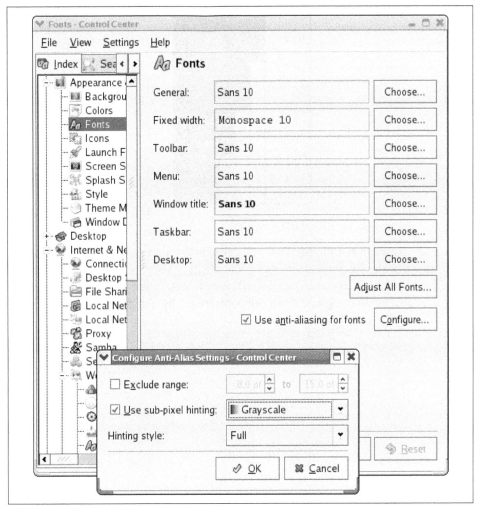

*Figure 11-6. KDE font rendering preferences tool*

Note that each pixel is comprised of a red, green, and a blue element; on this display, they are arranged horizontally in R-G-B order. In the first row, there is one white pixel. In the second row, there is a white pixel followed by one-third of a white pixel—which, in this case, means a red pixel. The third row consists of a white pixel followed by two-thirds of a pixel—a red and green pixel, which displays as yellow. The fourth row contains two white pixels.

It seems odd that a color pixel would be perceived as a partial pixel, but it works because the color pixel is a continuation of the R-G-B element pattern on the line.

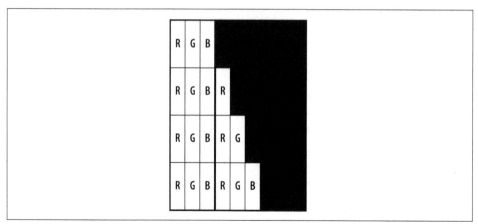

*Figure 11-7. Subpixel hinting on an LCD panel*

In order for subpixel hinting to work properly, the font renderer needs to know the arrangement of the subpixel elements on the display. This information is not documented for most LCD monitors, so the only way to determine the correct value is by using a large magnifying glass, or (more commonly) by experimenting to see what looks best.

# 12

# Keyboard Configuration

## 12.1  Keyboards and XKB

Keyboard configuration is a more complicated issue than it might at first appear. There are many different keyboards sold, each with a different number or arrangement of keys. Each of these keyboard models may be sold in different markets, with different key caps installed, and users may want their keyboard to operate in specific ways.

Together, this means that there are thousands of possible keyboard configurations. The XKB extension tries to simplify this by combining a small number of keyboard selection parameters to compose a particular configuration. The final configuration is called a *keyboard map*.

In addition to keys that type characters or perform actions directly, a keyboard map almost always includes modifiers—such as Alt, Ctrl, and Shift—which change the operation of the other keys. It may also contain dead keys, which don't actually type anything but cause the following character to be accented, so that pressing ´ by itself doesn't type an apostrophe (unless you type it twice), but pressing ´ then A types á.

The keyboard map can also include a compose key, which is pressed before a two-key sequence to generate special characters (for example, pressing Compose-/-C yields the cent symbol [¢]; Compose-O-R yields the registered trademark symbol [®]; and Compose-comma-C yields a C with cedilla [Ç]).

In these days of international communication, many users need to communicate in more than one language, so many keymaps have more than one keyboard group defined, with a key or key combination to temporarily switch or to cycle through the groups. Each keyboard group corresponds to one layout. Keyboard LEDs (particularly the ScrollLock LED) may be assigned to indicate the current group.

To load a keymap into the X server, you need to know how to specify that keymap (Sections 12.3 and 12.4), and you need to know how you can use that specification in a file or as command arguments (Sections 12.6, 12.7, and 12.8).

XKB has a special reputation in the X world for being under-documented. This reputation is not wholly deserved—there are other components of X that have less documentation—but for such a sophisticated system, the documentation is definitely thin.

## 12.2 The Location of XKB Files

XKB data is stored in a large number of files located in a directory tree. That tree may be located in any one of several different locations, as described next:

- In systems up to X11R6.9, the XKB data is usually in */usr/X11R6/lib/X11/xkb.*
- In Debian and Ubuntu Linux, it is in */etc/X11/xkb.*
- In SUSE and Fedora Linux, it is in */usr/share/X11/xkb.*

## 12.3 XKB Components

XKB keymaps are compiled from five components:

*keycodes*
   Provides a description of the scancodes that the hardware can produce. On PCs, these codes are fairly standard, but other (and older) hardware families—such as those produced by Unix workstation vendors—may use very different scancode values.

*types*
   Configures the modifiers that work with various key types. For example, this component configures the NumLock modifier to work with the keys on the numeric keypad—but the NumLock modifier has no effect on alphabetic keys. Each type of key (alphabetic, keypad, function key, and so forth) may have multiple levels accessed by various combinations of modifiers; for example, alphabetic keys on U.S. layouts produce different characters on each of two levels (unshifted and shifted) and have additional meaning when used with Ctrl or Alt modifiers. Many European layouts have an additional levels accessed with the AltGr (*alternate graphic*) modifier, which is not present in U.S. layouts.

*compat*
   Configures compatibility handling for programs that are not aware of the XKB extension. By now, almost all programs in widespread use are XKB-aware.

*symbols*
   Defines the key symbol produced by the current keyboard state (a combination of group, modifiers, and preceding keystrokes) and current keystroke.

*geometry*
   Describes the physical layout of the keyboard. This information may be used to draw a picture of the keyboard for documentation or an on-screen representation of the keyboard (which is useful for a very few applications such as typing tutorials). The geometry information is used by very few clients.

Each component is specified by a filename or by a filename followed by a section name in parentheses. For example, the default keymap for the X.org server is defined as:

```
keycodes:    xfree86+aliases(qwerty)
types:       complete
compat:      complete
symbols:     pc(pc105)+latin
geometry:    pc(pc105)
```

It's really tedious to determine which component values should be used, so XKB provides a rule-based system (Section 12.4) that combines more natural criteria determine the components to be used.

# 12.4  Selecting an XKB Keymap Using Rules

Rule-based keymap selection is much easier and more common than component-based selection. Rule-based selection uses five parameter values: Rules, Model, Layout, Variant, and Option.

The Rules value dictates the possible values for each of the other four parameters. For example, if the Rules value is sun, you can specify the Model type4, but that model name is not available if you are using the xorg rules.

The five parameters are described here:

Rules

Selects the rules used to compose the keyboard map based on the other parameters. The possible values for this parameter are listed in the text file *rules/rules.lst* or the multilanguage XML file *rules/rules.xml* (typically *xorg.lst* and *xorg.xml*). The *.lst* (or *.xml*) files are an essential reference when configuring a keyboard using XKB. As distributed, the possible values for this parameter are xorg (or base, the default), sun, sgi, and xfree98 (for computers that conform to the Japanese PC98 standard). XFree86 systems use the value xfree86 in place of xorg.

Model

Indicates the actual keyboard model installed. There are generic model numbers (such as pc105) for run-of-the-mill keyboards, and special model numbers for specific multimedia, wireless, and ergonomic keyboards.

Layout

Specifies the arrangement of keys on the keyboard. Usually, this corresponds to the labels on the physical key caps, but this is not a hard rule—you can use a French keyboard with a German layout, for example. The layout also specifies how modifiers work (such as Shift, Alt, and Ctrl), the operation of any dead keys, and the location of the compose key (if any).

Variant

Selects variations on the keyboard layout. This is commonly used to enable or disable deadkeys or use modified layouts (such as Dvorak).

Options

Applies options to the keyboard, such as special modifier behavior, compose keys, and keys and indicators for switching between layout groups.

To find available values, look in the *.lst* file. Here is the top of *rules/xorg.lst*:

```
! model
  pc101          Generic 101-key PC
  pc102          Generic 102-key (Intl) PC
  pc104          Generic 104-key PC
  pc105          Generic 105-key (Intl) PC
  dell101        Dell 101-key PC
  dellm65        Dell Precision M65
  everex         Everex STEPnote
  flexpro        Keytronic FlexPro
  microsoft      Microsoft Natural
```

The line starting with ! identifies the section for a particular parameter: model in this case. The first word on each of the following lines is a possible value for that parameter, and the rest of the line is a comment describing that value. Therefore, a value of pc105 for the XKB model parameter specifies a generic 105-key PC keyboard.

The same data is present in *rules/xorg.xml*, with translations of the descriptions. This is the top of the file, with some translations removed:

```
<?xml version="1.0" encoding="UTF-8"?>
<!DOCTYPE xkbConfigRegistry SYSTEM "xkb.dtd">
<xkbConfigRegistry>
  <modelList>
    <model>
      <configItem>
        <name>pc101</name>
        <description>Generic 101-key PC</description>
        <description xml:lang="af">Generies 101-sleutel PC</description>
        <description xml:lang="fr">PC générique 101 touches</description>
        <description xml:lang="hu">általános 101 gombos PC</description>
        <description xml:lang="it">Generica 101 tasti PC</description>
        <description xml:lang="nl">Algemeen 101-toetsen PC</description>
...lines snipped...
      </configItem>
```

The XML file can be easily parsed by a GUI configuration program, but it is so verbose that it's hard to browse by hand, so the *.lst* may be better for direct reading.

In addition to the model values, the *.lst* and *.xml* files contain values for the Layout, Variant, and Option parameters. This is the top part of the Layout section:

```
! layout
  us             U.S. English
  ad             Andorra
```

```
af              Afghanistan
ara             Arabic
al              Albania
am              Armenia
az              Azerbaijan
by              Belarus
be              Belgium
bd              Bangladesh
in              India
ba              Bosnia and Herzegovina
br              Brazil
bg              Bulgaria
mm              Myanmar
ca              Canada
```
*...lines snipped...*

The value in the first line, us, is the default layout. Obviously, there are multiple layouts that may be used in the United States, or Brazil, or Canada; these Layout values specify only the default layout, which is usually the most common. To specify another layout, the Variant parameter is added:

```
! variant
  intl          us: International (with dead keys)
  alt-intl      us: Alternative international (former us_intl)
  dvorak        us: Dvorak
  dvorak-l      us: Left handed Dvorak
  dvorak-r      us: Right handed Dvorak
  rus           us: Russian phonetic
  ps            af: Pashto
  uz            af: Southern Uzbek
  azerty        ara: azerty
  azerty_digits ara: azerty/digits
  digits        ara: digits
  qwerty        ara: qwerty
```
*...lines snipped...*

In this section of the file, the second column specifies the *layout* with which each variant may be used. For example, the dvorak variant will work with the us layout, but not the af layout.

The variant parameter is optional, and defaults to no variant.

The last section of the *.lst* file contains possible values for the Option parameter. Here are some common option values from the *xorg.lst* file:

```
! option
...lines snipped...
  ctrl            Ctrl key position
  ctrl:nocaps     Make CapsLock an additional Ctrl.
  ctrl:swapcaps   Swap Ctrl and CapsLock.
  ctrl:ctrl_ac    Ctrl key at left of 'A'
  ctrl:ctrl_aa    Ctrl key at bottom left
  ctrl:ctrl_ra    Right Ctrl key works as Right Alt.
...lines snipped...
```

| | |
|---|---|
| Compose key | Compose key position |
| compose:ralt | Right Alt is Compose. |
| compose:rwin | Right Win-key is Compose. |
| compose:menu | Menu is Compose. |
| compose:rctrl | Right Ctrl is Compose. |
| compose:caps | Caps Lock is Compose. |

*...lines snipped...*

Option values can be specified as a comma-delimited list, so ctrl:nocaps,compose:menu would configure the CapsLock key as an additional control key and the Menu key as a compose key.

## 12.5  Using Keyboard Groups

In today's globally connected environment, many users need to enter text in two or more languages, and these languages often require different keyboard layouts. XKB accommodates this need by providing up to four keyboard layout *groups*, along with mechanisms to switch between them and to indicate which group is active. Each group is effectively a keyboard layout that may be selected on-the-fly.

Groups are specified by listing multiple comma-delimited values for the layout and variant parameters. For example, these parameters specify group 1 as the international (intl) variant of the us layout, and group 2 as a ca (Canadian) layout with no variant:

```
rules:    xorg
model:    pc105
layout:   us,ca
variant:  intl,
```

The option parameter is used to specify which keys are used to switch between groups. These are the possible switching keys listed in the *xorg.list* file:

| | |
|---|---|
| grp:switch | R-Alt switches group while pressed. |
| grp:lswitch | Left Alt key switches group while pressed. |
| grp:lwin_switch | Left Win-key switches group while pressed. |
| grp:rwin_switch | Right Win-key switches group while pressed. |
| grp:win_switch | Both Win-keys switch group while pressed. |
| grp:rctrl_switch | Right Ctrl key switches group while pressed. |
| grp:toggle | Right Alt key changes group. |
| grp:lalt_toggle | Left Alt key changes group. |
| grp:caps_toggle | CapsLock key changes group. |
| grp:shift_caps_toggle | Shift+CapsLock changes group. |
| grp:shifts_toggle | Both Shift keys together change group. |
| grp:alts_toggle | Both Alt keys together change group. |
| grp:ctrls_toggle | Both Ctrl keys together change group. |
| grp:ctrl_shift_toggle | Ctrl+Shift changes group. |
| grp:ctrl_alt_toggle | Alt+Ctrl changes group. |
| grp:alt_shift_toggle | Alt+Shift changes group. |
| grp:menu_toggle | Menu key changes group. |
| grp:lwin_toggle | Left Win-key changes group. |
| grp:rwin_toggle | Right Win-key changes group. |

```
grp:lshift_toggle    Left Shift key changes group.
grp:rshift_toggle    Right Shift key changes group.
grp:lctrl_toggle     Left Ctrl key changes group.
grp:rctrl_toggle     Right Ctrl key changes group.
```

Note that the values marked with switch select group 2 while pressed, switching back to group 1 when the keys are released. This makes them usable only for 2-group configurations where group 1 is in effect most of the time. Entries marked toggle step through the available groups; if only two groups are defined, then toggle keys act like CapsLock—press once to switch, press again to switch back.

Since the Windows and Menu keys are often unused, they make good choices for switch or toggle keys. If you do not need to write in all-caps, the CapsLock key may also make a good toggle.

There are also options to display the group status on keyboard LEDs:

```
grp_led:num      NumLock LED shows alternative group.
grp_led:caps     CapsLock LED shows alternative group.
grp_led:scroll   ScrollLock LED shows alternative group.
```

Since the ScrollLock LED rarely displays useful information, it is a good candidate for a group indicator.

Unfortunately, the LEDs operate very simply: they are off when group 1 is active, and on when any other group is active—it's not possible to determine from the LEDs whether the alternative group is 2, 3, or 4.

A bug in some versions of the X.org server causes a new group LED setting to be added to a previous group LED setting instead of replacing it. For example, if you specify grp_led:scroll and later specify only grp_led:caps, then both the ScrollLock and CapsLock LEDs will light together when group 2, 3, or 4 is active.

To select the menu key as the group toggle and the ScrollLock LED as the group indicator, specify both option values in a comma-separated list:

```
rules:    xorg
model:    pc105
layout:   us,ca
variant:  intl,
option:   grp:menu_toggle,group. grp_led:scroll
```

# 12.6  Setting the Keymap in the xorg.conf File

If you're using the X.org server, the XKB keymap may be specified in the keyboard InputDevice section of the *xorg.conf* file, using a series of Option directives. Each options name is a concatenation of Xkb and a component or parameter name.

To specify an XKB keyboard map using rules, any combination of XkbRules, XkbModel, XkbLayout, XkbVariant, and XkbOption options may be specified:

```
Section "InputDevice"
        Identifier  "Keyboard0"
        Driver      "kbd"
        Option      "XkbRules"    "xorg"
        Option      "XkbModel"    "pc105"
        Option      "XkbLayout"   "us,ca"
        Option      "XkbVariant"  "intl,"
        Option      "XkbOption"   "grp:menu_toggle,grp_led:scroll"
EndSection
```

You may also specify the keymap using components, using the XkbKeycodes, XkbTypes, XkbCompat, XkbSymbols, and XkbGeometry option names:

```
Section "InputDevice"
        Identifier  "Keyboard0"
        Driver      "kbd"
        Option      "XkbKeycodes" "xfree86+aliases(qwerty)"
        Option      "XkbTypes"    "complete"
        Option      "XkbCompat"   "complete+ledscroll(group_lock)"
        Option      "XkbSymbols"  "pc(pc105)+us(intl)+ca:2+group(menu_toggle)"
        Option      "XkbGeometry" "pc(pc105)"
EndSection
```

## 12.7  Setting the Keymap from the Command Line

The *setxkbmap* command enables you to change the keymap at any time. The options -rules, -model, -layout, -variant, and -option are used to specify the parameters:

```
$ setxkbmap -rules xorg -model pc105 -layout us,ca -variant intl, \
    -option grp:menu_toggle,grp_led:scroll
```

If you specify the -v option, *setxkbmap* will print a list of the components used:

```
$ setxkbmap -rules xorg -model pc105 -layout us,ca -variant intl, \
    -option grp:menu_toggle,grp_led:scroll
keycodes:   xfree86+aliases(qwerty)
types:      complete
compat:     complete+ledscroll(group_lock)
symbols:    pc(pc105)+us(intl)+ca:2+group(menu_toggle)
geometry:   pc(pc105)
```

If you want only to see the components listed and do not wish to actually set the keyboard map, use the -print option. The output will be formatted for input to *xkbcomp*, which is the keymap compiler (Section 12.9):

```
$ setxkbmap -print -rules xorg -model pc105 -layout us,ca -variant intl, \
    -option grp:menu_toggle,grp_led:scroll
xkb_keymap {
        xkb_keycodes  { include "xfree86+aliases(qwerty)"       };
        xkb_types     { include "complete"      };
```

```
        xkb_compat    { include "complete+ledscroll(group_lock)"        };
        xkb_symbols   { include "pc(pc105)+us(intl)+ca:2+group(menu_toggle)"   };
        xkb_geometry  { include "pc(pc105)"       };
};
```

You can also configure the keymap using components. Using the values from the output above, the *xkbsetmap* command would look like this:

```
$ setxkbmap -keycodes "xfree86+aliases(qwerty)" \
    -types "complete" \
    -compat "complete" \
    -symbols "pc(pc105)+us(intl)+ca:2+group(menu_toggle)" \
    -geometry "pc(pc105)"
```

# 12.8   Setting the Keymap Using a Keyboard Configuration File

One *xorg.conf* configuration file may be shared between several server instances: for example, on a Linux system, you can start two (or more) X servers running on different virtual terminals and switch between them. You may want to use a common *xorg.conf* file for both servers, but specify different keyboard configurations.

You can do this by creating a per-server keyboard configuration file. These files are placed in the root of the XKB tree (Section 12.2) and are named *d*-config.keyboard, where *d* is the display number—so the configuration file for display :0 would be */etc/X11/xkb/X0-config.keyboard* or */usr/share/X11/xkb/X0-config.keyboard*.

This file contains name and value pairs, one per line, delimited by equal signs. The names may be component names or parameter names. For example:

```
rules = xorg
model = pc105
layout = us
variant = intl
```

Each keyboard configuration file may also specify how AccessX controls work as well as explain that some parameters are usually adjusted using *xset* (Section 6.4), such as the bell pitch and volume and the keyboard repeat rate, but these are rarely used.

 Many of XKBs features are poorly documented, but the keyboard configuration file is probably the worst—it is really documented only in the XKB source code. Ivan Pascal has made some notes about this feature at *http://pascal.tsu.ru/en/xkb/config.html*.

# 12.9   Compiling Keyboard Maps

XKB keyboard maps are compiled before use. Generally, the X server calls the *xkbcomp* program to compile the map based on information that either is in the server configuration file, in the keyboard configuration file, or passed to the server from *setxkbmap*.

The manpage for *setxkbmap* notes that it may fail if it is run on a system that has different XKB components than the server does, because *xkbcomp* may not find the components specified by *setxkbmap*. In that case, you may run *xkbcomp* on the client side:

```
$ setxkbmap -layout ca -print | xkbcomp - $DISPLAY
```

This will automatically upload the keymap to the server after compilation.

It is also possible to save a compiled keymap—but this is depreciated in favor of rules-based configuration.

## 12.10  Viewing or Printing a Keyboard Layout

If you're using a keyboard layout that doesn't match they physical keycaps on your keyboard, it may be useful to print (or view) a picture of the layout. The *xkbprint* program uses the XKB geometry component to generate Postscript or Encapsulated Postscript images of keyboard layouts.

The simplest way to run *xkbprint* is to provide a displayspec for the keymap source as well as a destination filename:

```
$ xkbprint $DISPLAY keyboard.ps
```

This will generate a single Postscript file containing an image of the first two levels of the first keyboard group, as shown in Figure 12-1.

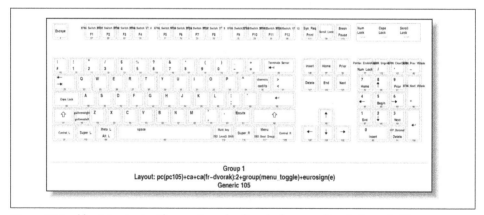

*Figure 12-1. xkbprint output with no options, loading the keymap directly from the X server*

If you defined more than two levels, use the -ll option to select the starting level; this is most commonly used to specify that the image should start with level 3, which causes the third and fourth level to be included:

```
$ xkbprint -ll 3 $DISPLAY keyboard.ps
```

In a similar way, you can select the starting group with -lg:

```
$ xkbprint -lg 2 $DISPLAY keyboard.ps
```

When reading the keymap from the server, *xkbprint* will show only one keyboard image. However, if you use a compiled keymap as input, *xkbprint* will draw multiple keyboard groups as separate images, which is usually ideal for a reference sheet. You can obtain the current keymap from the server and place it in a file using *xkbcomp*:

```
$ xkbcomp -xkm $DISPLAY -o keymap.xkm
$ xkbprint keymap.xkm keyboard.ps
```

The output is shown in Figure 12-2.

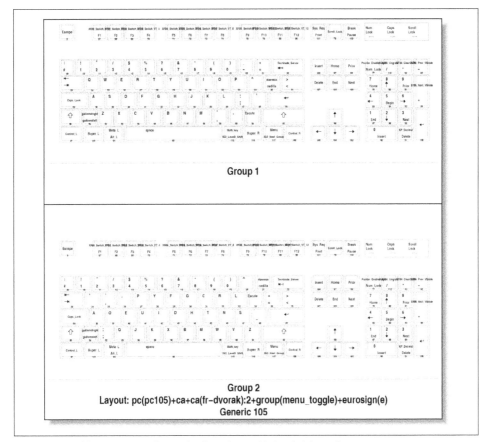

*Figure 12-2. xkbprint output from a keyboard map file loaded from the X server*

An additional page can be generated, showing the keyboard layout of the third and fourth levels, shown in Figure 12-3.

```
$ xkbprint -ll 3 keymap.xkm keyboard.ps
```

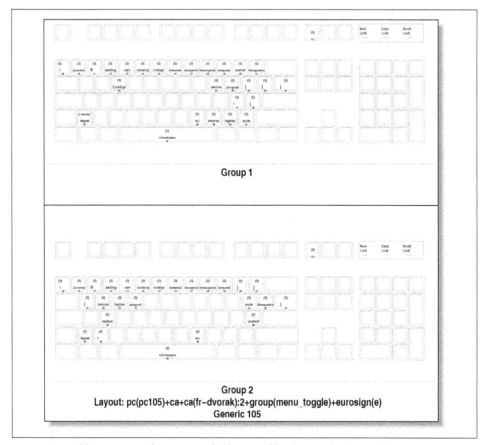

*Figure 12-3. xkbprint output from a compiled keymap file, showing levels 3 and 4*

# Part IV

# Using X Remotely

# 13

# Remote Access

## 13.1 Network Transparency

The manpage for X calls it a *portable, network-transparent window system*. The phrase *network-transparent* refers to the location-independence of the clients and server—the client may be on the same machine as the server or on machines spread all over the planet, as long as he has a network connection to the server.

In this chapter, we'll examine how to use remote clients and entire sessions, and the security and performance implications involved in remote access.

Remote access always involves two or more hosts, and when discussing this topic, it can be easy to confuse which machine is which. Throughout this chapter, I've adopted the convention of calling the computer on which the X server is running *blue*, and the computer on which the remote client is running *red*. The machine name is embedded into the shell prompt in the examples: blue$ is the shell prompt for the X server machine, and red$ is the shell prompt for the client machine.

 As virtualization and partitioning technologies such as *Xen*, Solaris *compartments*, and *VMware* grow into widespread use, X's network transparency gains new value. The ability to display windows from different machine partitions side-by-side on one display provides an important productivity boost for system administrators.

## 13.2 Displaying on a Remote Server

Causing an X client to display on a remote server is fairly straightforward: simply use the displayspec (Sections 1.12 and 7.1) to point to the desired server when starting the client.

Let's assume that the X display number on *blue* is :0 and the client you want to run on *red* is *xclock*.

For ease of experimentation, turn off access controls on *blue*—of course, don't do this on a production machine without understanding the consequences:

```
blue$ xhost +
access control disabled, clients can connect from any host
```

Now the client can simply be started on *red*, using the displayspec blue:0:

```
red$ xclock -display blue:0
```

The *xclock* window will appear on *blue*'s display.

> For this to work, you may need to check your firewall settings, both on your router/switch and on the host running the X server. On a Linux system, iptables -L will show you the current firewall rules; you can configure the settings with your distribution's tools (such as *lokkit* or *Yast*) or use the *iptables* command.

Telling a client to display across the network in this way does not address any of the three remote access challenges (Section 13.7): no attempt is made to reduce network bandwidth or latency requirements, no authentication is performed, and the data can be readily intercepted on the network.

> SUSE uses *KDM* as the default display manager and has configured it so that the local X servers accept connections only through Unix domain sockets and not through TCP/IP. This prevents the use of remote clients. To enable remote connections, remove the -nolisten tcp options from */opt/kde3/share/config/kdm* and restart *KDM*.

# 13.3  Enabling Remote Sessions

Display managers—such as *XDM*, *GDM*, and *KDM*—manage local X displays, but are also capable of managing remote displays through a protocol called *X Display Manager Control Protocol* (XDMCP).

XDMCP enables a user to remotely log in to a server using a graphical authentication dialog. After the user has logged in, a normal session is started (including the window manager, desktop environment, and so forth), as though the user was using a local X server.

XDMCP uses both TCP and UDP on port 177. It is disabled by default in most distributions and must be enabled before remote session can be used; the procedure to enable it varies according to the display manager in use.

# XDM

XDMCP is enabled or disabled by an entry in the *xdm-config* file (typically located at */etc/X11/xdm/xdm-config*). The entry of interest is DisplayManager.requestPort, usually configured like this:

```
DisplayManager.requestPort:    0
```

To enable XDMCP, change the port number to 177:

```
DisplayManager.requestPort:    177
```

You should also check your *Xaccess* file (usually */etc/X11/xdm/xaccess*) to ensure that it has two lines like this:

```
*
* CHOOSER BROADCAST
```

The first line enables any X server to connect directly to this XDMCP server (Section 13.4), and the second line enables indirect queries (Section 13.6).

Finish by restarting *XDM*.

# KDM

*KDM* uses the *kdmrc* file (usually */etc/X11/xdm/kdmrc* or */opt/kde3/share/config/kdm/kdmrc*) to control remote sessions. In this file, there is an [XDMCP] section, which typically looks like this:

```
[Xdmcp]
Enable=false
```

To enable XDMCP, simply change the value to true:

```
[Xdmcp]
Enable=true
```

The *Xaccess* file must be set up in the same way as for *XDM*.

Finally, restart *KDM*.

# GDM

*GDM*'s support for remote sessions is controlled by an entry in the [xdmcp] section of the local *GDM* configuration file (*/etc/gdm/gdm-custom.conf* or */etc/X11/gdm/custom.conf*):

```
[xdmcp]
Enable=false
HonorIndirect=false
```

To enable XDMCP, change the Enable line to true; it's also recommended that you enable HonorIndirect so that you can use indirect queries (Section 13.6):

```
[xdmcp]
Enable=true
HonorIndirect=true
```

Then restart *GDM*.

## 13.4  Accessing a Remote Session on a Specific Host

To access a remote session, command-line options are passed to the X server, which cause it to contact a remote system using XDMCP. The remote system, in turn, will draw an authentication screen using the standard X protocol.

To access a remote session on *red* using an X server on *blue*, start the X server with the option -query red:

```
blue$ X :8 -query red
```

The X server will attempt to contact the XDMCP server on *red*, and if successful, a session login prompt will appear on the display. This is called a *direct query* because a specific XDMCP server is contacted directly.

The advantage of directly querying a host in this way is that less network traffic is generated than when using the broadcast (Section 13.5) or indirect (Section 13.6) mechanisms.

## 13.5  Accessing a Remote Session on Any Available Host

Querying a specific host for a remote session works fine as long as you know the name of the host and that host is up—but if you're a guest on a network, or you want to connect to any of several hosts that provide similar services, you'll want to use a *broadcast query*.

This is even simpler to do than direct queries; just use the -broadcast option on the X server command line:

```
blue$ X :8 -broadcast
```

The X server will perform a XDMCP broadcast using UDP and present a session authentication prompt from the first server that responds.

This approach is particularly useful for load balancing. You can set up a bank of servers with identical services and files (typically sharing the home directories using NFS) and configure all of your users to connect using XDMCP broadcasts. Available servers only will respond; any server that is down or heavily loaded will not respond to broadcast requests.

The downside to this approach is that every X server will broadcast an XDMCP query, and every XDMCP server will respond. If you have 1,000 X servers and 50 XDMCP servers and the desktops are all turned on between 8:55 and 9:05 in the morning, there will be 1,000 broadcast queries and up to 50,000 replies in a 10-minute period. That would not be overwhelming to most networks but it is a significant amount of traffic.

# 13.6  Accessing a Remote Session from a List of Available Sessions

There is a compromise approach between direct XDMCP queries (Section 13.4) and XDMCP broadcasts (Section 13.5): a single host is designated as the host that decides which X server should connect to which XDMCP server. By default, that one system will broadcast a query to the network and present a graphical chooser to the user. When the user selects one of the available hosts, the X server and XDMCP server directly communicate, and the user is presented with an authentication dialog.

This technique is called an *indirect query* and is invoked with the -indirect *host* option on the X server command line. If the indirect host is *red*, you can send it an indirect query like this:

```
blue$ X :8 -indirect red
```

The appearance of the *chooser* display—the menu from which the user selects a host—varies according to the display manager in use on the indirect host. Figures 13-1 through 13-3 show the appearance of the standard choosers from *XDM*, *GDM*, and *KDM* hosted on a Fedora system.

Notice that in each case, the user is able to select a host by clicking on it. The hostname and status message come from each XDMCP host and may be customized; the host picture, if any, comes from the indirect host.

When the user selects a host, the indirect host instructs the X server to connect to that host, which it does directly. From that point on, the indirect host is not involved in any communication between the X server and the XDMCP host. However, if the XDMCP host's authentication dialog includes a Disconnect option, that option will cause the connection to the indirect host to be re-activated, and the host menu to once again be displayed.

Although the default configuration for all common display managers is to discover the list of hosts for the chooser list by broadcast, it is also possible to configure the chooser to present a list of selected hosts only. Those hosts will still be queried to ensure that they are accepting XDMCP connections, and only hosts that are available are shown in the chooser's list.

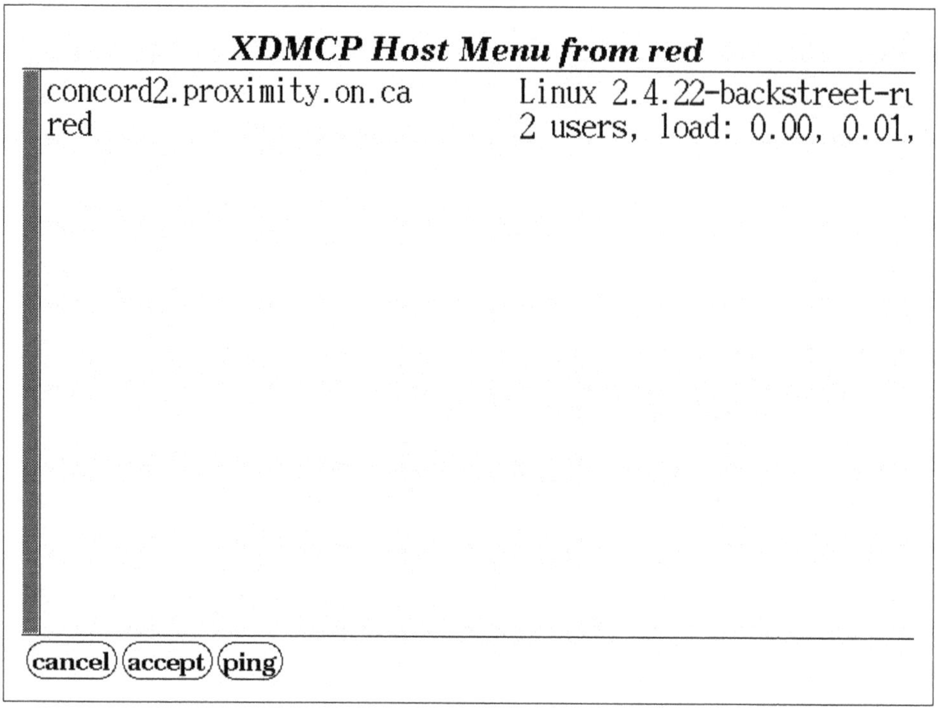

XDMCP Host Menu from red
concord2.proximity.on.ca
Linux 2.4.22-backstreet-ru
red
2 users, load: 0.00, 0.01,
cancel
accept
ping

*Figure 13-1. Standard xdm chooser*

Choose a host to connect to:
172.16.97.100
Linux 2.6.12-1.1398_FC4
concord2.proximity.on.ca (172.16.97.2)
Linux 2.4.22-backstreet-ruby
Add host:
Add
Help
Refresh
Cancel
Connect

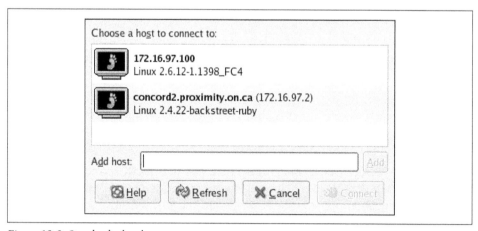

*Figure 13-2. Standard gdm chooser*

It is also possible to replace the chooser with a program or script that selects the target host using any criteria you care to code. For example, you could select the host on a round-robin basis, according to the time of day (East coast server early in the day, West coast server late in the day), or according to the user's IP address.

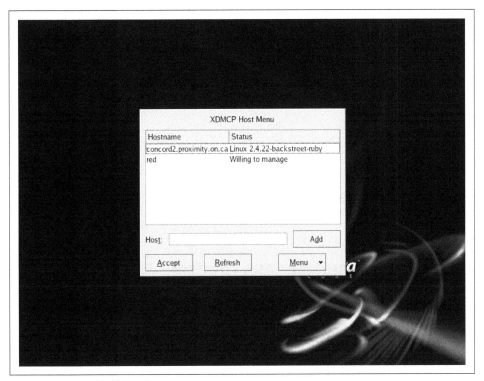

*Figure 13-3. Standard kdm chooser*

Using an indirect XDMCP query has several advantages over direct queries (Section 13.4) and broadcasts (Section 13.5): the user can select the host they wish to use, and the hosts can be discovered by broadcast without each X server system generating broadcast traffic. However, there is a single point of failure. iI the indirect host is down, the indirect query will fail. If a large number of X servers rely on a single indirect host, it may be wise to configure multiple machines to serve in that role with a failover system such as *Heartbeat* (*http://www.linux-ha.org/*).

# 13.7  The Three Challenges of Remote Access

Three are three challenges that any X remote access solution must address; one affects performance, and the remaining two affect security:

*Network bandwidth and latency*
> Bandwidth refers to the overall network data-delivery rate; latency refers to the round-trip delay. X requires moderate network bandwidth and low latency to deliver an effective user interface.

*Access control*
> Since unauthorized clients can access the screen (in the same way that *xwd* [Section 6.11] does), it's possible for a malicious client to snoop around your display and collect personal information, such as your bank account number and balance if displayed in a browser window. Therefore, it's important to ensure that only authorized clients can connect and perform certain operations.

*Privacy*
> Even if data can't be snooped on-screen, raw X protocol traffic can be captured on the network and analyzed to re-create the screen image (and user actions). Some form of encryption must be employed to circumvent this danger.

Many different programs, protocols, and techniques have been developed to address these issues, with varying degrees of success. In the remainder of this chapter, we'll examine a number of remote display techniques in the light of these three challenges.

# 13.8  Host-Based Access Control

You can allow or disallow client connections based on the IP address of the client's host. The *xhost* program manages host-based access control.

Running *xhost* by itself displays the current status:

```
blue$ xhost
access control enabled, only authorized clients can connect
```

The output indicates that host-based control is active, but since no hosts are listed, no hosts are authorized to connect.

You can grant access to a host by IP address or by name (which must resolve to an IP address), using the + symbol:

```
blue$ xhost +red
red being added to access control list
blue$ xhost +172.16.97.251
172.16.97.251 being added to access control list
```

The output of *xhost* (by itself) will now reflect the added hosts:

```
blue$ xhost
access control enabled, only authorized clients can connect
INET:172.16.97.251
INET:red
```

You can remove hosts with the - symbol:

```
blue$ xhost -172.16.97.251
blue$ xhost
access control enabled, only authorized clients can connect
INET:red
```

To disable access control altogether and permit any client to connect to the X server, use + by itself as an option:

```
blue$ xhost +
access control disabled, clients can connect from any host
```

Obviously, this is quite dangerous! But, I must admit, it's convenient when you're experimenting on a private, secure network. To re-enable access control, use a dash by itself as the option:

```
blue$ xhost -
access control enabled, only authorized clients can connect
```

It's possible to invoke the X server with access control entirely disabled—as though xhost + had been executed—using the -ac option:

```
blue$ X -ac
```

Host-based access control does not address network bandwidth and latency issues nor does it address privacy. It also suffers from two significant drawbacks:

- It grants access permission to *all* users of a particular host.
- It's relatively easy to spoof IP addresses.

These two faults led to the development of magic cookies (Section 13.9).

# 13.9  xauth and Magic Cookies

X provides a simple shared-secret access control protocol known as *MIT-MAGIC-COOKIE-1*.

*Magic cookies* or *tokens* are simply secret numbers. If a client attempting to connect to an X server knows the correct magic cookie value, it is permitted to connect; if it doesn't have the right number, the connection is denied.

Magic cookies are stored in the file *~/.Xauthority* and are cross-referenced to particular displays. This file is stored in a binary format and cannot be usefully viewed as text.

When a local client is executed, it takes the target displayspec, cross-references that against the *~/.Xauthority* file to get the appropriate magic cookie, and then presents that magic cookie to the server. If the permission mode on the *~/.Xauthority* file allows reading only by the owner, then other users on the local machine will not be able to read the token value and connect to the X server.

The *xauth* command is used to manipulate the *~/.Xauthority* file; it can operate interactively, accepting commands one-at-a-time from a user, or commands can be given as arguments. The examples in this article all use arguments.

To see the current magic cookies and the display associated with each token, use the *xauth* list command:

```
blue$ xauth list
blue/unix:0  MIT-MAGIC-COOKIE-1  63fa4c416da8b8c5b4d3ae32b3206486
blue:0  MIT-MAGIC-COOKIE-1 63fa4c416da8b8c5b4d3ae32b3206486
green:3  MIT-MAGIC-COOKIE-1  35abebfef1c159b75783a4f33e2610fd
orange:1  MIT-MAGIC-COOKIE-1  b6577a2f2b7af4d82a1321779468cd0f
```

In this case, there are two entries for the local machine *blue*: the first one is for Unix domain socket connections, and the second is for TCP/IP connections. The token value is identical (63fa4c416da8b8c5b4d3ae32b3206486 in each case). The syntax for the Unix domain socket in the *xauth* output (blue/unix:0 in this example) is slightly different from a normal displayspec (which would be :0). The last two entries in the output above are for displays on other hosts.

You may see some entries that use the *XDM-AUTHORIZATION-1* protocol; this is a variation on the magic cookie scheme that doesn't pass the token across the network in plaintext, and it is used by display managers.

You can view the magic cookie for one display by specifying a displayspec:

```
blue$ xauth list :0
blue/unix:0  MIT-MAGIC-COOKIE-1  63fa4c416da8b8c5b4d3ae32b3206486
```

If a client on *red* is going to connect to display :0 on *blue*, the magic cookie for that display needs to be placed into the *~/.Xauthority* file on *red*. Sharing the home directories via NFS will take care of this automatically; otherwise, this can be done with *xauth*'s add command, which accepts a displayspec, protocol, and token value as arguments:

```
red$ xauth add blue:0 MIT-MAGIC-COOKIE-1 63fa4c416da8b8c5b4d3ae32b3206486
red$ xauth list blue:0
blue:0  MIT-MAGIC-COOKIE-1  63fa4c416da8b8c5b4d3ae32b3206486
```

It's a pain typing in MIT-MAGIC-COOKIE-1 all the time, so *xauth* permits you to substitute the period character (.); therefore, the preceding add command could be rewritten as:

```
red$ xauth add blue:0 . 63fa4c416da8b8c5b4d3ae32b3206486
```

You can also use *xauth* to create an extract file, which can be sent to another machine and merged into the *~/.Xauth* file there:

```
blue$ xauth extract extractfile blue:0

...transfer extractfile from the host blue to red using the file
tranfer mechanism of your choice...

red$ xauth merge extractfile
```

Obviously, transporting cookies between hosts is a big nuisance. Don't despair; the process can be automated using SSH (Section 13.12).

Once the magic cookie has been copied to the remote machine (*red*), clients started there will be able to successfully connect to the X server regardless of the current host-based authentication settings (Section 13.8).

To remove a magic cookie from a ~/.*Xauthority* file, use the remove command:

```
red$ xauth remove blue:0
```

Initial cookies are generated by the display manager or by the program starting the X server (such as *startx*). If you wish to start an X server in your own script and use magic cookies for access control, use the *mcookie* command to make a cookie and then use *xauth* to store it in ~/.*Xauthority* before starting the X server. Here is an example:

```
#!/bin/bash
# Start an X server with a magic cookie

export DISPLAY=:8                    # Choose a display number
xauth add $DISPLAY . $(mcookie)      # Create cookie, save in ~/.Xauthority
X -terminate $DISPLAY &              # Start the X server
SERVERPID=$!                         # Remember the server process ID

# Run any clients here...
mwm &
kcalc &
soffice &

wait $SERVERPID                      # Wait for server to finish
xauth remove $DISPLAY                # Remove the cookie from the file
```

If your system doesn't have *mcookie*, you can make a random cookie from a hash of random data—just change the first *xauth* line to read:

```
xauth add $DISPLAY . $(dd if=/dev/random bs=10k count=1 2>/dev/null|
    md5sum|cut -c1-32)
```

Magic cookies are read by the X server from ~/.*Xauthority* only when the server starts up. Clients are subject to access control only when they first connect to the server; once connected, they can remain connected for any length of time without further access control checks.

Magic cookies do not address network bandwidth and latency issues, and they are a weak solution to the access control problem. The most significant issue with using magic cookies for access control is that they are passed across the network in plain text, and if the network traffic is intercepted, the magic cookie will be compromised. It can also be compromised if ~/.*Xauthority* can be read by an attacker.

If you are using *Kerberos* on your network, you can use the user-to-user authentication scheme to manage X access control. See the manpage for *Xsecurity* (Section 13.10) for more information.

# 13.10 The X Security Extension

Both host-based and magic cookie access control grant X server access on an all or nothing basis. A finer level of control is obviously desirable in some situations.

The X Security Extension (*SECURITY*) was introduced in 1996 but is only entering widespread use now, a decade later. It permits clients to be divided into two categories: *trusted* and *untrusted*. Trusted clients are permitted to use the entire X protocol; untrusted applications are limited in what they do—for example, they are prohibited from accessing window images of trusted clients, so *xwd* (Section 6.11) cannot usefully be used as an untrusted client.

Although having only two categories of applications doesn't provide much granularity of control, it strikes a pragmatic balance between functionality and complexity. The simplicity of this approach helps ensure that it is actually used, and used correctly.

*SECURITY* enables the X server itself to generate magic cookies, and those magic cookies can be associated with attributes. The two commonly used attributes are:

*trust status*
  Either trusted or untrusted.

*timeout*
  A time in seconds. If there are no connected clients authorized with the magic cookie for that length of time, then the cookie is invalidated.

(There is also a *group* attribute, but this is intended to be used with the *Application Group* extension, which is defunct.)

Any client that is trusted can ask the X server to create a new cookie. To create a new cookie from the command line, use the *xauth* command generate, which accepts a displayspec and a protocol as arguments. Optionally, you can include the keywords trusted or untrusted and the keyword timeout followed by a value in seconds. Here are some examples that generate tokens for display :2 on *blue*:

```
$ xauth generate blue:2 .                         # Untrusted, 60 second timeout.
$ xauth generate blue:2 . trusted timeout 300     # Trusted, 5 minute timeout
$ xauth generate blue:2 . timeout 0               # Untrusted, no timeout
```

The simplest way to use *SECURITY* is to leave the original, trusted magic cookie in place for local connections, and to generate a nonexpiring, untrusted key for remote TCP/IP connections. Running this command on the local display will set up the token for remote clients:

```
$ xauth generate "$(hostname -f):$DISPLAY" . untrusted timeout 0
```

Some versions of *hostname* don't accept the -f (fully qualified domain name) option.

*Xauth* will place the new magic cookie into the ~/.Xauthority file, leaving the local token unchanged.

One problem with the *generate* command is that it *replaces* any existing token (for the given display) with the newly generated value; therefore, the *xauth* list command will show only the most recently generated token for each displayspec.

To get around this problem, you can use the -f option to *xauth*, which enables you to specify an alternate authority file. To generate two untrusted keys and place them in separate files, you could use:

```
$ xauth -f ~/.Xauthority1 generate blue:2 . untrusted
$ xauth -f ~/.Xauthority2 generate blue:2 . untrusted
```

You can then query a specific authority file to get the token:

```
$ xauth -f ~/.Xauthority1 list blue:2
```

These tokens can be transferred to different remote machines as needed.

Effective use of the X Security extension mildly improves the basic cookie scheme to improve privacy, but the gains are minimal.

# 13.11 Low-Bandwidth X (LBX)

X provides a mechanism that is supposed to reduce bandwidth and latency requirements for X applications and that is called *LBX*—but it *doesn't make any appreciable difference* for most applications. Nonetheless, it's interesting to know how it works and why it's fallen into disuse.

LBX was part of the ill-fated *Broadway* remote-access initiative, and it consists of two parts:

*LBXproxy*
> A proxy server that runs on the client host. X clients connect to LBXproxy instead of the X server; LBXproxy then communicates with the server, using compression and caching in an attempt to reduce traffic.

*The LBX Extension*
> If data is being compressed on one end of the connection, it must be decompressed at the other end. The LBX extension to the X server provides the other end of the link.

Before attempting to use *LBX*, confirm that your server supports it. You can grep the output of *xdpyinfo* (Section 6.2):

```
blue$ xdpyinfo|grep LBX
```

Assuming the LBX extension is present—it is on most servers, though it may be dropped from the standard X distribution soon—you can set up the *lbxproxy*. This example sets up the proxy to receive X client connections directed to local display :5, and to forward the connections to the X server blue:2:

```
red$ lbxproxy -display blue:2 :5
```

Once *lbxproxy* is running, you should direct clients on the remote machine to connect to the *lbxproxy* instead of the X server. Setting the DISPLAY variable is the most convenient way to do this:

```
red$ export DISPLAY=:5
```

If you're using cookies, you'll notice that clients won't be able to connect to *lbxproxy*, even if they can successfully connect to the X server:

```
red$ xclock
Xlib: connection to ":5.0" refused by server
Xlib: No protocol specified

Error: Can't open display: :5
```

This happens because the magic cookie is cross-referenced against the server display-spec in ~/.Xauthority instead of against the client displayspec. To correct the problem, make a copy of the server's magic cookie (associated with blue:2 in this example) and cross-referenced it to *lbxproxy*'s display number (:5). The following command will automate the process:

```
red$ xauth add :5 . $(xauth list blue:2|sed "s/.*-1//")
```

Why doesn't *lbxproxy* make much difference? Its compression algorithm is weak, and the volume of cacheable data is insufficient to matter much.

There are some alternative packages available that work in a similar manner but offer somewhat better compression; the Differential X Protocol Compressor (*dxpc*) is one, but it must be executed on both the server host and client host.

However, in many cases, good general compression on the network link appears to be as effective as a proxy compression tool.

## 13.12  X Tunneling with SSH

Secure Shell (SSH) provides a simple and effective way to run X clients on a remote machine, addressing all three challenges of remote access. This is by far the preferred approach to running remote X clients.

At its most basic level, SSH provides remote shell access, acting like a secure version of *telnet*. But SSH also provides tunneling capability, which creates a listening port on one end of the connection and forwards any TCP/IP connections through the encrypted channel to a designated port on the remote host (or any system directly reachable from the remote host). Going one step further, SSH provides an enhanced version of the tunneling facility specifically for X traffic.

To connect to a remote host using SSH, simply specify a *username* (chris in this example) and *host* (red) in this format:

```
blue$ ssh chris@red
```

You may be prompted for your password on the remote host; you will then receive a shell prompt on that system.

X tunneling (called *X11 forwarding* in the SSH documentation) may be enabled or disabled by default, depending on the system configuration; to force it on, use the -X (uppercase) option:

```
blue$ ssh -X chris@red
```

You can use the -x (lowercase) option to force X11 forwarding off:

```
blue$ ssh -x chris@red
```

When an X11 forwarding connection is established, SSH generates a new magic cookie using the *SECURITY* extension (Sections 13.10 and 13.15), caches that on the originating machine, sets up the tunnel to the remote system, places a dummy magic cookie value in the remote ~/.Xauthority file, and sets the DISPLAY variable to point to the remote end of the tunnel. It then monitors traffic coming through the tunnel and changes any occurrence of the dummy cookie to the actual cookie.

This ensures that:

- The cookie value is never passed unencrypted over the network.
- If the remote ~/.Xauthority file is compromised, the cookie will not work for other connection paths to the server.
- All of the X traffic going through the tunnel is encrypted so it is protected against snooping.

Therefore, once you have connected to a remote system using SSH with X11 forwarding turned on, you can start X clients.

It's also possible to specify the name of the client directly on the SSH command line. For example, to run *kcalc* on *blue*:

```
blue$ ssh -X chris@red kcalc
```

In this case, no interactive remote shell will be started.

As they would say on late-night infomercials: "But wait—there's more!" SSH also has a compression feature, which is enabled with the -C option:

```
blue$ ssh -X -C chris@red kcalc
```

Although this is a simple data-stream compression (like *gzip*), it provides at least as much benefit as *LBX* (Section 13.11) in most use cases.

Use the SSH compression option even if your network connection is already compressed (for example, when using a modem), because compression is much more effective when applied *before* encryption.

# 13.13 Using Public Keys with SSH

SSH provides a simple way of starting a remote X client with a single command (Section 13.12). It's often convenient to place an SSH command in a *.desktop* file so that a menu option or icon will invoke a remote client automatically.

The user would probably not be aware that the application was running remotely— except that she will be prompted for a password each time she clicks on the icon.

It's possible to configure SSH to use public key cryptography for authentication instead of passwords. This eliminates the password prompt altogether and makes remote client execution beautifully seamless.

Public key cryptography and the intricacies of SSH are fascinating subjects, and I cannot do them justice in a few short articles. For detailed information on SSH, consult *SSH, The Secure Shell: The Definitive Guide* by Daniel J. Barrett et al. (O'Reilly).

There are several versions of SSH in use, but the most widely used is the open source *OpenSSH* package. It is included with BSD systems (where it originated) as well as most Linux distributions and some commercial Unix systems.

To set up public key authentication using *OpenSSH* (once again, I'm using *blue* to mean the host on which the X server is running, and *red* to mean the host on which the X client will be run):

1. On *blue*, create a public key, pressing ENTER to accept the default values for the various prompts:

   ```
   blue$ ssh-keygen -t rsa
   Generating public/private rsa key pair.
   Enter file in which to save the key (/home/chris/.ssh/id_rsa): ENTER
   Enter passphrase (empty for no passphrase): ENTER
   Enter same passphrase again: ENTER
   Your identification has been saved in /home/chris/.ssh/id_rsa.
   Your public key has been saved in /home/chris/.ssh/id_rsa.pub.
   The key fingerprint is:
   aa:bb:cc:dd:ee:ff:aa:bb:cc:dd:ee:ff:aa:bb:cc:dd chris@blue
   ```

2. Append the contents of the file *~/.ssh/id_rsa.pub* on *blue* to *~/.ssh/authorized_keys* on *red*:

   ```
   blue$ ssh chris@red "cat >>~/.ssh/authorized_keys" <~/.ssh/id_rsa.pub
   chris@red's password:
   ```

3. Ensure that ~/.ssh/authorized_keys on red has 0600 permission:

```
blue$ ssh chris@red chmod 0600 ~/.ssh/authorized_keys
chris@red's password:
```

4. Confirm that you can log in to the remote system without a password using SSH:

```
blue$ ssh red
red$
```

You can use the same public key with as many systems as you want; simply repeat step 2 for each additional system.

 The -v option to *ssh* is very useful when debugging connection problems. You can specify -v up to three times to increase the verbosity of the debugging information. Likewise, to debug the server side, stop the *sshd* daemon and run it from a shell using one to three -d (debug) options.

# 13.14 Using Passphrase Protection of SSH Keys

Using SSH without public key authentication results in a password request for each new SSH connection, but using SSH with public key authentication is only as secure as the ~/.ssh/id_rsa file. If that file is compromised—by a trojan program, account compromise, or even a stolen copy of a system backup—the accounts on other hosts will also be compromised. The challenge is balancing convenience against vulnerability.

SSH provides a solution to this problem too (of course!). Your private key file can be protected by a *passphrase*, and the *ssh-agent* program can be set up to request the passphrase *only once per session*, regardless of how many SSH connections are later established. If the private key file is stolen, it will be useless without the passphrase.

To set up a passphrase on your private key when using OpenSSH, execute *ssh-keygen* with the -p option. I used **TOPsecret** as the passphrase in this example:

```
blue$ ssh-keygen -p
Enter file in which the key is (/home/chris/.ssh/id_rsa): ENTER
Key has comment '/home/chris/.ssh/id_rsa'
Enter new passphrase (empty for no passphrase): TOPsecret
Enter same passphrase again: TOPsecret
Your identification has been saved with the new passphrase.
```

If you make only this change, then you will be prompted for your passphrase every time you use ssh to connect to *red*:

```
blue$ ssh red
Enter passphrase for key '/home/chris/.ssh/id_rsa': TOPsecret
red$
```

To set things up so that you are only prompted for the passphrase once per session, execute `ssh-agent` and `ssh-add` during session startup. There are many different places you can place these two commands—*startx, xinitrc, ~/.kde/env/ssh.sh*, and others—but the easiest place to put them is probably at the end of your shell startup script (*~/.bash_profile* for *bash* users, *~/.profile* for *sh, ksh, ash, and zsh* users, or *~/.login* for *csh* users).

The two lines to add are:

```
eval $(ssh-agent)
ssh-add
```

(Users with a genuine old-school Bourne shell—both of you!—should substitute `` `ssh-agent` `` for `$(ssh-agent).`)

Or, for CSH users:

```
eval `ssh-agent -c`
ssh-add
```

These two lines will be executed when you log in using character mode or start a session using a display manager. *Ssh-agent* will be started in daemon mode, and will then pass environment variables back to your login shell to tell later SSH clients how to connect to it; *ssh-add* then instructs *ssh-agent* to load your private keys, at which point you will be prompted for any necessary passphrases. The password prompt will appear as text or in a dialog box as appropriate.

# 13.15  OpenSSH and the SECURITY Extension

Recent versions of OpenSSH support the *SECURITY* Extension and can generate untrusted magic cookies on-the-fly. The -X option has been changed to use untrusted cookies by default.

Some other versions of SSH may use +X instead of -Y.

To use OpenSSH with trusted cookies, use the -Y option:

```
blue$ ssh -Y chris@red xwd -root >demo.xwd
```

SSH may be configured to use trusted connections all of the time. Check the `ForwardX11Trusted` option in /etc/ssh/ssh_config—it should be set to no if you wish to use untrusted clients.

# 14

# Using VNC

## 14.1  The VNC System

VNC (*Virtual Network Computer*) is a low-bandwidth cross-platform display system. It can be used to control and display a Windows XP desktop from a Mac, a Linux desktop from a Windows 2000 machine, or a Mac desktop from a Solaris workstation.

The VNC protocol is named RFB, for *Remote Frame Buffer*. In VNC terminology, the system on which the desktop is running is the *server*, and the system used to access the desktop is called the *viewer* (or *client*). Binary viewers are available for most platforms, including Windows, Mac OS X, Linux, Palm, Windows Mobile, and Symbian. There are also several Java viewers that can be run as web applets—therefore, allowing VNC access from any web-enabled browser.

This chapter covers some of the many ways in which VNC may be used in an X-based environment. In addition to the *red* (X client) and *blue* (X server) hostnames used in previous chapters, I'll use *green* to refer to the system on which the VNC client software is running.

Xvnc contains a very simple web server, which can be used to serve a Java applet version of the VNC viewer. This permits users to connect to the server from any Java-enabled browser—no special client is needed. The reason that the web server is built into Xvnc is so that the appropriate JavaScript parameters can be substituted into the web page before it is served.

Windows and Mac OS are both designed as single-user systems, so in those environments the VNC server software takes control of the one and only desktop. In an X environment, there are many more possibilities:

- The Xvnc server provides remote desktops *without* a local desktop display. In essence, Xvnc acts as a protocol converter, providing an X server on one side and a VNC server on the other side. This enables many remote users to work simultaneously, and also permits users to disconnect from and reconnect to a running session (even from another location). One standing server must be preconfigured for each remote user (Sections 14.4 and 14.6).

- Xvnc can be started on demand using *inetd/xinetd*. This permits any number of remote users to log in to the system without preconfiguring standing servers, and no resources will be used when there are no remote users connected. However, users will not be able to disconnect and reconnect (Sections 14.9 and 14.10).

- Xvnc can initiate a connection to a remote viewer or use SSH to create a secure tunnel to a remote machine. These techniques simplify connections to fire-walled or clustered server hosts (Sections 14.12 and 14.17).

- A Java viewer can be combined with Xvnc, *inetd/xinetd* and a glue script to embed one specific X application into a web page (Section 14.13).

- A VNC server that operates as an X client provides the same capabilities as the VNC server extension. It does not require server configuration and can be started only when needed, but it does not permit the remote user to start a new session—he can only connect after the local user has authenticated. Gnome's *vino* and KDE's *krfb* are examples of this type of X client/VNC server (Section 14.14).

- The VNC server can be an X server extension, operating in the same way as the Windows or Mac servers, where the remote and local displays are the same. This is a good solution for remote support, because the user can demonstrate a problem to the support technician, and the support technician can demonstrate a procedure to the user (Section 14.15).

## 14.2  So Many VNC Versions!

VNC was originally developed by the Oracle and Olivetti Research Lab in Cambridge, U.K., and released under the General Public License (GPL). The lab was eventually purchased by AT&T; when the lab was closed and the VNC project discontinued, a number of the original authors started their own company: RealVNC (*http://realvnc.com*). In the meantime, a fork of VNC was created, called TightVNC (*http://tightvnc.com*).

The number of VNC-related projects has proliferated to the point that there are now more than 75 listed on SourceForge (*http://sourceforge.net*). Some commercial products are also based on this technology (including several from RealVNC).

The RealVNC and TightVNC products are the most commonly deployed. These friendly competitors keep leapfrogging each other, and both versions continue to advance at a aggressive pace. Many Unix systems and Linux distributions contain one or the other (for example, Fedora includes the RealVNC software, and SUSE includes TightVNC). The server is called Xvnc in both cases.

Does it matter which one you use? Not really. Either RealVNC or TightVNC will work fine for most projects, so start with the one included with your OS or distribution. If you find yourself in need of a feature that that version does not have, then that's the time to go hunting.

---

# 14.3 Xvnc Basics

The Xvnc server is based on XFree86/X.org and therefore accepts most of the same command-line arguments, such as the display number, access control options, termination options, and XDMCP query commands. It does not use a *xorg.conf*-style configuration file because there is no hardware to configure; instead, the display depth and virtual screen size are specified on the command line. Table 14-1 lists the command-line options that may be used with Xvnc. These are in addition to those accepted by the XFree86/X.org server.

*Table 14-1. Xvnc command-line options in addition to X.org options*

| RealVNC | TightVNC | Description |
| --- | --- | --- |
| -depth *bits* | -depth *bits* | Color depth of the display. Some VNC clients (such as the TightVNVC binary viewer) will negotiate the color depth based on the performance of the network connection; for those clients, set the color depth high (24). For other clients, set the color depth to a low value (such as 8) for low-speed or congested network connections. |
| -geometry *XxY* | -geometry *XxY* | Size of the virtual display. |
| -rfbport *port* | -rfbport *port* | TCP/IP port for RFB protocol (default is 5900+display). |
| -httpport *port* | -httpport *port* | TCP/IP port for built-in web server. |
| -http *dir* | -http *dir* | Directory containing HTTP files (used for serving the Java applet version of the VNC client). Files in this directory include both the applet and the HTML page into which the applet is embedded. |
| -nevershared | -nevershared | Display is never shared between incoming clients (regardless of client-side settings). |
| -disconnectclients | -dontdisconnect | Do (don't) disconnect old clients when a new one connects. If disconnection is specified along with -nevershared, then new connections will close old ones (sometimes handy if you connect from one computer, then go to another and connect from there). If disconnection is not permitted and -nevershared is specified, then one connection is permitted only and other connections will be rejected. |
| -inetd | -inetd | Required when Xvnc is launched from *inetd/xinetd*. |
| -desktop *name* | -desktopname *name* | Name of the desktop as reported to clients. |
| -passwdfile *file*<br>-rfbauth *file* | -rfbauth *file* | Name of the password file for incoming connections (passwords are managed with *vncpasswd*). |

For example, to start up a VNC server with an 800×600 display and 24-bit color depth on display :5, while protecting the connection with a password and displaying a session prompt from the host *red*:

```
blue$ Xvnc -query red -once -rfbauth ~/myvncpasswd -geometry 800x600 -depth 24 :5
```

This server will send the XDMCP query immediately and will listen on port 5905 for incoming RFB connections. Before this command is run, the password file must be created with *vncpasswd*:

```
blue$ vncpasswd ~/myvncpasswd
Password: secret
Verify: secret
```

The password file is read at authentication time, not when the server is started, so it can be changed on-the-fly while the server is running and the change will take effect immediately.

## 14.4 The vncserver Script

The *vncserver* script is a wrapper for Xvnc, designed to be run by users. It provides a password-protected, persistent server; the user may connect to the server, disconnect, move to a different machine, and reconnect.

This script first checks to see whether the password file *~/.vnc/password* exists; if not, it runs *vncpasswd* to create it, prompting the user for the password value. It then searches for a free display number and sets the display geometry and depth to match the current screen size and depth (on the display on which the script is run, if one is present). The server number is reported to stdout, and Xvnc is started along with the clients specified in *~/.vnc/xstartup* (default settings are copied to this file if it is not already present). The internal mini-web server in Xvnc is also activated by default.

The default clients started by *xstartup* are pretty lame, so you will probably want to change *~/.vnc/xstartup* to read the following:

```
$!/bin/sh
unset SESSION_MANAGER
/etc/X11/xinit/xinitrc
```

These lines are present in the default RealVNC version of the *xstartup* file, but are commented out; they will start a normal session for your system (typically KDE or Gnome). Instead of */etc/X11/xinit/xinitrc*, you can specify a desktop startup command such as *startkde* or *gnome-session*.

 Setting a solid-color desktop background and using a visually simple window theme may improve remote display performance. A lightweight window manager/desktop environment such as Xfce (Section 8.6) may work better than KDE or Gnome on slow or congested network connections.

Running *vncserver* is straightforward, and may be done from a remote shell prompt (for example, via SSH). This is the output when *vncserver* is run for the first time:

```
blue$ vncserver

You will require a password to access your desktops.

Password: secret
Verify: secret

New 'blue:4 (chris)' desktop is blue:4

Creating default startup script /home/chris/.vnc/xstartup
Starting applications specified in /home/chris/.vnc/xstartup
Log file is /home/chris/.vnc/blue:4.log
```

To kill the RealVNC version of *vncserver*, use the -kill option with the display number reported by the server:

```
blue$ vncserver -kill :4
```

To kill the TightVNC version, kill Xvnc by name:

```
blue$ killall Xvnc
```

*vncserver* understands the same options as Xvnc. Some versions of this script access default values for command-line options from the configuration file */etc/vnc.conf*. If your system does not use */etc/vnc.conf*, you can modify the default configuration values by editing the actual *vncserver* script using a text editor. Most of the defaults are contained in global variables defined near the start of the script; for example, to change the default screen size from 1024×768 to 800×600 and the default color depth from 16 to 24 bits, change the geometry and depth variables:

```
#
# Global variables.  You may want to configure some of these for your site.
#

$geometry = "800x600";
$depth = 16;
$vncJavaFiles = (((-d "/usr/share/vnc/classes") && "/usr/share/vnc/classes") ||
                ((-d "/usr/local/vnc/classes") && "/usr/local/vnc/classes"));
$vncUserDir = "$ENV{HOME}/.vnc";
$xauthorityFile = "$ENV{XAUTHORITY}" || "$ENV{HOME}/.Xauthority";
```

## 14.5  Using the VNC Viewers

To connect to a server from another system, execute *vncviewer* and specify the host and display:

```
green$ vncviewer blue:4
Password: secret
```

If you leave the connection information (host and display number) out, you will be prompted for it; if the *vncviewer* command is not run from a terminal, the host/display prompt and the password prompt will be presented graphically. The viewers for other platforms operate in the same way.

> To connect to a nonstandard port number, specify *host::port* (note the double colon) instead of *host:display*—for example, to connect to a server running on port 6120 on blue, use:
>
> green$ **vncviewer *blue::6120***

You can also connect to the Xvnc web server at port 5800+display using any Java-enabled web browser; since the server in this example is on display :4, the port number will be 5804:

green$ **firefox *http://blue:5804/***

The web server will send you a predefined HTML page containing an embedded Java applet; the applet geometry and the port number of the RFB connection will be substituted into the HTML page by Xvnc.

The X version of *vncviewer* is the exact counterpart of Xvnc—it's a client to both VNC and X, whereas Xvnc is server to both VNC and X.

> The KDE Remote Desktop Connection (*krdc*) and Gnome-oriented Terminal Server Client (*tsclient*) programs offer a graphical method of connecting to a VNC server as well as a Windows Terminal Server. You can also create desktop or panel icons to connect to frequently used VNC servers.

# 14.6  Using Standing VNC Servers

Although the *vncserver* script permits any user to easily start a VNC server, it is sometimes desirable to have VNC servers start up automatically when the system boots. Users can connect to those servers remotely and then later disconnect, reconnecting at will from any location. For example, users can start a task from work, disconnect, reconnect from an Internet cafe to check on the progress of the task, disconnect, and then finally connect from home to finish the operation. However, since they remain logged in while disconnected, it's imperative that password protection be used on the VNC server.

Although standing servers can be started with any clients, it is easiest and most common to start them with a connection to a display manager, which will then start a normal session. This requires that XDMCP be enabled (Section 13.3).

Before enabling standing servers, create password files using *vncpasswd*. I recommend placing these in the directory */etc/vncpasswd.d*:

```
blue# mkdir /etc/vncpasswd.d
blue# vncpasswd /etc/vncpasswd.d/p0
Password: secret0
Verify: secret0
blue# vncpasswd /etc/vncpasswd.d/p1
Password: secret1
Verify: secret1
blue# vncpasswd /etc/vncpasswd.d/p2
Password: secret2
Verify: secret2
```

Entries to start standing VNC servers can then be added to */etc/inittab*:

```
v0:5:respawn:/usr/bin/Xvnc -rfbauth /etc/vncpasswd.d/p0 -query localhost :20
v1:5:respawn:/usr/bin/Xvnc -rfbauth /etc/vncpasswd.d/p1 -query localhost :21
v2:5:respawn:/usr/bin/Xvnc -rfbauth /etc/vncpasswd.d/p2 -query localhost :22
```

Note that these servers are started only in runlevel 5. I've used display numbers :20 through :22 here to avoid conflict with local displays and ssh port forwarding (Section 14.12).

These servers will default to 1024×768 pixels in size, with 16-bit color depth. You can override these defaults with the -geometry and -depth options (Section 14.3).

# 14.7  Configuring the Xvnc Web Server

To make remote sessions available to users through browsers, Xvnc reads a set of HTML and Java files. When running Xvnc, add the -httpd argument to indicate where the files are stored. Typically, this is */usr/share/vnc/classes*, so you could execute:

```
blue$ Xvnc -httpd /usr/share/vnc/classes -rfbauth pwfile -query localhost :8
```

The HTTP port defaults to 5800+*display*. This example uses display :8, so the Java applet could be viewed at:

```
green$ firefox http://blue:5808/
```

The HTTP port can be overridden and set to any arbitrary value using the -httpport option:

```
blue$ Xvnc -httpd /usr/share/vnc/classes -httpport 1900 \
         -rfbauth pwfile -query localhost :8
```

In this case, the URI becomes *http://blue:1900/*.

# 14.8  Customizing the VNC Java Applet Web Page

The default web page included with the Xvnc server is very simple. There are two versions: the version included with the current TightVNC and older RealVNC Java viewer embeds the viewer applet into the web page, whereas the newer version of the RealVNC Java viewer opens in a separate window.

You can customize the web page by adding a company logo, instructive text, or links to other pages (perhaps even a link to a binary viewer software for higher performance). It's not a bad idea to rewrite it into standard XHTML at the same time. The default page included with the TightVNC distribution, usually installed as */usr/share/vnc/classes/index.vnc*, looks like this:

```
<!--
    index.vnc - default HTML page for TightVNC Java viewer applet, to be
    used with Xvnc. On any file ending in .vnc, the HTTP server embedded in
    Xvnc will substitute the following variables when preceded by a dollar:
    USER, DESKTOP, DISPLAY, APPLETWIDTH, APPLETHEIGHT, WIDTH, HEIGHT, PORT,
    PARAMS. Use two dollar signs ($$) to get a dollar sign in the generated
    HTML page.

    NOTE: the $PARAMS variable is not supported by the standard VNC, so
    make sure you have TightVNC on the server side, if you're using this
    variable.
-->

<HTML>
<TITLE>
$USER's $DESKTOP desktop ($DISPLAY)
</TITLE>
<APPLET CODE=VncViewer.class ARCHIVE=VncViewer.jar
        WIDTH=$APPLETWIDTH HEIGHT=$APPLETHEIGHT>
<param name=PORT value=$PORT>
$PARAMS
</APPLET>
<BR>
<A href="http://www.tightvnc.com/">TightVNC site</A>
</HTML>
```

Notice the presence of the $USER, $DESKTOP, $DISPLAY, $APPLETWIDTH, $APPLETHEIGHT, $PORT, and $PARAMS variables, which will be replaced by appropriate values by Xvnc.

Rewritten in XHTML with a company logo, company title, and links to the Windows *vncviewer* and a help page, the file looks like this:

```
<?xml version='1.0' encoding='UTF-8'?>
<!DOCTYPE html PUBLIC
    '-//W3C//DTD XHTML 1.0 Transitional//EN'
    'http://www.w3.org/TR/xhtml1/DTD/xhtml1-transitional.dtd'>

<html xmlns='http://www.w3.org/1999/xhtml' xml:lang='en'>
  <head>
    <title>
      Foo Corporation - Remote Employee Access
    </title>
  </head>
  <body>
    <img src="company.png" alt="" />
```

```
        <applet code="VncViewer.class" archive="VncViewer.jar"
            width="$APPLETWIDTH" height="$APPLETHEIGHT">
          <param name="PORT" value="$PORT" />
        </applet>
        <p>
          <a href="vncviewer.exe">Windows VNC viewer program.</a>
          <a href="http://foocorp/help.html">Help!</a>
        </p>
      </body>
    </html>
```

The Java applets accept parameters, using the <param ...> tag as shown earlier. The
TightVNC applet seems to be a little more flexible than the RealVNC applet (and is
certainly better-documented); these are some of the key parameters:

PORT
> Port to connect to (not the display number). Usually set to $PORT when using
> Xvnc's built-in web server.

PASSWORD
> Password in plain text. Dangerous to use, since anyone can see the password
> using the View Source option in the browser; however, this can also be used to
> specify that there is no password and the user should not be asked for one.

RESTRICTED COLORS
> Set to No for 24-bit color, or Yes for 8-bit color (default).

VIEW ONLY
> Set to Yes to disable sending keyboard and mouse events to the remote system,
> or No for normal operation.

SHARE DESKTOP
> Controls whether a shared or exclusive connection is requested. This parameter
> interacts with the -disconnectclients or -dontdisconnect options given to the
> server (see Table 14-1). Possible values are Yes (request a shared connection) or
> No (request an exclusive connection).

OPEN NEW WINDOW
> Set to Yes, this opens a new window for the VNC display; set to No, it embeds the
> display in the web page.

SHOW CONTROLS
> Displays control buttons at the top of the screen (Yes/No).

OFFER RELOGIN
> Presents a reconnection button in the event of a disconnection (Yes/No).

SHOW OFFLINE DESKTOP
> Controls whether the desktop image remains visible after disconnection from the
> server (Yes) or the image is erased (No).

For example, to configure the applet to run in 24-bit mode, request an exclusive connection to the server, and disable the controls at the top of the applet, use this code in your *index.vnc* file:

```
<applet code="VncViewer.class" archive="VncViewer.jar"
    width="$APPLETWIDTH" height="$APPLETHEIGHT">
  <param name="PORT"               value="$PORT" />
  <param name="RESTRICTED COLORS" value="No"    />
  <param name="SHARE DESKTOP"      value="No"    />
  <param name="SHOW CONROLS"       value="No"    />
</applet>
```

TightVNC's Xvnc can generate some of the *param* tags based on the server settings; insert the variable $PARAM into your code after your last <param ...> tag and before the closing </applet> tag.

## 14.9  Starting VNC On Demand Using xinetd

Instead of using standing VNC servers, it's possible to use *inetd/xinetd* to start Xvnc only when an incoming connection request is made. This has a number of advantages over standing servers:

- Any (reasonable) number of VNC servers can be used, without configuring in advance how many servers should be started.

- Servers are started only when needed, and terminated when not in use, so no system resources are used unnecessarily.

- All of the servers use the same port number, so all the users have the same connection details (simplifying support).

- Since it's not possible to connect to a logged-in session, no VNC passwords are required—you can use display manager authentication alone.

- X display numbers are automatically assigned.

The downside to this approach is that it is not possible to disconnect from the server and reconnect at a later time or from another location and pick up where you left off.

To configure *xinetd* and Xvnc to work together, you must first select at least one port number. It's often useful to define a few port numbers for different VNC server resolutions. These numbers should be appended to the end of the */etc/services* file along with service names of your choice; in this example, I'm using port 5940 (VNC display number 40) for 800×600 resolution, 5941 for 1024×768, and 5942 for 1280×1024:

```
# VNC servers started by xinetd
vnc-800x600     5940/tcp
vnc-1024x768    5941/tcp
vnc-1280x1024   5942/tcp
```

It's also a good idea to create a unique user for these services, so that damage to the system is limited if a vulnerability in Xvnc is found and exploited. The following command suffices to add a new user on most Linux/Unix systems:

```
blue# useradd vnc
```

Once this has been done, corresponding service files can be added to */etc/xinetd/xinetd.d*. Here is the file for the 800×600 service, placed in */etc/xinetd/xinetd.d/vnc-800x600*:

```
# default: on
# description: Local Xvnc sessions @ 800x600 resolution via xinetd
service vnc-800x600
{
  flags           = REUSE
  socket_type     = stream
  wait            = no
  user            = vnc
  server          = /usr/bin/Xvnc
  # The following two lines must be one line in the file.
  server_args     = -inetd -query localhost -once -terminate
                    -depth 24 -geometry 800x600 -securitytypes none
  log_on_failure  += USERID
  disable         = no
}
```

 Note that the server_args line, which has been broken into two lines here due to space constraints, must be a single line in the file.

The service files for the other resolutions are identical, except that the three occurrences of 800x600 are replaced by 1024x768 or 1280x1024.

Notice that the -securitytypes argument is used to disable VNC passwords (since the user must log in through the display manager's login dialog); to enable VNC passwords, replace -securitytypes none with -rfbauth *passwordfile*.

Assuming that your display manager has *xdmcp* enabled, you can now enable the servers by instructing *xinetd* to reload its configuration file. On Fedora systems, this can be done using the *service* script:

```
blue# service xinetd reload
```

Or you can manually signal *xinetd* to reload the configuration:

```
blue# killall -HUP xinetd
```

You can then connect to *xinetd* using a VNC viewer, and a copy of Xvnc will be started for you automatically:

```
green$ vncviewer blue:40
```

Each time you connect with a VNC viewer, you will see the display manager's authentication dialog. All of the connections share the same VNC display number, but a different X display number—the Xvnc server automatically assigns the X display number by successively attempting to open ports starting at 6000 and going up to 6099. If it doesn't find an available port by that point, your server is probably too heavily loaded to handle another connection anyway!

 Recent versions of SUSE Linux ship with a configuration that is similar to the one described here, but that is disabled by default. To enable on-demand VNC service in SUSE, edit */etc/xinetd.d/vnc*, change the disabled=yes lines to disabled=no, and restart *xinetd* (you'll also need to enable XDMCP if you haven't already done so). 800×600 resolution will be available on port 5901, 1024×768 on port 5902, and 1280 ×1024 on port 5903.

## 14.10  Starting VNC On Demand Using inetd

If you are using a system that has a traditional *inetd* server instead of *xinetd*, the configuration for the on-demand VNC servers is slightly different. After setting up the *vnc* user and the */etc/services* entries as you would for *xinetd*, append these entries to the */etc/inetd.conf* file (each of these three entries must be contained on a single line):

```
vnc-800x600 stream tcp nowait vnc /usr/bin/Xvnc -inetd -query localhost -once -
terminate -depth 24 -geometry 800x600 -securitytypes none

vnc-1024x768 stream tcp nowait vnc /usr/bin/Xvnc -inetd -query localhost -once -
terminate -depth 24 -geometry 1024x768 -securitytypes none

vnc-1280x1024 stream tcp nowait vnc /usr/bin/Xvnc -inetd -query localhost -once -
terminate -depth 24 -geometry 1280x1024 -securitytypes none
```

To activate the new services, signal *inetd* to reload its configuration:

```
blue# killall -HUP inetd
```

## 14.11  Using the Java Applet with On-Demand VNC Servers

When Xvnc is configured to work with *xinetd* or *inetd*, the server is started when an incoming RFB connection is detected. This connection is initiated by the viewer program. But if you're using the Java viewer applet along with the Xvnc web server, then the applet is served by Xvnc…which hasn't started yet! It's the classic chicken-and-egg problem.

The solution is to serve the web page and Java applet from a normal web server. In order to run as an applet in the default Java security model, the VNC server will have to be on the same system as the web server.

To configure this using Apache:

1. Create a new subdirectory within your Apache *DocumentRoot* (or any directory served by Apache):

   ```
   blue$ mkdir vnc
   ```

2. Copy the VNC Java applet files to that directory:

   ```
   blue$ cp /usr/share/vnc/classes/* vnc
   ```

3. Rename the *index.vnc* file to *index.html* and hardcode any values that would normally be substituted if the page was served by the Xvnc web server—so, all of the strings starting with $. For the applet HEIGHT, use the height of the Xvnc server geometry, plus 20 pixels for the Java applet's controls (which will appear at the top of the display). For example, to adjust the TightVNC version of the page for use with an 800×600 server on port 5940:

   ```
   <HTML>
   <TITLE>
   VNC Remote Acces
   </TITLE>
   <APPLET CODE=VncViewer.class ARCHIVE=VncViewer.jar
           WIDTH=800 HEIGHT=620>
   <param name=PORT value=5940>
   </APPLET>
   <BR>
   <A href="http://www.tightvnc.com/">TightVNC site</A>
   </HTML>
   ```

4. You can now access the Java applet page at http://*blue*/vnc/ (adjust the URI if you placed the VNC directory in a location other than the DocumentRoot).

# 14.12 Accessing VNC Securely Using SSH

VNC addresses two of the three remote access challenges (Section 13.7): access control and network bandwidth and latency. It doesn't protect your data in transit, although it does avoid sending VNC passwords in plain text across the network.

To use VNC securely, it is necessary to add an encryption layer. There are several ways to do this, but the most common is to tunnel the RFB protocol through an SSH tunnel.

Most binary VNC viewers can automatically start an SSH client to create a tunnel. This is done with the -via argument:

```
green$ vncviewer -via user@blue localhost:40
```

*vncviewer* will launch ssh with the appropriate arguments to log in to *blue* with the user ID *vncuser* and open a pipe from *green* to *blue*. The VNC server contacted is specified as localhost:40, but since that is written from the perspective of the remote end of the connection, *localhost* refers to the host *blue*.

The standard Java viewers do not provide SSH tunneling capability. An SSH-enhanced version of the TightVNC Java applet is available from the SSHTools project at *http://sourceforge.net/projects/sshtools/*—however, that project is not currently being maintained.

# 14.13 Embedding an X Application in a Web Page

Web applications have traditionally been designed around page-based interaction: the server sends a page, the user fills in a form or clicks on a link, and then the server sends another page. Ajax and similar approaches provide a more interactive approach, but sometimes it would be ideal if we could embed remote access to a single existing application into a web page—for example, an interactive database lookup application or a system monitoring tool. With a little scripting, VNC can do the job.

Figure 14-1 shows an example: *xboard* and *gnuchess* embedded in a web page.

Any graphical X client can be embedded into a web page this way as long as Xvnc runs on the same host as the web server in order to conform to the default Java applet security model. Embedding the program requires you to define the embedded program as a service on the host.

First, to set up the web page, create a subdirectory that is served by your web server and place the VNC Java applet files in that subdirectory:

```
blue$ mkdir /ApacheDocumentRoot/chess
blue$ cp /usr/share/vnc/classes/* /ApacheDocumentRoot/chess
```

Create an index page (*index.html*) in that directory, and have it contain <applet ...> and <param ...> tags for the Java VNC viewer applet:

```
<?xml version='1.0' encoding='UTF-8'?>
<!DOCTYPE html PUBLIC
    '-//W3C//DTD XHTML 1.0 Transitional//EN'
    'http://www.w3.org/TR/xhtml1/DTD/xhtml1-transitional.dtd'>

<html xmlns='http://www.w3.org/1999/xhtml' xml:lang='en'>
  <head>
    <title>
      VNC Embedded Application Demo
    </title>
  </head>
  <body>
    <div style="float: right">
      <applet code="VncViewer.class" archive="VncViewer.jar"
          width="348" height="437">
        <param name="port"          value="5930" />
        <param name="password"      value=""     />
        <param name="show controls" value="no"   />
        </applet>
```

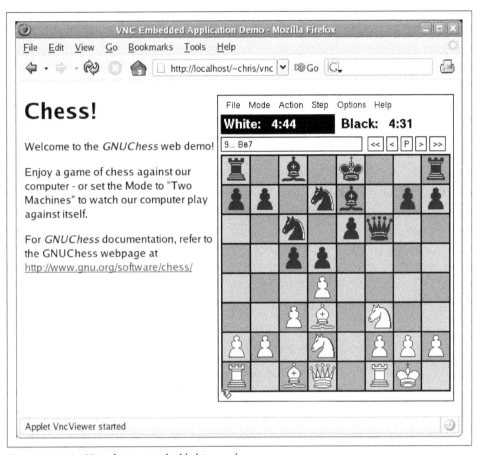

*Figure 14-1. An X application embedded in a web page*

```
    </div>

    <h1>Chess!</h1>

    <p>Welcome to the <i>GNUChess</i> web demo!</p>

    <p>Enjoy a game of chess against our computer -
    or set the Mode to "Two Machines" to watch our
    computer play against itself.</p>

    <p>For <i>GNUChess</i> documentation, refer
    to the GNUChess webpage at
    <a href="http://www.gnu.org/software/chess/"
    >http://www.gnu.org/software/chess/</a></p>
  </body>
</html>
```

In this example, I've used the TightVNC Java applet. I've used the parameters to specify the port 5930, set the password to blank (so that the applet does not ask for a password to be entered), and disabled the controls at the top of the applet. The applet width and height have been matched to the size of the application window.

The next step is to configure *xinetd/inetd* for this new service. Append a service entry to */etc/services*:

```
vnc-gnuchess    5930/tcp
```

Match the port number to the port number used in the applet parameters in *index.html*.

It's also a good idea to create a new user for this service, so that you can limit access through this service (and identify any files created by it):

```
blue# useradd vnc-gnuchess
```

Next, create a service in */etc/xinetd.d/*—use the service name as the filename (*/etc/xinetd.d/vnc-gnuchess*):

```
# default: on
# description: gnuchess via Xvnc
service vnc-gnuchess
{
        flags           = REUSE
        socket_type     = stream
        wait            = no
        user            = vnc-gnuchess

        server          = /usr/local/bin/vnc-gnuchess
        log_on_failure  += USERID
        disable         = no
}
```

If you're using *inetd* instead of *xinetd*, add an entry to */etc/inetd.conf* instead:

```
vnc-gnuchess stream tcp nowait vnc-gnuchess /usr/local/bin/vnc-gnuchess
```

Finally, create a script which will start Xvnc, determine the display provided by that copy of Xvnc, and then connect the client (*gnuchess* in this example) to that display:

```
#!/bin/bash
#
# /usr/local/bin/vnc-gnuchess :: start Xvnc and gnuchess
#
# This script is called by xinetd.

SCRIPTPID=$$

# Create an .Xauthority file if necessary
export XAUTHORITY=/home/$(whoami)/.Xauthority

if [ ! -f $XAUTHORITY ]
then
    COOKIE=$(mcookie)
    for ((D=0;D<100;D++))
    do
```

```
        xauth -q add :$D . $COOKIE >/dev/null 2>&1
    done
fi

# Run commands to set up the client in the background
(
    # Wait for the Xvnc server to start (may not be required)
    sleep 1

    # Get the PID of the Xvnc server
    XVNCPID=$(ps --ppid $SCRIPTPID|grep Xvnc|sed -n "s/^ *\([0-9]*\) .*$/\1/p")

    # Get the display specification from the port number
    # identified by netstat
    DISPLAY=:$(/bin/netstat -ap 2>/dev/null|
        sed -n "s=^[^:]*:60\([0-9][0-9]\).*LISTEN *${XVNCPID}/Xvnc.*$=\1=p" \
        2>/dev/null|head -1|sed "s/^0//")
    export DISPLAY

    # Start the client - 'nice' lowers the priority because gnuchess
    # tends to use the CPU heavily.
    nice /usr/bin/xboard  -geometry 346x435+0+0 -size small >/dev/null 2>&1

)&

# Start the VNC server - must be foreground for socket connection to work
/usr/bin/Xvnc -terminate -inetd -securitytypes none -depth 24 -geometry 348x437

# Tidy up - when the VNC server dies, kill all child processes
kill 0
sleep 3
kill -KILL 0
```

The key is the subshell code within the parenthesis: this code determines the Xvnc PID by finding a child of the parent script with Xvnc as the program name, and then using *netstat* to discover which TCP/IP port in the 6000–6099 range has been opened by that copy of Xvnc. The port number is manipulated to get the display number, and then the client is started, instructed to connect to that display.

This code is needed because when *inetd* is used to start Xvnc, it automatically picks the X display number but does not communicate that number to X client programs—because it's intended to be used with an XDMCP query or broadcast.

The *.Xauthority* file has entries for all displays from :0 to :99 because we don't know what the final display number will be. The file is shared among all of the Xvnc servers for this service. The client and server both pick up the *.Xauthority* filename from the XAUTHORITY environment variable.

Finally, you can access the web page with the embedded application using a Java-enabled browser—in this example, the URI is:

```
http://blue/chess/
```

Be very careful about providing remote access to local applications! In the example given here, *xboard* offers load and save options on its File menu. If the vnc-gnuchess user is inadvertently given write access to an important file, it could be obliterated by an accidental or malicious save performed by a remote user. If you are using a client that provides *any* file operations, you should run it in a *chroot* jail. Although you can password-protect web pages, the web page can be bypassed by using a binary VNC viewer to directly access the Xvnc port. Using a VNC password file (with the -rfbauth option) and matching the `<param password="...">` tag in the HTML can help reduce this vulnerability—only users with access to the web page will have the password for VNC access.

You can take this concept and extend it as far as you want, perhaps incorporating elements of a kiosk configuration (see Section 15.1). For example, if you want to give live software demos of complex applications on the Web, you could require users to register through a web-based facility, and then create a *chroot* jail specifically for each user's instance of the program. The application could be started with a simple window manager such as *mwm* or *fvwm*, and the user could create, save, and open files, but not start any other applications; when the user finishes the demo, the *chroot* environment could be destroyed automatically.

# 14.14  Using KDE and Gnome Remote Desktop Access Tools

Both KDE and Gnome provide X clients that are VNC servers. These tools read the X desktop continuously, using the DAMAGE extension (Section 1.15) in order to identify the areas of the display that have changed, and then present that information to remote VNC displays. These programs are similar to the *x0vncserver* program provided by RealVNC, and produce an effect similar to the VNC servers used on Windows and Macintosh systems where the only desktop display is shared to a remote user.

The KDE desktop sharing tool is named *KRfb* and is configured through the KDE Control Center; it's under Internet & Network → Desktop Sharing. The configuration dialog is shown in Figure 14-2.

KRfb can be used in two ways: through *invitations*, which are temporary passwords valid for one hour, and by allowing uninvited connections, which act like normal VNC connections and may optionally be password-protected.

To manage invited connections, click on the Create & Manage Invitations button; you will be shown the current invitations and given options for creating new invitations, creating and emailing them, and deleting them. The invitation system is ideal for some support applications when you want to permit temporary remote access.

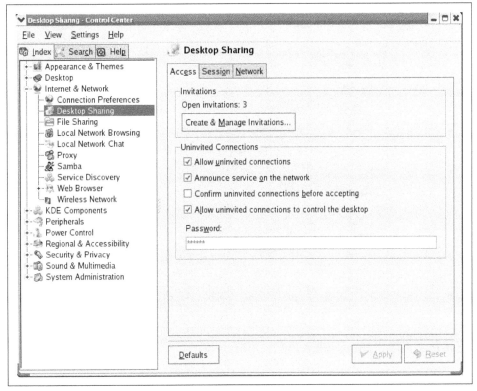

*Figure 14-2. KRfb configuration in the KDE Control Center*

If the "Allow uninvited connections" checkbox is selected, users will be able to connect without one of the temporary passwords generated by the invitation system. You can still impose a password by entering one in the password field.

It's possible to allow both invited and uninvited connections at the same time; however, only one connection can be active at a time (other connection attempts are denied), and KRfb takes a few seconds to reset when a connection is dropped before it will accept new ones.

If any invitations are outstanding *or* if uninvited connections are enabled and the "Confirm uninvited connections before accepting" checkbox is selected, the local user will be prompted with a confirmation dialog before the remote connection is accepted. This will prevent connections to an unattended KRfb system from succeeding, so check the configuration if you intend to use KRfb unattended.

 Some versions of KRfb have a bug in the XRLE encoding that may prevent clients from connecting. Specifying *hextile* encoding on the viewer command line will work around the problem and enable the connection to succeed:

```
green$ vncviewer -preferredencoding hextile blue:0
```

Gnome's remote access tool is named *Vino* and is configured using the Remote Desktop preference, as shown in Figure 14-3.

*Figure 14-3. Vino configuration dialog*

Vino does not have the invitation mechanism present in KRfb, but the other features are basically the same. Vino does permit multiple simultaneous connections, and there is no reset time after a disconnection. Vino ignores the client's request for an exclusive connection—so there is no way to "bump" an existing connection as you can with other VNC servers (which is useful if you forget to disconnect from one location and later connect from another).

# 14.15 Using the VNC Extension to the X.Org Server

VNC is also available as an extension for the standard X.org server. This extension makes the image on the X display available to VNC clients; unlike KRfb or Vino (which are started by the session manager), the VNC extension is present whenever the X server is running, which means that you can authenticate using the display manager through VNC and start a new session. The server extension also provides better performance.

RealVNC includes a loadable X module for the X.org server; it installs as */usr/lib/xorg/modules/extensions/libvnc.so*.

To use the VNC extension module, add an entry to the Modules section of the X server configuration file:

```
Section "Module"
        Load  "vnc"
        ...Other Modules...
EndSection
```

If you execute X -configure when the *vnc.so* module is present, an entry for it should be created automatically. You can confirm that the VNC extension is loaded by examining the output of *xdpyinfo* (Section 6.2).

You must add a SecurityTypes option entry to the Screen section to turn VNC passwords on or off; without this option, all RFB connections will be rejected.

If you want passwords turned off—which is unwise, unless you're on a very secure, closed network—set SecurityTypes to None:

```
Section "Screen"
        Option              "SecurityTypes"         "None"
        ...Remainder of Screen section...
EndSection
```

Otherwise, to use passwords, create a VNC password file using *vncpasswd*:

```
blue# vncpasswd /etc/vncpasswd
Password: bigsecret
Verify: bigsecret
```

Then add these two entries to the Screen section:

```
Section "Screen"
        Option              "SecurityTypes"       "VncAuth"
        Option              "PasswordFile"        "/etc/vncpasswd"
        ...Remainder of Screen section...
EndSection
```

Almost any option accepted by the Xvnc server can be passed to the VNC extension by adding Option entries in the Screen section. For example, to specify that the incoming VNC connections should be accepted on port 5907 (VNC display number :7):

```
Section "Screen"
        Option              "SecurityTypes"       "VncAuth"
        Option              "PasswordFile"        "/etc/vncpasswd"
        Option          "RFBport"           "5907"
        ...Remainder of Screen section...
EndSection
```

# 14.16  Using VNC to Share a Presentation

About two years ago, I led a introductory workshop on the use of *LAMP* (Linux, Apache, MySQL, and Perl/PHP). I had prepared some slides, but knew that during some parts of the presentation the slides would be obscured by live demos. The participants would also be performing hands-on experimentation and would have to refer to the slides, so I needed some way of enabling them to see the slides regardless of what I was doing on the screen. Although my presentation software (MagicPoint) had a web-based follow-along mode, it didn't scale well enough for this workshop.

The solution I used was to start an Xvnc server with a geometry smaller than my screen size and to run the presentation software on that display. I then used a VNC viewer to display that window on my screen, and I provided each of the participant workstations with an icon that started a VNC viewer on the workstation with appropriate arguments to prevent updates (so they could see the current slide, but not terminate the presentation or change the slide).

This is the script used on the podium computer:

```
#!/bin/bash
#
# govnc :: start a VNC server with mgp inside
#                use index.mgp as the slideset
#                use display 20 for VNC

VNCDISPLAY=20                        # VNC display number
HOST=''                             # VNC hostname
SLIDESET="index.mgp"                 # slide set to be used
MGPARGS="-t210"                      # mgp arguments, if desired (e.g., -G, -t)
GEOMETRY="800x600"                   # mgp geometry

# If an Xvnc server is already running, this will silently fail
Xvnc -securitytypes none -geometry $GEOMETRY \
    -depth 24 :$VNCDISPLAY >/dev/null 2>&1 &
sleep 1

# Kill the existing mgp and vncviewer processes
killall mgp vncviewer

# Start a new mgp and vncviewer process
DISPLAY=$HOST:$VNCDISPLAY mgp $MGPARGS $SLIDESET &
MGPPID=$!

vncviewer $HOST:$VNCDISPLAY&

echo "MGP Process ID: $MGPPID" >/tmp/x

# Kill the server and viewer when mgp dies
wait $MGPPIG
killall Xvnc vncviewer
```

On the client machines, the script looked like this:

```
#!/bin/bash
#
# showvnc :: start a VNC viewer to follow podium presentation

VNCDISPLAY=20                        # VNC display number
HOST='blue'                         # VNC hostname

exec vncviewer -viewonly $HOST:$VNCDISPLAY
```

It would also be possible to use the Java VNC viewer and give out the URI to participants at the start of the presentation if they're using their own equipment (such as wireless laptops).

# 14.17 Bypassing a Firewall

Firewalls can pose a problem when using VNC. By far, the simplest and most secure way to get around a firewall when using VNC is through SSH tunneling (Section 14.12).

But if the machine you're connecting to is a cluster of computers—or if SSH is not configured—then SSH is not an option. However, you may be able to create the connection if you reverse the direction: make the VNC server connect to the VNC viewer.

To set up the viewer side of a reverse connection, run *vncviewer* with the -listen argument. You can specify a port, or omit it and use the default of 5500 like this:

```
green$ vncviewer -listen
```

The server side is then set up in two steps. First, start the Xvnc server; here I'm specifying display :1 and instructing the server to connect to the display manager on *red*:

```
blue$ Xvnc -query red :1
```

If you're using a recent version of RealVNC, use the *vncconfig* command to instruct the VNC server to connect to the viewer:

```
blue$ vncconfig -display :1 -connect blue:5500
```

If you're using TightVNC or an older version of RealVNC, the command is *vncconnect*:

```
blue$ vncconnect -display :1 blue:5500
```

The port can be omitted if the default (5500) is used.

# Part V

# Special Configurations

# 15

# Building a Kiosk

## 15.1  What Is a Kiosk, and Why Do I Want One?

A kiosk is a publicly accessible computer display dedicated to a specific task or group of tasks. Here are some examples:

- An electronic catalog station in a library
- An automated teller machine
- A ticket-vending machine
- A video wall
- A browsing and word-processing system in an Internet café

Many of these applications—including the library card catalog and ticket-vending machine—are most easily developed and deployed using a restricted, browser-based interface.

Kiosks differ from normal user-interface configurations in the way that they are managed. Many kiosks do not offer normal windows, and instead run a single application that takes up the entire display; others offer a limited selection of applications in a normal window environment. The user-interface hardware may also be more limited than in a desktop configuration—for example, there may be no keyboard—and it may be more rugged: a trackball or touchscreen to control the pointer instead of a mouse.

In all cases, a kiosk configuration will strictly limit what the user can do and be robust enough that it will handle most error situations without intervention. This chapter covers configuring a kiosk using standard applications and tools.

## 15.2  Selecting Kiosk Hardware

If your kiosk will be used only by selected, trusted users (e.g., staff) or in a light-duty environment (Internet café), you may be able to get by with regular PC hardware.

For any other purpose, you will probably want to invest in specialized hardware. Kiosk hardware is usually similar to desktop hardware but is typically more rugged and is often mounted in a custom-built case. Obviously, the wide range of kiosk applications means that there is also a wide range of possible kiosk hardware configurations: what is suitable for a vending machine is not suitable for an Internet café.

## Monitor

Although LCDs have long life, low-power consumption, and a flat surface, they usually have a soft plastic surface that is not sufficiently durable for public operation. Therefore, many kiosks use an LCD display covered by a glass, acrylic, or polycarbonate sheet, or a traditional CRT display. Since most kiosks are used from a standing position, the display may be farther from the user than a normal desktop display. Because some users may have visual impairment, it is best to use a large, bright, high-contrast display. The monitor should be positioned to accommodate users of many different heights, including people in wheelchairs.

For some applications such as public information displays or video walls, you may want to consider using a rear-projection screen and one or more LCD or DLP video projectors.

## Pointer

Mice are inappropriate for most kiosks, because the cord and position sensor are susceptible to damage. When the kiosk application requires pointer positioning (not always the case), a touchscreen, touchpad, or trackball are usually used.

## Keyboard

Some kiosk applications require a full keyboard. Keyboards are susceptible to dirt, abraded labels, and liquids; to deal with this, some kiosk builders use cheap keyboards that can be replaced inexpensively, while others choose rugged keyboards that resist liquids and can be easily cleaned. The keyboard can be mounted behind a metal or acrylic panel cut to shape.

If your application does not require a full keyboard, you may be able to use a USB numeric keypad instead; these are commonly marketed for use with laptops.

There are a number of companies that make custom keycaps for use with keyboards or keypads; you can order standard sets of specialized symbols, blank keycaps (for unused keys on the keyboard), or custom legends. Another possibility is mounting heavy-duty pushbuttons adjacent to the screen and wiring those pushbuttons in parallel with the keys on a keypad or keyboard; the application can then present *soft keys*—on-screen options that can be selected by pressing one of the adjacent buttons.

For applications that require only limited keyboard input, consider using a touch-screen and presenting the keyboard on-screen when necessary.

 Avoid using a touchscreen for password or PIN entries, since it's too easy for someone else to view (or video-record) the password as it being entered.

## System Unit, Power Supply, and Ventilation

Most kiosks have an *inner* and outer case; the outer case is visible to the user and takes the form of a vending machine, podium, recessed wall unit, or whatever is suited to the application. The inner case is usually a standard or rackmount PC chassis. Because kiosks may run without inspection for weeks or months at a time, it is wise to select a basic but rugged chassis with a good power supply and extra fans for the system unit. Easily washed air filters which are oversized (in case they become partially clogged) will help prolong the life of the unit, and airflow through the outer case or cabinet of the kiosk should also be carefully planned. Ventilation louvers should be positioned to allow good airflow while eliminating the possibility of liquids or foreign objects reaching internal components (an internal baffle can prove helpful). A good UPS with temperature monitoring is highly recommended. Depending on the application, the external power supply cable, network cable, and (if necessary) alarm cables may need to be armored.

# 15.3  Configure X for a Kiosk

Configuring X for a kiosk involves removing features to limit what the user can do. The three main configuration entries for this can be placed in the ServerFlags section:

```
Section "ServerFlags"
    Option    "DontZoom"
    Option    "DontZap"
    Option    "DontVTSwitch"
EndSection
```

This prevents the user from changing the display resolution, terminating the X server, or switching virtual terminals.

During the development and testing of the kiosk, you may want to store the kiosk X configuration in a separate file (such as */etc/X11/xorg.kiosk.conf*) so that the default X server retains its original configuration. To start X with the kiosk configuration, supply the -config argument on the command line:

```
blue$ X -config /etc/X11/xorg.kiosk.conf
```

# 15.4 Controlling the Keyboard

Many programs have special functions that can be invoked using function keys, Alt- or Ctrl-key combinations, or Alt-Ctrl-Shift-modified mouse clicks. To prevent the users from accessing these functions, you can modify the keyboard map using the *X Keyboard Extension* or the *xmodmap* command. In most cases, the *xmodmap* command provides the simplest solution.

Here is an *xmodmap* file that will disable the Ctrl, Alt, and CapsLock keys as well as function keys F1–F12:

```
! clear unneeded modifier keys
clear CTRL
clear mod1
clear mod2
clear mod3
clear mod4
clear mod5
clear lock

! clear the function keys (F1-F12)
keysym 0xffbe =
keysym 0xffbf =
keysym 0xffc0 =
keysym 0xffc1 =
keysym 0xffc2 =
keysym 0xffc3 =
keysym 0xffc4 =
keysym 0xffc5 =
keysym 0xffc6 =
keysym 0xffc7 =
keysym 0xffc8 =
keysym 0xffc9 =
```

To use this file, pass the filename (*/usr/local/kiosk/xmodmap.txt* in this case) to *xmodmap* as an argument:

```
$ xmodmap /usr/local/kiosk/xmodmap.txt
```

To disable other keys, discover the keycode by running the *xev* utility, then add additional lines to clear out the key symbols (also called *keysyms*) associated with that keycode. For example, to disable the A key, run *xev* and press the A key. *xev* will output a message like this on *stdout*:

```
KeyPress event, serial 29, synthetic NO, window 0x3a00001,
    root 0x119, subw 0x0, time 342476839, (176,174), root:(1062,320),
    state 0x10, keycode 38 (keysym 0x61, a), same_screen YES,
    XLookupString gives 1 bytes: (61) "a"
    XmbLookupString gives 1 bytes: (61) "a"
    XFilterEvent returns: False

KeyRelease event, serial 29, synthetic NO, window 0x3a00001,
    root 0x119, subw 0x0, time 342476939, (176,174), root:(1062,320),
```

```
    state 0x10, keycode 38 (keysym 0x61, a), same_screen YES,
    XLookupString gives 1 bytes: (61) "a"
```

From this output you can see that the keysym for A is 0x0061; append a line to the *xmodmap* file disabling that key:

```
    keysym 0x0061 =
```

# 15.5  Controlling the Mouse

The middle and left mouse buttons can be used to access special features of some programs. For example, if you highlight a URI in *Firefox* and press the middle mouse button on a nonlink portion of a web page, the browser will load the page at that URI. Likewise, the right mouse button provides a pop-up menu of features that you may not want your users to access, such as saving onto the local filesystem.

You can configure which physical mouse buttons generate which button event using *xmodmap*. Normally, button 1 generates a button 1 event, button 2 generates a button 2 event, and so forth.

To change the mouse button mapping, first find out how many mouse buttons are configured by your X server:

```
$ xmodmap -pp
There are 5 pointer buttons defined.
```

| Physical<br>Button | Button<br>Code |
|:---:|:---:|
| 1 | 1 |
| 2 | 2 |
| 3 | 3 |
| 4 | 4 |
| 5 | 5 |

In normal operation, buttons 1–3 correspond to the left, middle, and right mouse buttons; button 4 and 5 are scrollwheel up and down; and buttons 6 and 7 are scroll-wheel left and right (for mice that have two scrollwheels, a tiltable scrollwheel, or buttons on the side of the mouse and typically used for browser history navigation).

You can use the *xmodmap* pointer command to specify the button event code for each physical button:

```
$ xmodmap -e "pointer = 1 10 11 4 5"
```

You must specify a code for each button defined on the mouse (five for this mouse).

In this example, button 1 (left button) and buttons 4 and 5 (scrollwheel up and down) retain their original meaning, but button 2 will generate a button 10 event, and button 3 will generate a button 11 event, both of which are ignored by most applications. This effectively disables buttons 2 and 3.

If you are using *xmodmap* to change the keyboard, you can append the pointer line to the end of the *xmodmap* input file:

```
pointer = 1 10 11 4 5
```

Some applications may not use the pointer mapping set by *xmodmap* and may continue to recognize all of the mouse buttons. In that case, you can disable all but the first mouse button by using the Buttons option in the mouse's InputDevice section of the X server configuration file:

```
Section "InputDevice"
        Identifier  "Mouse0"
        Driver      "mouse"
        Option      "Buttons" "1"
        Option      "Protocol" "IMPS/2"
        Option      "Device" "/dev/input/mice"
EndSection
```

## 15.6 Starting a Single Fullscreen Application

For a kiosk that runs only one application, it makes sense to omit the window manager and just start that one application in fullscreen mode.

For many applications, this can be done with a command-line geometry specification; on a $1024 \times 768$ screen, this opens a full-screen *xclock*:

```
$ xclock -geometry 1024x768+0+0
```

It is common to use a web browser as a kiosk application. Unfortunately, most of the current generation of web browsers ignores command-line geometry specifications, and, although they have a fullscreen mode, this mode is not accessible from the command line. In that case, it may be necessary to use a browser extension or chrome file; alternately, you can use JavaScript to invoke a full-screen browser window, using a file such as this:

```
<?xml version='1.0' encoding='UTF-8'?>
<!DOCTYPE html PUBLIC
        '-//W3C//DTD XHTML 1.0 Transitional//EN'
        'http://www.w3.org/TR/xhtml1/DTD/xhtml1-transitional.dtd'>

<html xmlns='http://www.w3.org/1999/xhtml' xml:lang='en'>
  <head>
        <title>Kiosk Startup</title>
  </head>
  <body>
    <script language="JavaScript">
        window.open('http://yellow/','master','width=1024,height=768,menubar=no');
    </script>
  </body>
</html>
```

This script requires that pop-up blocking be disabled in the browser.

Insert the desired URI, width, and height into the window.open line, save the file locally (e.g., at */usr/local/kiosk/index.html*) and then invoke the browser with the script:

```
$ firefox file:/usr/local/kiosk/index.html
```

This will start a second window on top of the first, with a 1024×768 geometry and no menu bar. Since no window manager is running, the user cannot close, minimize, or move the top window to return to the first window. To disable the status bar, navigation bar, and other user interface features on a browser such as Mozilla or Firefox, start the browser normally and deselect those features using the View menu, then exit the browser. The browser configuration files will automatically be updated with your preferences.

 You may also be able to configure a kiosk mode for a browser using the browser's *chrome* capability, theming, or an extension.

# 15.7  Network Status Monitoring

Impaired or broken kiosk operation can be very frustrating to users, so automatic monitoring (and notification) of network status may help prevent users from taking out their frustration on your hardware.

If you're using a browser as your kiosk application, you can use a command such as *wget* to periodically poll the server and determine whether it is available. For example, if the main index page for the kiosk is http://yellow/, you could check whether the remote server is prepared to serve that page with this command:

```
blue$ wget http://yellow/ --spider -t 1
```

The exit status will be 0 if the page is available, or 1 if it is not. The --spider argument instructs *wget* to check the page availability (using the HTTP HEAD command) rather than retrieve the page (using HTTP GET), therefore reducing the amount of data transferred over the network.

If you're using another network-based service, you can use any other appropriate tool (such as ping for general server connectivity, showmount -e for NFS servers, or a netcat or a Perl script for a custom service) to test whether the service the kiosk needs is available.

Using the *wget* command, we can create a script that will place a message on the kiosk display when the remote server becomes unavailable and removes it when the remote server comes back online:

```
#!/bin/bash
#
# monitor.sh :: monitor server availability, warn user if service unavailable
#

# === Configuration variables

# Seconds between service availability tests
SECONDS=15

# Command to test the server availability
CHECK="wget http://yellow/ --spider -t 1"

# URIs for warning message (should be file://...) and kiosk's homepage
WARN="file:/usr/local/kiosk/outage_warning.html"
HOMEPAGE="http://yellow/"

# === End of configuration variables

STATE="UP"
while sleep $SECONDS
do

    $CHECK
    RESULT=$?

    case "$STATE" in
    "UP")
        if [ "$RESULT" -ne "0" ]
        then
            firefox -remote "openurl($WARN)"
            STATE="DOWN"
        fi
        ;;

    "DOWN")
        if [ "$RESULT" -eq 0 ]
        then
            firefox -remote "openurl($HOMEPAGE)"
            STATE="UP"
        fi
        ;;
    esac

done
```

This script uses the Firefox -remote argument to instruct a running instance of Firefox to load a local error message page ($WARN) or the kiosk's home page on the remote server ($HOMEPAGE) when connectivity to the remote server is lost or restored.

If you're setting up a kiosk that uses an application other than a browser, substitute another command to check that the remote server is accessible and replace the browser messages with a graphic image that will fill the screen when the server is down:

```
#!/bin/bash
#
# monitor.sh :: monitor server availability, warn user if service unavailable
#

# === Configuration variables

# Seconds between service availability tests
SECONDS=15

# Command to test the server availability
CHECK="ping yellow"

# File containing a full-screen warning image
WARN="file:/usr/local/kiosk/outage_warning.tiff"

# === End of configuration variables

STATE="UP"
while sleep $SECONDS
do

    $CHECK
    RESULT=$?

    case "$STATE" in
    "UP")
        if [ "$RESULT" -ne "0" ]
        then
            xloadimage -fullscreen $WARN
            STATE="DOWN"
        fi
        ;;

    "DOWN")
        if [ "$RESULT" -eq 0 ]
        then
            killall xloadimage
            # Add any application-reset commands here
            STATE="UP"
        fi
        ;;
    esac

done
```

If *xloadimage* is not included with your distribution/system, you can obtain it from *ftp://ftp.x.org/R5contrib/* or use a similar application such as ImageMagick's *display*. Note that both *xloadimage* and *display* can be exited by pressing Q, so they may not be appropriate for desktops that are equipped with a full keyboard (but will work fine on kiosks that have only a keypad, soft keys, or a pointer device).

## 15.8  Using xscreensaver to Reset a Kiosk

It's often desirable to reset a kiosk after a period of inactivity. For example, if a kiosk is presenting a library catalog, it should return to the library home page after a few minutes of idle time.

Although there are many ways to detect kiosk inactivity, *xscreensaver* (Section 6.13) already contains the required logic and can be easily put to use.

*xscreensaver* uses various graphics *hacks* to present screensaver effects—whether bouncing cows, fractals, or floating text. You can add, as an additional hack, a script that simply resets your kiosk application and deactivates the screensaver, or you can create a script that resets your application and then executes an existing graphics hack.

To simply reset your application and the disable the screensaver, create a script like this:

```
#!/bin/bash
#
# kiosk-reset :: xscreensaver 'hack' to reset the kiosk

# Reset the kiosk application (Firefox browser in this case)
firefox -remote 'openURL(http://yellow/)' &

# Deactivate the screensaver to return to normal display mode
/usr/bin/xscreensaver-command -deactivate
```

The location of the *xscreensaver* command varies between operating systems/distributions.

Name this script *kiosk-reset*, add execute permission, and save it in */usr/libexec/ xscreensaver* (or whatever location is used by your version of *xscreensaver*).

Next, add a line configuring this hack into */usr/share/X11/app-defaults/XScreenSaver*, in the *programs section:

```
*programs:
  "Kiosk reset"  /usr/libexec/xscreensaver/kiosk-reset \n\
  "Qix (solid)"  /usr/libexec/xscreensaver/qix -root -solid -segments 100 \n\
```

If you have an existing ~/.xscreensaver file, delete it so that the changes to /usr/share/X11/app-defaults/XScreenSaver are detected.

Use the xscreensaver-demo application to configure xscreensaver, specifying the length of idle time before the screensaver should kick in and denoting Kiosk reset as the one and only screensaver to be used.

The script above will reset the Firefox browser to the specified page, and then resume normal operation; however, the screen will go black briefly when xscreensaver kicks in.

Instead of this unpolished blanking effect, it may be better to run one of the existing hacks to present a message to users while the kiosk is idle; for example, the GLslideshow hack can very attractively zoom around and cross-fade between product images, or fontglide can present advertising messages or announcements in an attention-getting manner.

To invoke another hack from your script, you need to find the command line for that hack; this can most easily be done by copying (or modifying) the command line for the hack from /usr/share/X11/app-defaults/XScreenSaver, or configuring the hack using the Settings feature in /usr/share/X11/app-defaults/XScreenSaver and then using the Advanced tab to view the command line.

Replace the xscreensaver-command line in the earlier kiosk-reset script with the command line for your selected hack:

```
#!/bin/bash
#
# kiosk-reset :: xscreensaver 'hack' to reset the kiosk

# Reset the kiosk application (Firefox browser in this case)
firefox -remote 'openURL(http://yellow/)' &

# Execute an existing xscreensaver hack
exec /usr/libexec/xscreensaver/phosphor -program 'echo -e "\fX Power Tools
\nby Chris Tyler\nO\'Reilly Media, 2007\n\nEverything you ever wanted\nto know
about X - and then\n some\n-Slashdot Anonymous Coward\n\nTouch the mouse to
begin..."' -root
```

# 15.9  Refining the Kiosk Appearance

The default X cursor (which is a thick X, visible whenever an application has not taken overridden the default cursor shape) and the root window appearance (either solid black or a stippled grayscale pattern) are ugly. You can control both using the xsetroot command:

```
blue$ xsetroot -cursor_name left_ptr -solid steelblue
```

left_ptr is the name of the standard, northwest-pointing arrow cursor; to see other possible cursor names, read /usr/include/X11/cursorfont.h. To see the cursor shapes, use the X font display program, and match up the character numbers (seen at the top of the window when you click on a shape) with the numbers in */usr/include/X11/cursorfont.h*:

```
$ xfd -fn cursor
```

The -solid argument takes a color name (Section 3.13) or a color code (hex digits in the form #rrbbgg) as its argument.

# 15.10  Putting It All Together: Scripting a Kiosk

The core of most kiosk systems is a script (or group of scripts) that start the X server, kiosk applications, and any related services, and then monitor the kiosk application, restarting the X sever or applications when necessary.

Here is an example of a basic kiosk script, combining the ideas from the other articles in this chapter:

```
#!/bin/bash
#
# kiosk.sh :: start a web browser in Kiosk mode
#

# --- Configuration variables
export DISPLAY=":1"
BROWSER="/usr/bin/mozilla"
STARTPAGE="file:/usr/local/kiosk/index.html"
HOMEPAGE="http://yellow/"
WARN="file:/usr/local/kiosk/outage_warning.html"
XSERVER="/usr/bin/X"
XMODMAP="/usr/bin/xmodmap /usr/local/kiosk/xmodmap.txt"
SCREENSAVER="/usr/bin/xscreensaver -nosplash"
SCREENSETUP="xsetroot -cursor_name left_ptr -solid blue"
SECONDS="15"
CHECK="wget $HOMEPAGE --spider -t 1"
# --- End of configuration variables

while true
do

    # Step 1: Start the X server, allowing local connections only
    $XSERVER $DISPLAY -nolisten tcp -ac -terminate &
    XPID=$!

    # Step 2: Start the screensaver
    $SCREENSAVER &

    # Step 3: Adjust the keymapping, pointer configuration, mouse shape,
    # and root window color
    $XMODMAP
    $SCREENSETUP
```

```
# Step 4: Start the browser
$BROWSER $STARTPAGE &
BROWSERPID=$!

# Step 5: Start the network monitoring code
(
    sleep 10        # Give the browser a chance to start

    STATE="UP"
    while sleep $SECONDS
    do

        $CHECK
        RESULT=$?

        case "$STATE" in
        "UP")
            if [ "$RESULT" -ne "0" ]
            then
                firefox -remote "openurl($WARN)"
                STATE="DOWN"
            fi
            ;;

        "DOWN")
            if [ "$RESULT" -eq 0 ]
            then
                firefox -remote "openurl($HOMEPAGE)"
                STATE="UP"
            fi
            ;;
        esac

    done
)&

# Step 6: Wait until the application dies
wait $BROWSERPID

# Step 7: Kill everything and start over
killall -KILL $BROWSERPID $XPID

done
```

The core of the script is a loop, which will restart the kiosk if it stops. The X server is started without access controls, but only local connections are accepted; in most cases, that should be sufficient to prevent external clients from connecting.

After the X server is started, the screensaver is started. This is done first to ensure that the X server always has a connected client, so that it does not reset prematurely—or terminate in this case, due to the -terminate option on the X command line. This enables the script to run *xmodmap* without the server resetting and clearing out the *xmodmap* settings as soon as it's done. The script then runs the browser program—which could just as easily be any other full-screen program of your choosing—and then the network monitoring code in the background.

Finally, the script monitors the application (Firefox) to see if it terminates—which shouldn't happen, but many programs have slow memory leaks or other problems that may cause them to fail after extended periods of use. An X server failure should automatically cause the application to terminate. Nonetheless, the script watches for this condition, and rather than leave anything to chance, it kills off all of the child processes and restarts all of them.

Note that display :1 is used here; this facilitates testing of the kiosk script while display :0 is active on the system.

## 15.11  Booting a Kiosk

Most kiosk systems boot directly into the configured kiosk application. This can easily be configured and tested on a system that supports runlevels.

Traditionally, runlevel 4 is unused, so it is a perfect candidate for a kiosk mode. It's easiest to start off by copying the scripts for a working runlevel. On a Fedora system, you could copy the runlevel 5 configuration with this command:

```
blue$ cp -l /etc/rc.d/rc5.d /etc/rc.d/rc4.d
```

Other systems may use other directories; for example, Debian/Ubuntu uses /etc/rc4.d and /etc/rc5.d.

Next, disable all unnecessary services (this will depend on the kiosk application). For example, to delete the bluetooth services:

```
blue# chkconfig bluetooth off
```

 It is a good idea to leave ssh enabled, so that you can log in to the kiosk remotely for diagnostic and maintenance work.

You can also use your system- or distribution-specific configuration tools, but they will have the same effect: deleting symlinks from the directory for runlevel 4.

You will then need to modify /etc/inittab to disable character-mode logins in runlevel 4. Here are the affected lines:

```
# Run gettys in standard runlevels
1:2345:respawn:/sbin/mingetty tty1
2:2345:respawn:/sbin/mingetty tty2
3:2345:respawn:/sbin/mingetty tty3
4:2345:respawn:/sbin/mingetty tty4
5:2345:respawn:/sbin/mingetty tty5
6:2345:respawn:/sbin/mingetty tty6
```

In each line, the character 4 in the second field must be removed:

```
# Run gettys in standard runlevels
1:235:respawn:/sbin/mingetty tty1
2:235:respawn:/sbin/mingetty tty2
3:235:respawn:/sbin/mingetty tty3
4:235:respawn:/sbin/mingetty tty4
5:235:respawn:/sbin/mingetty tty5
6:235:respawn:/sbin/mingetty tty6
```

Finally, append a line to this file to configure *init* to start the kiosk script (and respawn it if it dies) only in runlevel 4:

```
ks:4:respawn:/usr/local/kiosk/kiosk.sh
```

Whenever you change */etc/inittab*, you must inform *init* of the change:

```
# init q
```

You can then test the kiosk mode by switching into from your current runlevel:

```
# init 4
```

Once you are confident that the kiosk is properly configured, you can change the default system boot runlevel by changing the `initdefault` line in */etc/inittab*. To temporarily boot into runlevel 3 or 5 for maintenance, append the desired runlevel to the boot parameters (Section 2.5).

 Remember to add a password to the boot manager configuration before deploying the kiosk, in order to prevent unauthorized booting into any runlevel other than 4.

# 15.12 Creating a Video Wall

Video walls—huge grids of monitor or projection screens set up to show large images—are always impressive. Xinerama can be used to create displays that span as many screens as you have video cards, but typical PC motherboard design limits you to six or seven video cards. For larger displays, DMX provides a way of merging displays from multiple hosts into one giant display.

DMX stands for *Distributed Multihead X*. The DMX server, *Xdmx*, is an X server that uses other X servers as screens. This permits you to combine almost any number of monitors into one giant display.

To use *Xdmx* in its most basic form, start it with two or more -display arguments, a display number for the *Xdmx* server itself and any other standard X server options:

```
blue$ Xdmx -display blue:0 -display  red:0 -ac +xinerama :35
```

In this example, the *Xdmx* server is display :35, and it uses blue:0 (left) and red:0 (right) as screens in a Xinerama configuration with no access control. If blue:0 and red:0 are both 800×600 in size, then the *Xdmx* server will have a display resolution of 1600×600 pixels.

In order to configure the spatial relationship of the constituent displays/screens, *Xdmx* provides a configuration file option. A simple config file looks like this:

```
virtual testconfig 1600x600 {
    display blue:0  800x600 @0x0;
    display red:0   800x600 @800x0;
}
```

The file consists of one or more configurations, each of which consists of the keyword `virtual`, a name assigned to this configuration, and a list of displays enclosed in braces. Each display entry starts with the keyword `display` followed by the displayspec (Section 1.12), display geometry, and the position of that display within the *Xdmx* display space. Semicolons separate the `display` entries. This example is the same as the *Xdmx* command shown earlier, and it configures two 800×600 displays into one 1600×600 display.

The configuration file is used with the `-configfile` option to *Xdmx*:

```
blue$ Xdmx -configfile dmxconfigfile -ac +xinerama :35
```

If the config file includes multiple configurations, select one with the `-config` option:

```
blue$ Xdmx -configfile dmxconfigfile -config testconfig -ac +xinerama :35
```

If you're going to configure multiple screens on each host, I recommend that the screens be configured using Xinerama at the host level, so that *Xdmx* has only one entry for each display. For example, to build a 16-monitor grid where four 800×600 monitors are controlled by each of four hosts (*host0* through *host3*), the four monitors on each host should be configured using Xinerama (Section 4.2) to present a single 3200×600 display (one row of the grid). The *Xdmx* configuration would then look like this:

```
virtual grid 3200x2400 {
    display host0:0  3200x600 @0x0;
    display host1:0  3200x600 @0x600;
    display host2:0  3200x600 @0x1200;
    display host3:0  3200x600 @0x1800;
}
```

*Xdmx* will take its input from the first display specified, unless the `-input` option is used. The argument to `-input` can be any of the backend (hardware) displays in the configuration, or it can be a separate X server, in which case a *DMX Console* is drawn that shows outlines of the various backend displays and an outline of each window. Figure 15-1 shows a DMX Console window; note that there are inaccessible areas in this Xinerama configuration.

There are several things to keep in mind when configuring DMX:

* Performance will be degraded by the simple fact that multiple X servers will be processing the command and reply streams and the amount of network traffic that will be generated.

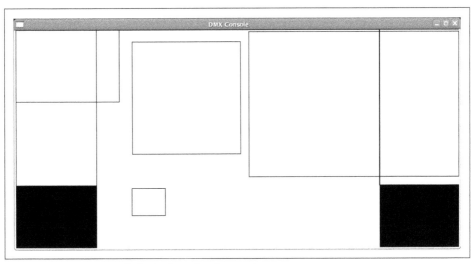

*Figure 15-1. DMX Console for keyboard and mouse input*

- *Xvideo* and *XVideo-MotionCompensation* extensions will not be available through DMX. Video and animation will have to be drawn using traditional X operations or through the RENDER extension. If you're using *mplayer*, this can be configured using the -vo x11 option.
- GLX is available through DMX if all of the backend displays support it.
- DRI will not be available.

 There is a graphical configuration tool that is shipped with *Xdmx* named *xdmxconfig*, but the configuration files generated by that program may need editing before they are used. Specifically, some versions will insert slash characters which the *Xdmx* server will parse incorrectly. Deleting the slashes will clear up the problem.

# Index

## Symbols

& (ampersand), background operation of
    commands, 112
* (asterisk), mouse key, 38
# (hash mark) beginning comment lines, 32
- (minus) mouse key, 38
+ (plus sign) mouse key, 38
/ (slash) mouse key, 38

## Numbers

0 key (mouse key), 38
32-bit systems, 19
    using 24-bit RGB values, 138
5 key (mouse keys), 38

## A

Above keyword (screen positioning), 72
absolute pointing devices, 12
absolute X-Y pixel position (screens), 71
accelerated graphics port (AGP), 17
acceleration
    accel option (video driver), 57
    mouse, 103
acceleration factor, 103
accented characters, 13
access control, 182
    host-based, 182
    magic cookies and xauth utility, 183–185
    SECURITY extension, 186
    tunneling with SSH, 188
additive color systems, 135

additive primaries, 135
AGP (accelerated graphics port), 17
AGP bus, scanning, 48
AIX and HP/UX systems, CDE desktop, 118
aliasing (monochrome fonts), 142
AllowClosedownGrabs option, 92
AllowDeactivateGrabs option, 92
AllowMouseOpenFail option, 81
Alt, Ctrl, and Shift keys, 161
AlwaysCore argument, 80
analog connection, video cards, 18
antialiasing, 142
    enabling/disabling or adjusting, 158
Apache web server, configuring Java applet
    VNC servers, 205
applet tags (Java VNC viewer), 202, 206
application clients, 8
ARGB visuals, 138
Argyll (color management system), 140
ASCII-based terminal emulators, 116
Asian languages, keyboard input
    methods, 13
Athena project widgets, 11
ATI drivers, 56
    closed-source driver fglrx, multiple
      outputs, 77
    open-source driver radeon, multiple
      outputs, 77
audio feedback scripts, 102
autologin, 30
AZERTY keyboards, 13

We'd like to hear your suggestions for improving our indexes. Send email to *index@oreilly.com*.

---

## About the Author

**Chris Tyler** is a computer consultant, author, and professor in the School of Computer Studies at Seneca College in Toronto, where he teaches courses on open source software development, Linux system administration, and the X Window system. Chris has been using, configuring, and administering graphical interfaces based on X since 1993. He is the author of *Fedora Linux: A Complete Guide to Red Hat's Community Distribution* (O'Reilly). He also blogs from time to time on the O'Reilly Network (*http://oreillynet.com*) and on his personal web site (*http://chris.tylers.info*). Chris is the main author of the Fedora Daily Package (*http://dailypackage.fedorabook.com*).

## Colophon

The image on the cover of *X Power Tools* is a power sander. A power sander is an electric tool that is used to smooth surfaces of wood and wood finishes. When using a power sander, it is wise to always make sure to take basic safety precautions. For example, tie back long hair so there is no chance of it being caught in the machinery, wear goggles to protect your eyes from sawdust, and cover your ears to protect them from the loud sound and from the sawdust as well.

The cover image is a photograph taken by Frank Deras. The cover font is Adobe ITC Garamond. The text font is Linotype Birka; the heading font is Adobe Helvetica Neue Condensed; and the code font is LucasFont's TheSans Mono Condensed.

# Learn from experts.
# Find the answers you need.

Sign up for a **10-day free trial** to get **unlimited access** to all of the content on Safari, including Learning Paths, interactive tutorials, and curated playlists that draw from thousands of ebooks and training videos on a wide range of topics, including data, design, DevOps, management, business—and much more.

## Start your free trial at:

## oreilly.com/safari